Enlightenment and Exploration
in the North Pacific, 1741–1805

Port Dick near Cook Inlet as sketched by H. Humphreys on Vancouver's 1794
northern survey (*Hydrographic Office, Taunton, Somerset*).

The original sketch included no ethnographic detail. In the published version
reproduced on the cover of this book, engraver B. T. Pouncy added canoes and
Native hunters. The explorers had seen such a flotilla in the area.

ENLIGHTENMENT
AND
EXPLORATION
IN THE
NORTH PACIFIC
1741–1805

EDITED BY

Stephen Haycox

James K. Barnett

Caedmon A. Liburd

Published for the Cook Inlet Historical Society

in the Anchorage Museum of History and Art *by the*

University of Washington Press   *Seattle and London*

Library of Congress Cataloging-in-Publication Data

Enlightenment and exploration in the North Pacific, 1741–1805

edited by Stephen Haycox, James Barnett, Caedmon Liburd.

p. cm.

Includes index.

ISBN 0-295-97583-0 (alk. paper)

1. Alaska—Discovery and exploration—European.   2. Alaska—
History—To 1867.   3. Explorers—Alaska—History—18th century.
4. Explorers—Northwest, Pacific—History—18th century.
5. Northwest, Pacific—Discovery and exploration—European.
I. Haycox, Stephen W.   II. Barnett, James, 1947-   .   III. Liburd,
Caedmon.   IV. Cook Inlet Historical Society.   V. Anchorage Museum
of History and Art.

F907.E55   1997

979.8'01—dc21   96-37993

                             CIP

The paper used in this publication meets the minimum requirements of American
National Standard for Information Sciences—Permanence of Paper for Printed Library
Materials, ANSI Z39.48-1984.

Cover photo: Port Dick near Cook Inlet, engraving by B. T. Pouncy, based on a sketch
made by H. Humphreys on Vancouver's 1794 northern survey (The Anchorage
Museum of History and Art)

Contents

Preface   vii

Introduction   xi

Alaska and the North Pacific: A Crossroads of Empires   **James K. Barnett**   3

PART 1: MOTIVES AND OBJECTIVES

Spain's Role in Pacific Exploration during the Age of Enlightenment
Iris H. W. Engstrand   25

George Vancouver, the Admiralty, and Exploration   **Glyndwr Williams**   38

Lapérouse 1786: A French Naval Visit to Alaska   **Robin Inglis**   49

Ethnology in the Enlightenment: The Voyage of Alejandro Malaspina in the Pacific   **Phyllis S. Herda**   65

PART 2: SCIENCE AND TECHNOLOGY

The Health of Mariners: Vancouver's Achievement   **John M. Naish**   79

The Evolution of Shipbuilding in the Eighteenth Century   **John Kendrick**   88

Testing a New Technology: Vancouver's Survey and Navigation in Alaskan Waters, 1794   **Alun C. Davies**   103

From Cook to Vancouver: The British Contribution to the Cartography of Alaska **Andrew David**   116

Russian Mapping of the North Pacific to 1792   **Carol Urness**   132

PART 3: OUTCOMES AND CONSEQUENCES

Vancouver: Cautious Collector   **J. C. H. King**   149

Images of Native Alaskans in the Work of Explorer Artists

Kesler E. Woodward   161

The Publication and Readership of Voyage Journals in the Age of Vancouver,

1730–1830   **Anthony Payne**   176

Efforts at Humane Engagement: Indian-Spanish Encounters in Bucareli Bay, 1779

Stephen J. Langdon   187

George Vancouver and the Native Peoples of the Northwest Coast

Robin Fisher   198

Contributors   211

Index   213

Preface

I n October 1994, the Cook Inlet Historical Society of Anchorage, Alaska, hosted sixteen international scholars at an invitational symposium commemorating the bicentennial of the survey voyage of George Vancouver on the Northwest Coast as far north as Cook Inlet in 1792–94. Expanding the work of James Cook in 1778–79, Vancouver began work in the south each of the first two years but started the third season's endeavors at Eagle River, several miles above Point Woronzof in Knik Arm, one of two branches that form the head of Cook Inlet and that today embrace the city of Anchorage, a modern metropolis of more than a quarter million people. In recognition of the bicentennial of Cook's first charting of Cook Inlet waters, the City of Anchorage in 1978 commissioned a James Cook statue. Today the likeness stands on the bluff overlooking those waters just at the apex of downtown Anchorage, a source of pride and respect for the city's residents and of interest and information for its visitors. This publication of scholarly papers constitutes Anchorage's tangible recognition of the significance of Vancouver's voyage, as well as the legacy of the Cook Inlet Historical Society's 1994 Vancouver Symposium.

The Cook Inlet Historical Society is dedicated to the collection and interpretation of regional history. It is headquartered in the Anchorage Museum of History and Art and is a support group for that museum, which is a principal cultural institution for the city, region, and state. All of the activities associated with the Symposium, "Exploration in the North Pacific, 1741–1805," were held at the Anchorage Museum of History and Art.

The audience for the symposium was the general public, which has responded enthusiastically to the efforts of the society through many years, and did so again for this event. Attendees included visitors from a number of states and countries, as well as many local residents, including interested faculty and students from the Anchorage campus of the University of Alaska and from private Alaska Pacific University.

In preparation for the symposium, the society hosted a series of monthly lectures on the history of European exploration of the Northwest Coast. Professor Richard Pierce of the University of Alaska Fairbanks (UAF) reviewed Russian discovery and exploitation of the northern reaches of the coast; Professor Marvin Falk of the Rasmuson Library at UAF surveyed the cartographic context of North Pacific exploration; Professor Donald Cutter of the University of New Mexico recounted the Spanish voyages along the coast; Dee Longenbaugh of *The Observatory* bookstore in Juneau noted the beginnings of the maritime fur trade with the arrival of James Hanna on the coast in the *Sea Otter* in 1785 and of James Strange with the *Captain Cook* and *Experiment* the following year. Kathryn Arndt of Fairbanks presented a paper on Russian exploration of and contact with the Natives of the Yukon-Kuskokwim Delta region; Dr. Nancy Yaw Davis of Anchorage discussed general European and Native responses to contact, while Professor Steve Langdon of the University of Alaska Anchorage discussed Spanish-Tlingit relations in Bucareli Bay in the context of Native social maturity. Finally, James Barnett of Anchorage summarized the significance of Vancouver's role in the broader context of Enlightenment maritime exploration, noting the convergence on the Northwest Coast of diverse European energies and a variety of sophisticated Native cultures. This series provided a useful context for the original contributions of the scholars who convened in Anchorage in October. Two of the preparatory lectures, by Langdon and Barnett, are included in the present anthology.

Drawing upon current analysis of Vancouver's achievements, symposium planners solicited papers for the October meeting in several specific research areas. The salient factors that motivated the several European nations to dispatch expeditions to the coast seemed a significant arena of discussion. These included the peculiar conditions and leaders in each country, which bore on planning and financing. Some recent scholarship has addressed the role of capitalist and imperial expansion and competition in the European advance upon the Americas, which at the same time drew the aboriginal inhabitants of the Americas into the developing world market system. And while national economic interest as well as personal glory and religious fervor were major incentives, few explorers manifested or elaborated clear and conscious insight into the role of capitalist expansion in the European Enlightenment, and those who did took for granted its validity. Several papers in this collection address economic motivation and its implications in the changing world of the eighteenth century.

Encounters with American aborigines constituted one of the more significant of the explorers' activities. Several papers dealt with Native contact from diverse points of view, including comparative analysis of Spanish understanding of aborigines in Tonga, the manipulation of images of Natives by European artists and their publishers, the approach to collecting Native artifacts, and an assessment of the interpretive paradigms historians have brought to the study of contact.

Understanding the nature of Native contact was part of a larger enterprise: gathering, and also applying, new knowledge. The planners thus sought papers on the technologies of exploration, including the cartographic context, especially of Vancouver's survey, as well as advances in shipbuilding and medicine, which were substantial. Increasingly, interest in science occupied the attentions of planners of the great maritime expeditions to the Northwest Coast. The editorial committee sought papers that elucidated this theme as well. One paper demonstrates that publication of official expedition journals symbiotically showed this increasing interest while simultaneously encouraging it. The experiences of the explorers were captured not only in the written accounts but also in artists' images, and one of the papers addresses the nature of those images and their impact. In all, the papers presented cover a broad range of interpretation of Vancouver's work and its principal focus, the Northwest Coast.

The Cook Inlet Historical Society is pleased with the support of the University of Washington Press in publishing a selection of papers from the symposium. This involvement is a further reflection of that press's commitment to work that treats the broader Alaskan and international context of Pacific Northwest history.

All of the papers included in this collection represent important commentary on the significance and role of Vancouver's epic contribution. As well, they present analysis absent from current historical interpretation. The society hopes that their publication will advance scholarship and understanding. Several papers presented at the symposium could not be included in the present volume because of space limitations and the guidelines agreed upon with the University of Washington Press. These include presentations by Dr. Eric Groves of Surrey, England, Dr. Victoria Ibañez of the University of Madrid, and Dr. Mary Malloy of the Sea Education Association at Woods Hole, Massachusetts.

The editors thank the Board of Directors of the Cook Inlet Historical Society and Patricia B. Wolf, Director of the Anchorage Museum of History and Art, and her staff, for their encouragement and support of the symposium, *Exploration in the North Pacific, 1741–1805,* held in Anchorage at the Museum on October 14 and 15, 1994. The symposium and lecture series leading to the publication of this volume were overseen by the Vancouver Committee of the society, chaired by Wilda Marston, whose tireless work was essential to the success of the project. In addition to the editors, the committee members included Joan M. Antonson, Eva R. Trautmann, and Gwynneth Wilson, with staff support from Barbara Geib, the museum registrar.

The symposium enjoyed the generous financial support of many corporations and individuals. The principal donors were Robert B. Atwood, National Bank of Alaska, Alaska Railroad Corporation, First National Bank of Anchorage, Cook Inlet Historical Society, Alaska Humanities Forum, Alaska Commercial Company, Hotel Captain Cook, Elmer and Mary Louise Rasmuson, Larry and Wilma Carr, Brooke and Wilda Marston, Key Bank of Alaska, Anchorage Telephone Utility, BP Exploration (Alaska), Incorporated, Cook Inlet Region, Incorporated, the Herb Hilscher Memorial Lecture Fund, Alaska Airlines, and the Anchorage Daily News.

The editors are grateful to Julidta Tarver and Pat Soden of the University of Washington Press for their support in the development of this volume, as well as to the faculty and staff of the History Department of the University of Alaska Anchorage, who provided invaluable assistance in the editorial process. Finally, we thank the participants and attendees of the symposium and its monthly lecture series. This was a truly international conference, with significant support from the local community. Without such extensive support, this volume would not have been possible.

Introduction

This volume examines the large theme of the Enlightenment and exploration in the North Pacific under three organizing principles: the motives and objectives of the European explorers; the contribution of science and technology to the success of European exploration; and the outcomes and consequences resulting from the contacts of Europeans with the Native peoples of the North Pacific.

The drive to explore the North Pacific is the central concern of the first section. The motivations of European explorers in the Pacific are too complex and too diverse to be explained solely by imperial desire and market forces. The empirical spirit inherent in late eighteenth-century Enlightenment Europe was in part motivated by the hegemonic needs and desires of European governments and economies. As exploration progressed, there developed an increasing awareness among political and commercial men of the intimate relationship between knowledge, power, dominion, and profit. Thus imperial and colonizing impulses were nurtured by a parallel objective: to reduce the unknowns in the North Pacific region—its peoples, lands and seas, and resources—to the comprehensible, the tangible, and ultimately, the malleable.

The primary theme scrutinized in the section "Science and Technology" is that exploration of the North Pacific and international rivalry for overseas empire were undergirded by significant technological and scientific discoveries and innovations that took place away from public acclamation. Advances in public medicine and hygiene, instrumentation, ship design, navigation, and cartography significantly increased knowledge of the North Pacific and contributed to the establishment of European hegemony there and elsewhere throughout the world. The scholars here examine the advances that increased the endurance, strength, and reach of eighteenth-century European explorers.

Under the rubric "Outcomes and Consequences" several writers explore separate but significantly interrelated issues. As befits a conference occasioned by his voyage to the North Pacific, they assess Captain Vancouver's achievements as an ethnographer of and emissary to the Native people of the North

Pacific. A principal focus of inquiry is concentrated upon the fact that Europeans intruded into not a *terra nullius* but a land already occupied by indigenous peoples who had highly developed political and social systems, well-established economic systems, and strongly held ideas about property in lands, woods, and waters. Contacts were made with different peoples, each of whom was asserting its own perceived, indisputable, cultural prerogatives. The consequences of these contacts initiated profound cultural changes in European as well as indigenous societies. European representational practices in art as well as literature are examined as instruments through which Europeans not only projected their own narcissism but also appropriated and relegated the indigenous "Other" to permanent subordination in a hierarchy that in their eyes confirmed European superiority. The authors also examine Native reactions to the European interlopers. A final critical theme is the need for a new paradigm of exploration and contact history that moves beyond the reductionism that largely produces little more than the language of blame, panegyrics to innocence, and obsession with power relationships.

Enlightenment and Exploration in the North Pacific, 1741–1805

The North Pacific

JAMES K. BARNETT

Alaska and the North Pacific: A Crossroads of Empires

The voyage of Captain George Vancouver two centuries ago was crucial to Europeans, as for all practical purposes it disproved stories of the Northwest Passage and mapped the coastal contours of the last uncharted temperate region of the world. It also was the culmination of a series of adventures in the drama of exploration by the major seafaring nations that led to the conquest and colonization of the west coast of North America.

Vancouver was just thirty-six years old when he and his men sailed into Cook Inlet in April 1794. Traveling north along the western shore, they saw an awe-inspiring vista of high, snowcapped mountains. A wisp of volcanic steam rose from one of the loftiest peaks. But the journey was treacherous, as the vessels encountered boulders, mud flats, shoals, and strong tides. Snow fell. The temperature dropped to seven degrees. Ship hulls shuddered and anchor cables snapped as chunks of ice drifted in the ebb and flow of the tide. Vancouver had spent the winter in Hawaii; now he was returning to Alaskan waters to begin his third year surveying the Northwest Coast. According to British admiralty requirements, he was to give special attention to Cook's River, as the armchair geographers speculated this might be the outlet of Canada's Mackenzie River.

After anchoring in an estuary to take on fresh water, Vancouver repositioned his ships near what would one day become the downtown area of Anchorage. Joseph Whidbey left with two boats to explore the eastern arm that Captain Cook in his journal had earlier named the Turnagain River, and in two days he returned to report that it was "no longer entitled to the name of a river." Vancouver himself then surveyed the northern branch of the river and soon sighted the end of today's Knik Arm. He decided to substitute the name "Cook's Inlet" for "Cook's River," frustrated that Cook had been so careless. He wrote that, had Cook "dedicated one more day to its further examination, he would have spared the theoretical navigators . . . the task of ingeniously ascribing to this arm . . . a channel, through which the north-west passage . . . might ultimately be discovered."[1]

Vancouver's voyage into Cook Inlet was the culmination of a series of voyages and other opportunities for interaction between Europeans and Natives in the region that began in the seventeenth century. Alaska had long served as a crossroads of human contact in the North Pacific, even before the time of European exploration. Anthropologists believe that Alaska provided the land bridge for man's entry into America some 20,000 years ago.[2] The people of the First Nations settled in America and developed unique and varied cultures, uninfluenced by their European contemporaries. Centuries later, European explorers were driven to "discover" the region for scientific, religious, and capitalist motives. After Christopher Columbus reached the Caribbean, many Spanish expeditions concentrated on exploring North America. It took just fifty years for Spain to conquer the mainland, establish ports on the Pacific coast, and, anticipating a short distance to the wealth of the Orient, begin its search to the north.[3] After many failed expeditions, Juan Cabrillo was the first to reach modern-day California, arriving at the site of present-day San Diego on September 28, 1542. After he died from a gangrene infection, his pilot ran to the north along the coast before rough seas and violent winds turned him back at Cape Mendocino.[4] The Spanish found that prevailing Pacific trade winds could fetch the treasures of Cathay to the capitals of Europe via Mexico in the Manila Galleons. These voyages were undertaken annually until 1815, yet in the course of hundreds of sailings, making landfall on the west coast of North America on each return, little was learned about the North Pacific, as the ships quickly turned south and headed for the safety of Mexico.[5]

The English made the greatest headway toward the North Pacific when the privateer Francis Drake struck at the Spanish New World colonies' unprotected western flank in 1579. After entering the Pacific at Cape Horn, Drake raided several Spanish towns and ships, capturing considerable loot. To avoid capture, he decided to escape to the north through the fabled Strait of Anian. The farthest reach of his trip was probably in the latitude of Seattle.[6] Given the cold conditions encountered in June, his voyage may have ended even farther north. When he abandoned his search, he returned to refit his ships near San Francisco Bay, at a place he called New Albion ("New England"). He then returned home with a fortune in treasure.

The only Spanish voyage north from Mexico for two centuries after Cabrillo was by Sebastián Vizcaíno, who sought a harbor in California for the galleons on their return from the Orient. His crews were so overcome with scurvy that only a few could walk, but they reached the latitude of Oregon, observing "Aguilar's River."[7] This legend stimulated armchair geographers anticipating a Northwest Passage. Although all of Vizcaíno's boats returned to Mexico, the death by scurvy of two-thirds of the crew confirmed that the price of searching for ports or treasure in the North Pacific was too high.

The Russian empire, the least experienced and most unlikely competitor in the drama of European conquest, was the first exploring nation to actually reach the North Pacific. When Peter the Great came to power in 1685, the Russians were not seafarers, but the new czar created a modern navy. He then chose a Dane, Vitus Bering, to determine Russia's proximity to America. The appalling hardships of Siberian travel, extending more than 6,000 miles from the Russian capital, far overshadow Bering's accomplishments at sea. In his first expedition, Bering sailed north from Kamchatka in 1728 and rounded the tip of Siberia. In rain and fog, he rarely saw the Russian coastline, passing Alaska unknowingly. Sailing farther north, he feared encountering ice, so he turned back to Kamchatka before reaching the Arctic ice pack.[8]

On his return, there was criticism for his judgment on the expedition, but Bering had no trouble generating support for a second expedition, this time to find Europeans in America. This was no modest proposal. His first expedition used 100 men; the second required more than 3,000. His plans were burdened with assignments to find the northern reach of Siberian rivers and to make contact with imperial Japan. But on June 4, 1741, the *St. Peter,* under the command of Captain Commander Bering, and the *St. Paul,* under the command of Captain Aleksei Chirikov, set out for America. The ships sailed to the southeast to search in vain for the imagined Juan de Gama Land. As they did, Chirikov's vessel was driven away by strong winds. Unable to regain contact, each captain continued toward America alone.

Six weeks after leaving Siberia, Chirikov and his men raised the west side of Prince of Wales Island. They found the shoreline steep and rocky, so they went north, finally entering a large bay near Sitka. A landing party was sent to secure fresh water. The ship's crew watched them row out of sight around a headland, but no landing signal was given and they did not return. After five days, crewmen on the ship thought they spotted a fire on shore, so a carpenter and caulker were sent to the same place in the remaining shore boat. They followed the same route, but, like the first party, they vanished. Indians came out in two canoes, but after shouting something unintelligible, they paddled away. Chirikov was certain they had killed his men, or held them captive, but thousands of miles from home, with no shore boats and limited water supplies, he retreated to Kamchatka. The Russians who later dominated the region sought the fate of these men, but found little. Today scholars assume that a tidal rip, and not a hostile Native encounter, caused the loss.[9]

As the *St. Paul* made its first landfall in southern Alaska, the *St. Peter* was several hundred miles to the north. A day after Chirikov sighted land, Bering's crew saw a high, snow-covered volcano appear out of the haze; the peak was later called Mount St. Elias. The crew was elated, but Bering was not. In his journal, the German naturalist Georg Steller wrote that the captain accepted the discovery "very indifferently and without particular pleasure . . . he even shrugged his shoulders while looking at the land." Although this was his crowning life achievement, Bering was already fearful of the return to Kamchatka through the vast ocean, its rain, fog, and winds.[10] The explorers found a large island, and Bering sent his boats to shore. The one sent for water also carried Steller, who in just ten hours conducted considerable scientific exploration, feverishly collecting plants and tracing evidence of human habitation. He concluded that the North Americans were related to the Natives of Kamchatka and speculated on their ancestral crossing.[11]

Bering's ship was quickly underway, but progress was slow. In a month, scurvy broke out, and by September the log of the ship recorded increasing sickness and death. In November, suffering from exhaustion, the crew took an uninhabited island to be Siberia. When they approached, the tides drove the ship mercilessly onto a reef. During the winter ashore, most of the men slowly regained their health, but the captain was too weak. He died on December 8, 1741. The survivors built a driftwood cross, and named the forbidding place Bering Island.[12] They soon found plenty of sea otters on the island, killing far more than they could eat, aware that the skins were of high value in China. In the spring, they built a small boat from the wrecked *St. Peter* and returned safely to Kamchatka.[13] Despite the travail, Steller's brief foray onto Kayak Island and his time on Bering Island provided new and valuable information about the flora and fauna of the North Pacific. Further, the sea otter pelts brought back from Bering Island emboldened Russian hunters to return to these islands.

In 1743 the Cossack Emelian Basov sailed to Bering Island in a small *koche*, a crude Russian sailing vessel. Spending the winter ashore, he turned the island into a virtual killing ground, returning to Kamchatka the following spring with thousands of sea otter and fur seal pelts. He made other voyages, all wildly successful, and other hunters soon followed.[14] As each island's treasure of accessible furs was exhausted, the crews passed east along the Aleutian chain, enlisting the Aleut people to hunt otters in their remarkable *bidarkas* (modern-day kayaks).

This advancing Russian fleet had the attention of the other seafaring nations, particularly Spain, who maintained long-standing claims to both Americas. To augment these claims the Spanish enlisted Friar Junípero Serra to establish missions in Alta California. They assumed settlements of Christianized Indians would repel Russian efforts to colonize the coast. Two ships left Mexico in the spring of 1769, and two overland expeditions followed, led by Serra and Gaspar de Portolá, governor of the Californias. The ships' crews were so overcome by scurvy that they lay disabled in San Diego harbor when the overland elements arrived. As Portolá continued north to find San Francisco Bay, on Sunday, July 16, 1769, Father Serra founded Mission San Diego de Alcalá. When

James K.
Barnett

6

Serra died in 1784, nine missions and four presidios had been established in Alta California, stretching from San Diego to San Francisco.[15]

Not satisfied with these meager colonies, the Mexican Viceroy Antonio María de Bucareli sent out ships to take possession of lands north of California. The *Santiago,* under Juan Pérez, sailed from Mexico early in 1774, first resupplying the beleaguered colonies, then sailing north to the region of the Queen Charlotte Islands. Three Haida canoes approached at once, and a lively trade developed. The Spanish acquired sea otter skins in exchange for knives, bits of metal, and old clothes. Pérez later anchored the *Santiago* at Nootka Sound. Indians in canoes approached to trade, but a strong wind came up, and Pérez had to leave without landing. Scurvy soon broke out, and winds, rain, and seas prevented further exploration. Pérez took possession of no land, but Viceroy Bucareli was glad to learn he also did not find any Russians.[16]

The *Santiago* was quickly recommissioned in 1775 for a second expedition, under Bruno de Hezeta. It was accompanied by the thirty-six-foot schooner *Sonora,* under the command of Juan Francisco de Bodega y Quadra. Near the mouth of Washington's Quinault River, the ships were separated in coastal shoals. As the *Santiago* began trade with the Natives, six men on a watering mission from the *Sonora* were ambushed and killed. Bodega retreated, the small swivel gun in the bow his only protection from advancing war canoes. Once free, he set course to the north. In three weeks he sighted Mount Edgecumbe, where he came into an inlet he called Bucareli Bay, spending several days in fruitless search for the Strait of Anian and Russian outposts. The small craft then reached the latitude of Lituya Bay before winds, high seas, depleted rations, and scurvy forced a retreat. The viceroy was gratified both by Bodega's seamanship and because no Russians were encountered on the voyage.[17]

Although the Russian occupation of the North Pacific was not as extensive as the Spanish had feared, their advance soon led to permanent colonies. In 1776, the same year the United States declared its independence from Great Britain and when Hezeta returned to Mexico, Grigor Ivanovich Shelikov arrived in Kamchatka to enter the sea otter trade. Shelikov fell in with prosperous merchants and, in 1783, outfitted three ships for the largest Russian venture up to that time. In a year, he stood in a bay off the southeast coast of Kodiak Island, which he named after his ship, "Three Saints Bay." Here he decided to build the first permanent European settlement in Alaska.[18] The closest settlement to the south was the tiny presidio and mission of San Francisco, in Spanish California, founded just eight years earlier.

Three Saints Bay was a small village of seven or eight dwellings. A school was constructed, then an Orthodox church, and the Russians began teaching first the local children and later the adults. Shelikov decided the education and conversion of the Alutig (Kodiak Island) people would lead to peaceful and permanent colonization. But his primary interest was furs, and he mounted expeditions into the far corners of the island, then into Prince William Sound and Cook Inlet. When he later discharged his bountiful cargo of sea otter pelts in Kamchatka, he petitioned for a trading monopoly that would eventually become the Russian American Company.[19]

The domination of the North Pacific by Spain and Russia did not last. In the final decades of the eighteenth century, the greatest seafaring nations, England and France, developed an interest in this unexplored region of the Pacific, stimulated by the intellectual fervor of the Enlightenment. The great explorer James Cook sailed at the height of this era. No one matched his exploits in three separate voyages as he charted much of the Pacific, finding the Hawaiian Islands and establishing that New Zealand consisted of two large islands. He was the first to traverse the fertile eastern shore of Australia, opening the way for British settlements near modern-day Sydney, and he disproved the existence of a great temperate southern continent, finding Antarctica instead.[20]

Cook came to the Northwest Coast in 1778 on his third voyage of exploration. He was instructed to follow the coast from Drake's New Albion to the Arctic, to determine whether the fabled Northwest Passage existed. Among his crew were William Bligh, who later gained infamy during the troubled voyage of the *Bounty,* as well as George Vancouver, Nathaniel Portlock, George Dixon, and Joseph Billings, each of whom would gain fame as captains in the North Pacific. Charles Clerke was the captain of the consort, and John Webber the official artist. It was a roster of the finest English seamen and scientists, many of whom wrote of their exploits after Cook's untimely death at Kealakekua Bay, Hawaii, in February 1779.

After reaching the Oregon coast, Cook missed the Columbia River and Strait of Juan de Fuca before arriving at Nootka Sound. As they came to shore, his two ships were surrounded by the cedar plank canoes of the Nootka people. He found these Natives less attractive than the Polynesians, as they were covered with dirt and grease, but their music was pleasing, especially when they paddled in cadence, and their carved wooden masks reflected extraordinary craftsmanship. Their principal interest was trade, and they engaged Cook and his crew with animal skins, fishhooks, weapons, and carved masks. In return, they accepted anything the English offered, but they preferred iron, often pilfering items not offered in trade.[21]

As the ship sailed north, at Sitka the sun broke out, and a snowcapped peak was named Mount Edgecumbe. After passing Mount St. Elias, Cook was disappointed to find the coastline trending first to the west, then to the southwest. The maps he carried indicated that he could travel straight north to the Arctic, but they were wrong. Soon he entered a large bay, which was later called Prince William Sound. A leak required repair, so in a snug cove his ships were hauled

The *Resolution* and *Discovery* in Snug Corner Cove, Prince William Sound, Alaska, 1778. Drawing by John Webber. Webber was one of the most highly regarded of early exploration artists, sailing on Captain James Cook's third voyage. *State Library of New South Wales, Sydney*

out. Here the crew met several dozen Natives, who reminded Cook of Greenland Eskimos. They wore sealskin clothing but had unusual bone labrets on their lower lips, which the English sailors found unsightly. Their vessels were the sleek *bidarkas* and larger, skin-clad *umiaks*.[22]

Leaving Snug Corner Cove, Cook soon came to a wide gap of open water fifty or sixty miles across. He and Bligh were certain it was not a passage to the Arctic, but the other officers were buoyant, assuming this was the start of a great inland sea. Cook was supposed to sail to the Arctic and not lose time exploring rivers along the way. But now he was unsure whether he was in a river or a northern sea. So he entered the water and sailed north. The crew watched with anticipation, expecting at any moment to exit a strait as Magellan did when he entered the Pacific at Cape Horn. As they reached Fire Island, they were impressed by the snowcapped peaks in the distance, but the near shore landscape suggested they were at a dead end. Bligh went off to examine the northeast arm and returned to report a deep and navigable river between ridges of mountains. King then went up the southeast arm, but the tide prevented progress, and Cook, disappointed, named the passage the River Turnagain.[23]

So the travelers headed down the inlet, then to the west, deeper into the Pacific. Passing the Alaska Peninsula, they turned north, able finally to reach Norton Sound, Bering Strait, and the long-sought Arctic Ocean. Here Vitus Bering had turned around in his first expedition, but Cook continued, soon reaching an impassable ice pack, which he said was "as compact as a wall." Cook's crew returned the following year to chart the ice pack, but it was a mission without spirit—they had since lost Cook in a dispute over a shore boat in Hawaii.[24]

Cook's final voyage was of critical importance to the European exploration of the region. He was the first captain to sail the full reach of the coast and record its principal features, setting the standard for those who followed. The French were the first to return, with the ill-fated voyage of Jean François Galaup, Count of Lapérouse. His principal geographic discoveries were near Japan, but Lapérouse was also the second European to visit Hawaii. He also gained new knowledge of the Gulf of Alaska and was the first foreigner to visit the Spanish colonies of Alta California.[25]

Lapérouse traveled to the Gulf of Alaska in July 1786, coming within sight of Mount St. Elias. His ships sailed east, entering Lituya Bay, which the crew called Port des Français. The local inhabitants commenced trade that was so intense the crew posted a continuous guard to prevent theft. The people lived in large wooden sheds with fires in the center over which fish were smoked. The women adorned themselves with stone labrets. The Natives had extensive skill in woodcarving, building canoes, and working with iron and copper. While the crew replenished wood and water supplies, the commander charted glaciers in the bay. As Lapérouse and his crew prepared to leave, two longboats were engulfed at the outlet of the bay and twenty-one men drowned. In profound anguish, the survivors erected a monument with the inscription: "Twenty-one brave sailors perished at the entrance to this harbor; whosoever you may be, mingle your tears with ours."[26]

Overcome by the disaster, Lapérouse did not investigate Alaska further but sailed for Monterey Bay, where he was warmly received by the friars. The French were surprised at how few Spaniards lived in the colony, and they commented extensively on Spanish efforts to Christianize the Indians.[27] They soon sailed for Kamchatka, where a crew member was dispatched over land to return the journals to France. After a brief stop at Botany Bay, Australia, in 1788, Lapérouse was never seen again. For more than forty years, the whereabouts of his ships was unknown until wreckage was found at Vanikoro near the Fiji Islands.[28]

The Age of Enlightenment was not lost in New Spain. Aware of Cook's departure from Europe in 1776, Viceroy Bucareli decided to intercept him as he reached America. In 1779 he sent two frigates north, commanded by Lieutenant Ignacio de Arteaga, with Juan Francisco de Bodega y Quadra his second. In May, when Cook was in Prince William Sound, Arteaga put into Bucareli Bay, where conflict with the Natives limited trade. In July the frigates advanced to Prince William Sound, taking formal possession at Port Etches, the northernmost point ever claimed by Spain. They were then driven by a storm along the Kenai Peninsula to Afognak Island, where they finally gave up the search for Cook. Despite Cook's presence in these waters, neither fleet sighted the other, and the Spanish returned confident that Cook had not reached the coast and that the Russians were still confined to the Aleutians.[29]

Official accounts of the Cook and Lapérouse expeditions challenged Spanish claims to the region, so a royal expedition was sent to New Spain in 1785, and a second, more expansive expedition was soon undertaken by Alejandro Malaspina. His two corvettes, the *Descubierta* and the *Atrevida,* were well outfitted for coastal examinations, and botanists, cartographers, astronomers, and artists were gathered to record events. Malaspina arrived at Port Mulgrave, or Yakutat Bay, in late June 1791. He had hoped to find the elusive Northwest Passage in the bay, but he was stopped by glaciers, one of which was later named for him. He named the inlet Bahia del Desengaño (Disappointment Bay). Hundreds of Tlingit Indians arrived in canoes to trade, offering fishing implements and domestic articles for old clothing, nails, buttons, and other commodities. The Natives favored iron goods, and those not proffered by the Spanish were soon pilfered. Still the Spanish persevered, collecting weapons, articles of dress, manufactured items, and artifacts for display in Madrid.[30]

Coasting to the south, Malaspina passed Bucareli Bay, then entered Nootka Sound, site of a short-lived Spanish colony. He then sailed to California, con-

"The Corvettes *Descubierta* and *Atrevida* and a View of Mount St. Elias," 1791.
Drawing by Tomás de Suría. Snow-covered Mount St. Elias, viewed by Captain Vitus
Bering fifty years earlier, dominates this portion of the Alaskan coastline. It was
drawn during Captain Malaspina's entry into Port Mulgrave (Yakutat Bay). *Museo de
America, Madrid*

tinuing by way of the Philippines to Spain. Upon his return, he was embroiled in political intrigue when he criticized Spain's inattention to its New World colonies. Tried and convicted of treason, he was imprisoned, then banished, and the expedition manuscripts went unpublished. Spain's role in scientific maritime exploration during the Enlightenment thus came to an abrupt end.[31]

The Russian government also attempted formal expeditions to the North Pacific, although it is unclear whether they were for the lofty objectives of the Enlightenment or to assure the proper collection of tribute. The most notable voyage was that of an Englishman who had sailed with Cook, Joseph Billings. Authorized in 1785, the journey required an overland march from the Baltic and construction of new ships on the Siberian coast. So the expedition did not reach Three Saints Bay until 1790. Once there, the explorers made a careful record of the Native people, as well as Russian commerce. More than six hundred *bidarkas* were in the waters surrounding Kodiak Island at the time, hunting sea otters, sea lions, and fur seals. In Prince William Sound, while Billings engaged the Natives in trade, Gavriil Sarychev went to Kayak Island. There he spoke with an old Native man who remembered Steller's brief visit.[32]

In 1784 the official publication of accounts of Cook's last voyage sent merchants and traders from a host of nations to the Northwest Coast in search of sea otter furs. The English came first, with the arrival of James Hanna in the *Sea Otter* in 1785. The following year, Nathaniel Portlock and George Dixon, who had sailed with Cook's last voyage, left in companion trading vessels the same month that Lapérouse left France. Later, James Strange and John Meares were dispatched from India. In all, seven English trading expeditions arrived in 1786. Dixon and Portlock spent the winter in Hawaii. Meares, unaware of the severity of Alaskan winters, decided to pass it in Prince William Sound. His desperate condition the next spring made it clear that the traders needed a more temperate port on the coast, distant from the Russian settlements in Alaska. Slowly the merchant fleet centered its activities at Nootka Sound. Although most traders were British, soon Americans, Spanish, even Portuguese and Swedes stopped at Nootka. The local chieftain, Maquinna, became a virtual gatekeeper of the trade, acquiring treasures of Europe in exchange for sea otter furs.[33]

In 1788 the Spanish launched an expedition under Estéban José Martínez to determine the extent of this fur trade. Martínez reached several Russian outposts, including the colony at Three Saints Bay. The Russian manager there told him of the growing British merchant fleet in the China-Nootka trade.[34] These reports alarmed the viceroy, who sought to protect Spain's claims to the coast against British, and even Russian, designs. Martínez was instructed to establish fortifications at Nootka the following year. Although Meares had already erected a building there, Martínez constructed a fort and permanent dwellings. James Colnett, Meares's partner, later entered the bay. Outraged by the presence of the Spanish fort, he confronted Martínez, insisting that the port belonged to Britain, by virtue of the discoveries of Captain Cook. Martínez had been at Nootka with Pérez four years earlier than Cook, so he knew of Spain's prior claim. Martínez arrested Colnett, and the Englishman and his ship were hauled back to Mexico.[35]

The incident in Nootka now became an international crisis. The British were enraged by the insult and, sensing a weakening Spanish position, threatened war. Although Spain had a prior right to Nootka, it agreed to a truce. In the Nootka Sound Convention of 1790, each country abandoned its claim, agreeing instead to restore the structure and land to Meares.[36]

The British admiralty was already planning an expedition to follow Cook, but the Nootka Sound Convention gave added impetus, since someone had to supervise the restoration of Meares's possessions. Because of his experience with Captain Cook, George Vancouver was chosen to command two ships, the *Discovery* and the *Chatham,* which carried one hundred forty-five men, forty fewer than on Cook's final voyage. He was to assist at Nootka, then undertake a detailed survey from California to Cook's River in Alaska. The theoretical geographers were still at work, particularly at Cook's River, and the admiralty wanted to put all the theories to rest. The most capable mapmakers and surveyors were instructed to chart every inlet on the coast. This formidable task was scheduled to take two years but ultimately required a third.[37]

The ships sailed April 1, 1791, around the Cape of Good Hope to Australia, then New Zealand, Tahiti, and finally Hawaii, which they reached after eleven months. During the first survey season on the Northwest Coast, the explorers made landfall in April 1792, north of San Francisco Bay. They saw the mouth of the Columbia River, but in flood stage it was not approachable. In the Strait of Juan de Fuca, they met the Boston trader *Columbia,* commanded by Robert Gray. Gray had spent several days in the strait but was now within days of the first entry into the Columbia River, which was named after his ship.[38]

When Vancouver reached the end of the strait, he began the first of dozens of coastal surveys in the shore boats. Lieutenant Peter Puget was in command, so his name was bestowed on Puget Sound, the first of more than three hundred names given to coastal features. Vancouver shortly encountered the Spanish schooners *Sútil* and *Mexicana,* whose commanders were seeking a new site for fortifications. The four ships surveyed the narrows separating Vancouver Island from the mainland, but the Spaniards turned back, leaving to Vancouver the first circumnavigation of the island that bears his name.[39]

After fruitless negotiations with the Spanish at Nootka, Vancouver turned for California. While he sailed ahead, his consort struggled past dangerous breakers and entered the Columbia River. Gray had accomplished this task in May, traveling twenty miles upriver. Now the *Chatham* anchored, and its shore boats went one hundred miles upriver. Meanwhile, Vancouver entered San Francisco Bay in November, the first foreign ship to visit the Spanish mission and presidio there. Like Lapérouse, he was amazed by the undermanned California garrisons. In January he sailed to Hawaii, where he persuaded King Kamehameha to cede the Hawaiian Islands to Great Britain.[40]

The second survey season began in April 1793. From Vancouver Island, the ships proceeded north during the summer months into southeast Alaska, all the while conducting the laborious coastal examinations. The following year, Vancouver began surveying in Cook Inlet, where he and his crew disproved the existence of the Northwest Passage in that latitude. He then passed Resurrection Bay and entered Prince William Sound, where local fur hunters explained the proximity of the sound to Turnagain River and described the Kenai Peninsula as nearly an island. He then charted the perimeter of the sound, sailing afterward for Yakutat Bay. As the season progressed, Vancouver made several efforts to contact the Russian manager, Alexander Baranov, without success. He and his crew did encounter one of Bananov's men, George Purtov, in Cook Inlet, in Prince William Sound, and again at Yakutat Bay, as Purtov was leading a Russian expedition of nine hundred Koniags in *bidarkas* hunting sea otters. Leaving the range of these hunting ventures, Vancouver's survey progressed south, where it finished in August at Port Conclusion, on the inner coast of Baranov Island. After stopping briefly at Nootka that fall, Vancouver and his men returned to England the following September.[41]

At four years, six months, the expedition was the longest in the annals of British exploration, covering an estimated 65,000 miles. Despite minor outbreaks of scurvy and a few skirmishes with Natives, the crew suffered just six fatalities, a mortality rate one-third of that in England.[42] The accuracy of the resulting survey has always been well regarded. William Dall, the Alaskan explorer, stated in 1870 that Vancouver's explorations "have not been excelled by any other navigator," and he found in the 1880s that the charts remained the most trusted authority on Alaskan waters. Indeed, these charts were still the official maps of the coast a century after their initial publication.[43]

During Vancouver's voyage, Russian hunting ventures were haphazard, conducted by several competing trading companies. In 1799 the Russian American Company was formed to conduct all hunting in the region. Alexander Baranov was forty-three when he was hired in Siberia, and from 1790 to 1818 he was the chief manager in Alaska. Shelikov's operations were loosely knit and limited to Kodiak, Afognak, and parts of Cook Inlet when Baranov arrived. In fifteen years, Baranov consolidated operations, relocating them first to St. Paul Harbor (present-day Kodiak), and then to the realm of the Tlingit at New Archangel (present-day Sitka).[44] The Russian population was small. Baranov had one hundred forty-nine men in Kodiak when he arrived, and in 1794 another one hundred twenty-three were sent by the imperial government. By the time the capital moved to Sitka, there were perhaps four hundred Russians in the two cities, and far more Aleuts and Koniags, who conducted the fur hunting expeditions.

Early in the nineteenth century, the Russian government launched an expedition to establish commercial relations with Japan and resupply the Alaska colonies. This expedition, commanded by Ivan Krusenstern, avoided the difficulties of a transcontinental march by sailing from the Baltic in 1803. Accompanying the voyage was Nicholas Rezanov, Shelikov's son-in-law, who had been named the new Russian ambassador to Japan. When they reached Hawaii, Krusenstern's consort, the *Neva,* commanded by Urey Lisiansky, sailed for Kodiak. Lisiansky soon learned that the Tlingit had overrun the Sitka settlement in 1802, so he sailed to support Baranov's efforts to retake the capital. His attack on the Tlingit encampment was fierce, with frequent cannon salvos. Although the Natives had firearms provided by American and English traders, they could not withstand the bombardment and they abandoned Sitka to the Russians.[45]

Rezanov and Krusenstern were unsuccessful in Japan, rejected in favor of the traditional isolation. So Rezanov left the expedition and sailed for Kodiak and Sitka with the naturalist and physician G. H. von Langsdorff. They were aghast at the conditions at Sitka. In October 1805 the American ship *Juno* was purchased outright for its provisions. Soon these supplies were exhausted, so Rezanov sailed in the *Juno* for San Francisco. He returned in three months, having bartered furs for wheat, oats, flour, and other supplies, thus saving Sitka from starvation, if not outright abandonment.[46]

The Spanish colonies of Alta California were as simple as those of Russian America. By 1805 there were just a few hundred Spaniards between San Diego and San Francisco, mostly soldiers in the presidios. In the twenty years since Serra's death, ten more missions had been established, and nearly 20,000 Indians were confined. But the California ports were sealed from foreign visits, and trade was officially banned. Vancouver and Lapérouse were accepted as ambassadors from their countries, but only a few other ships were admitted.[47] When they arrived in San Francisco, von Langsdorff wrote of the stark contrast between the privation of the Russian settlements and the abundance of California. Rezanov himself was certain of his long-held plans for expansion of company operations into Oregon, California, and Hawaii and wrote the czar of a joint Russian and Spanish enterprise on the coast. Almost to seal the scheme, he was soon captivated by the Spanish governor's fifteen-year-old daughter, the Doña Concepción Argüello. The courtship was intense, and in six weeks they agreed to be wed, providing they received consent from the papal authorities in Rome. Rezanov quickly returned to Kamchatka and set off for St. Petersburg

James K.
Barnett

16

"View of the Establishments at Norfolk Sound," 1805–6. Drawing by G. H. von Langsdorff. The Russian settlement at Sitka had just been reestablished after prolonged battles with the Kolosh Tlingit when Rezanov and von Langsdorff arrived. *Bancroft Library, University of California, Berkeley*

and Rome. But he soon fell ill, and in March 1807 he died. With his death his plans for coastal empire were abandoned.[48]

Rezanov's death may have been the last opportunity for the survival of the Spanish and Russian colonies in North America. The first step in that inevitable downfall came at Nootka, as Madrid, reflecting the shift of power in Europe, backed away from its only fortress north of California. Spanish exploration culminated in 1792, when Vancouver met Alcalá Galiano and Cayetano Valdés in the Strait of Juan de Fuca and when Jacinto Caamaño charted southeast Alaska.[49] In the next two decades the Spanish were ousted from America in a series of colonial revolutions.

The Russians enjoyed their Alaskan colonies longer. Within a few years of Rezanov's visit to San Francisco, a colony was founded north of San Francisco at Fort Ross; it lasted three decades. Another colony was established in Hawaii, but it survived for just three years.[50] Naval expeditions produced extensive information about the coast and its Native people, offering the timeless drawings of Louis Choris and Mikhail Tikhanov. Ultimately the Russian government—tired of supporting a colony with dwindling fur populations, plagued by provisioning problems, and pressed by more immediate geopolitical concerns—lost interest in Alaska as well.

The British and Americans persevered. In its westward compulsion, the United States sent Lewis and Clark on their overland expedition, reaching the Oregon coast in November 1805. The fur merchant John Jacob Astor established the first American colony, Astoria, on the coast in 1812. At the time of Vancouver's epic voyage, a British fur trader, Alexander Mackenzie, made the first transcontinental crossing, reaching the coast from central Canada in July 1793. Soon the vast fur-trapping network of the Hudson's Bay Company crossed into the Oregon Territory, occupying the vast region from the Rocky Mountains to the Pacific coast. When the Russians lost interest in Alaska, the Hudson's Bay Company hunted for them, virtually supporting the Russian colonies in their final years.

In 1848 John Marshall discovered gold in a mill race on the American River near Sacramento, California. The subsequent rush for gold overwhelmed the new Mexican nation and the Natives of California. Half a world away, the Crimean War burdened the Russian empire with debts that could be repaid from the sale of its Alaskan colony. Intent on its western destiny, the United States seized upon these prospects to secure new lands. It is alluring to speculate on what might have happened if Rezanov had returned to San Francisco to wed the lovely Doña Concepción. That union might have established an impenetrable empire that forever preserved the Spanish and Russian flags. But he never returned. Even so, the rich history of the North Pacific and Alaska includes the many European voyages of exploration that sought the great uncharted coast-line and established the first fledgling colonies on its distant shores.

NOTES

1. George Vancouver, *A Voyage of Discovery to the North Pacific Ocean and round the World, 1791-95,* ed. W. Kaye Lamb, 4 vols. (London: Hakluyt Society, 1984), 4:1243 (hereafter Lamb, *Vancouver's Voyage*). Weather conditions in Cook Inlet are reported by Archibald Menzies, the botanist on the voyage, in Wallace M. Olson, ed., *The Alaska Travel Journal of Archibald Menzies, 1793-1794* (Fairbanks: University of Alaska Press, 1993), p. 91.

2. Brian M. Fagan, *The Great Journey, the Peopling of Ancient America* (London: Thames & Hudson, 1987), pp. 101–18.

3. Bernal Díaz, *The Conquest of New Spain, 1568*, ed. J. M. Cohen (London: Penguin Books, 1963). Díaz was with Cortés during the siege and capture of Mexico City.

4. Henry R. Wagner, *Spanish Voyages to the Northwest Coast of America in the Sixteenth Century* (San Francisco: California Historical Society, 1929), p. 92.

5. *Ibid.,* pp. 94–120.

6. Francis Fletcher, *The World Encompassed by Sir Francis Drake* (London: N. Bourne, 1628), p. 67. Drake left no records, and the northern reach of his voyage is in dispute. This report says he reached forty-eight degrees, the latitude of the Strait of Juan de Fuca.

7. Wagner, *Spanish Voyages,* chapters 9–11.

8. E. G. Kushnarev, *Bering's Search for the Strait: The First Kamchatka Expedition, 1725-1730,* ed. E. A. P. Crownhart-Vaughn (Portland: Oregon Historical Society, 1990). Bering's apprehensions that ended the brief, fifty-one-day expedition at sea are described on pp. 101–12.

9. F. A. Golder, *Bering's Voyages* (New York: American Geographical Society, 1928), Vol. 1. The journal of the *St. Paul* is in chapter 7. On July 27 Chirikov decided to retreat without his men, as he had only forty-five casks of water remaining. Consult the Note on the Loss of Chirikov's Men (p. 311), where tidal rips are offered as the likely explanation for the loss.

10. Georg Wilhelm Steller, *Journal of a Voyage with Bering, 1741-1742,* ed. O. W. Frost (Stanford: Stanford University Press, 1988), p. 61 (hereafter Steller, *Journal*). See also Golder, *Bering's Voyages,* 2:34.

11. Steller, *Journal,* pp. 65–72; Sven Waxell, *The American Expedition* (London: Hodge & Company, 1952), p. 106.

12. Waxell, *American Expedition,* p. 135; Golder, *Bering's Voyages,* 1:230; Steller, *Journal,* pp. 134–41.

13. Waxell, *American Expedition,* pp. 136–58; Golder, *Bering's Voyages,* 1:231–61; Steller, *Journal,* pp. 142–69.

14. V. N. Berkh, *A Chronological History of the Discovery of the Aleutian Islands,* ed. R. A. Pierce (Kingston, Ont.: Limestone Press, 1974), pp. 2, 98–105.

15. C. E. Chapman, *The Founding of Spanish California, 1687-1783* (New York: Macmillan, 1916), pp. 96–101. See also H. E. Bolton, *Fray Juan Crespi, Missionary Explorer*

on the Pacific Coast, 1769-1774 (Berkeley: University of California Press, 1927). Crespi was with Portolá, then with Pérez in 1774.

16. Herbert K. Beals, trans., *Juan Pérez on the Northwest Coast* (Portland: Oregon Historical Society, 1989), pp. 33, 75-117. The crew observed an old bayonet and pieces of other iron implements in the hands of the Natives. Because Pérez was the first European in these waters since Chirikov, the Spanish assumed these implements were from Chirikov's lost boats (pp. 111, 247 n. 17).

17. Warren L. Cook, *Flood Tide of Empire: Spain and the Pacific Northwest, 1543-1819* (New Haven: Yale University Press, 1973), pp. 69-84. Bodega had frequent contact with the local Tlingit, which may have caused a smallpox epidemic that killed a substantial part of the population. See p. 80, n. 69, describing Portlock's evidence from his voyage ten years later.

18. P. A. Tikhmenev, *A History of the Russian-American Company,* ed. R. A. Pierce and A. S. Donnelly (Seattle: University of Washington Press, 1978), pp. 9-15 (hereafter Tikhmenev, *Russian-American Company*).

19. *Ibid.,* pp. 15-24; S. B. Okun, *The Russian-American Company* (Cambridge: Harvard University Press, 1951), pp. 22-34. See also B. Dmytryshyn, E. A. P. Crownhart-Vaughan, and T. Vaughan, *Russian Penetration of the North Pacific Ocean, 1700-1797* (Portland: Oregon Historical Society, 1988), pp. 296-320, offering Shelikov's account of the establishment of the settlement and his description of the local population. His account omits reference to a horrible and controversial battle that occurred soon after his arrival on the island and that left hundreds of Koniags dead.

20. J. C. Beaglehole, *The Life of Captain James Cook* (Stanford: Stanford University Press, 1974), pp. 689-714.

21. *Ibid.,* pp. 583-87.

22. *Ibid.,* pp. 592-97.

23. *Ibid.,* pp. 599-602.

24. *Ibid.,* pp. 607-22, 660-72.

25. F. Valentin, *Voyages and Adventures of LaPérouse,* trans. Julius S. Gassner (Honolulu: University of Hawaii, 1969); John Dunmore, *Pacific Explorer: The Life of Jean-François de La Pérouse, 1741-1788* (Palmerston North, N.Z.: Dunmore Press, 1985).

26. Valentin, *Voyages and Adventures,* p. 34; Dunmore, *Pacific Explorer,* p. 232.

27. Valentin, *Voyages and Adventures,* pp. 46-51; Dunmore, *Pacific Explorer,* pp. 238-42.

28. Jules Sebastien César Dumont d'Urville's account of the discovery of the lost ships is found in Valentin, *Voyages and Adventures,* pp. 135-56, and in Dunmore, *Pacific Explorer,* pp. 292-95.

29. Cook, *Flood Tide,* pp. 93-98.

30. *Ibid.,* pp. 306-309.

31. *Ibid.,* pp. 314-20.

32. Martin Sauer, *An Account of a Geographical and Astronomical Expedition to the Northern Parts of Russia* (London: T. Cadell, 1802), pp. 148-209. See also G. Sarychev, *Voyage of Discovery to the Northeast of Siberia, the Frozen Ocean and the North-East Sea* (London: Richard Phillips, 1806), 2:19-28.

33. Cook, *Flood Tide,* pp. 100-106; Derek Pethick, *The Nootka Connection: Europe and the Northwest Coast, 1790-95* (Vancouver: Douglas & McIntyre, 1980), pp. 12-23. See

the introduction to José Mariano Moziño, *Noticias de Nutka,* ed. Iris H. W. Engstrand (Seattle: University of Washington Press, 1970), which documents the maritime history of Nootka Sound. Finally, an excellent summary of this period of exploration and conquest of the Northwest Coast is found in the introduction of Lamb, *Vancouver's Voyage,* 1:15-27.

34. Cook, *Flood Tide,* pp. 119-25.

35. *Ibid.,* pp. 129-99; Pethick, *Nootka Connection,* pp. 22-23.

36. Pethick, pp. 200-49.

37. Lamb, *Vancouver's Voyage,* 1:27-54. See Bern Anderson, *Surveyor of the Sea: The Life and Voyages of Captain George Vancouver* (Toronto: University of Toronto Press, 1960), pp. 44-48 (hereafter Anderson, *Vancouver*).

38. Lamb, *Vancouver's Voyage,* 2:502-03. See also Frederic W. Howay, *Voyages of the Columbia to the Northwest Coast, 1787-1790 and 1790-1793* (Boston: Massachusetts Historical Society, 1941), pp. 336-96.

39. Lamb, *Vancouver's Voyage,* 2:658-87.

40. *Ibid.,* pp. 747-70, gives Lieutenant Broughton's account of the Columbia River voyage. Kamehameha ceded the Hawaiian Islands to Vancouver the following winter, but the British never acted upon this diplomatic achievement.

41. *Ibid.,* 4:1231-1391, which covers the third survey season in Alaska. Contacts with Purtov in Yakutat Bay are described on pp. 1313, 1329-31. Baranov apparently sent three messages to Vancouver via Purtov suggesting that they meet, but Baranov never kept the appointments. (pp. 1259-60).

42. Anderson, *Vancouver,* p. 213. Cook's longest expedition was his second, but it covered 10,000 fewer miles than Vancouver's voyage.

43. *Ibid.,* p. 232; William H. Dall, *Alaska and Its Resources* (Boston: Lee and Shepard, 1870), p. 316.

44. Tikhmenev, *Russian-American Company,* pp. 41-80; Okun, *Russian-American Company,* pp. 50-54.

45. Urey Lisiansky, *A Voyage round the World in 1803 . . . 1806 Performed . . . in the Ship Neva* (London: John Booth, 1814). The attack and flight of the Tlingit are at pp. 157-63.

46. G. H. von Langsdorff, *Voyages and Travels in Various Parts of the World* (London: Henry Colburn, 1814), 2:87-91, 220-24 (hereafter von Langsdorff, *Travels*).

47. Charles E. Chapman, *A History of California, the Spanish Period* (New York: Macmillan, 1921), pp. 397-417. The Rezanov visit, and the courtship of the Doña Concepción Argüello, is discussed on pages 411-17.

48. Cook, *Flood Tide,* pp. 498-99; von Langsdorff, *Travels,* 2:182-86. The young Doña Concepción was long unaware of Rezanov's death, but remained faithful to his promised return. She rejected all suitors and, at length, took the robes of a nun and devoted her life to charity. Not until 1842 did she learn of the death from Sir George Simpson of the Hudson's Bay Company. The story is remembered in a 1902 Bret Harte ballad. Hector Chevigny, *Lost Empire* (New York: Macmillan, 1937), offers a popular and sentimental look at Rezanov's grand plans for coastal empire.

49. Cook, *Flood Tide,* pp. 345-49, 353-56.

50. Tikhmenev, *Russian-American Company,* pp. 131-42; Richard A. Pierce, *Russia's Hawaiian Adventure, 1815-17* (Kingston, Ont.: Limestone Press, 1976).

Part 1 Motives and Objectives

IRIS H. W. ENGSTRAND

Spain's Role in Pacific Exploration during the Age of Enlightenment

By the latter half of the eighteenth century, scientific inquiry had joined the established motives of territorial acquisition, commercial gain, and religious conversion as dominant themes for European exploration. The work of the Swedish botanist Carolus Linnaeus,[1] the writings of the French encyclopedists, the activities of the Royal Society of London, the founding of the American Philosophical Society, and worldwide interest in the transit of Venus had all left their imprint on the intellectual climate of the times. Europeans were similarly influenced by the concept of naturalism, the assumption that the whole universe of mind and matter was subject to and controlled by natural law. Its acceptance caused men of the Enlightenment to turn with enthusiasm to rediscovering their own lands: studying and recording natural resources and noting the customs and history of a region. Ancient authority was no longer sufficient to establish the truth of long-accepted propositions; everything on earth, and even beyond, was submitted to questioning and new investigation.

Men of the eighteenth century broke with Aristotelian tradition and adopted a method of inquiry based upon direct observation and reason. The critical spirit of the age inspired intellectuals to reevaluate previous knowledge and propose a geographical, historical, and statistical survey of the New World, one that would leave no corner uncataloged. This kind of scientific zeal existed in the leading countries of Europe, especially in England and France, and to a lesser extent in Sweden, Russia, Germany, Prussia, Italy, and the Netherlands. The young United States also participated. All had explorers and scientists in the field cataloging and pictorially reproducing the zoology, botany, and geography of the Old and New Worlds.[2]

Although much of this intellectual enthusiasm is well documented, general works on the European Enlightenment seldom include the accomplishments of Spain. Several factors combined to prevent Spanish scientists from receiving recognition for their achievements in discovering and classifying fauna and flora during the late eighteenth century. Even though expeditions started out

El Cacique de Mulgrave acompañado de otras Canoas pide la paz á las Corbetas

Chief of Mulgrave and his delegation greet Malaspina's corvettes, seeking peace.
Sketch probably by José Cardero, 1791. *Museo de America, Madrid*

with full government support, by the time of their return, the vacillating policies of Carlos IV (1788–1808) had resulted in court intrigues and international disputes. These problems plus the Napoleonic invasion all but ensured the obscurity of Spanish efforts, while those of England and France became better known throughout the world. Recently, however, as a result of the quincentenary and bicentennial celebrations of the voyages of Columbus and Malaspina, much has been done by Spanish researchers, as well as historians in Canada, Mexico, and the United States, to remedy the lack of information about Spain's contributions. At the same time, with research continuing by scholars concentrating on English, French, Russian, American, and other nations' activities, it is possible to show the interrelationships of the European and American scientific communities during the Age of Enlightenment.[3]

In Spain, the subject of botany had commanded royal attention since the first Bourbon king, Felipe V (1700–1746), had requested all state officials in the Spanish empire to watch for unusual specimens of plants, animals, and minerals and send them to Madrid. He had also required two Spaniards, Jorge Juan and Antonio de Ulloa, to accompany a French scientific expedition to South America in 1735.[4] Fernando VI (1746–1759) continued the crown's interest in scientific inquiry and encouraged Ulloa to found a museum of natural history in Madrid in 1752. Fernando VI also saw to it that the Swedish botanist Pehr Loefling, a student of Linnaeus's who had promoted his mentor's works in Spain in 1751, be allowed to accompany a botanical expedition to Venezuela in 1754.[5] Loefling followed the path set by Pehr Kalm, a fellow botanist who traveled through North America in 1748–51 seeking plants adaptable to the Swedish climate.[6]

Although the major reforming efforts of Carlos III were directed toward political and economic development, the enlightened Spanish king encouraged intellectual pursuits by sponsoring the establishment in Madrid of the Royal Botanical Garden, the Royal Academy of Medicine, and an astronomical observatory. Staff members of these centers assessed the accuracy of new knowledge and passed judgment on the new truths. Inspired by the work of Linnaeus and excited by the amount of information contained in Buffon's encyclopedic *Natural History of Animals*,[7] Spanish naturalists especially desired to apply new methods of identification to the botanical, zoological, and mineralogical resources of North and South America.

In France, the high regard for knowledge was shown by the publication during the years from 1751 to 1772 of the *Encyclopédie; ou, dictionnaire raisoné des sciences, des arts et des métiers,* generally edited by Diderot and d'Alembert and completed in seventeen large folio volumes. Throughout the work there was "an implication that the cause of humanity would be promoted not by the right theological doctrines, but by the right secular knowledge. Quietly and

The chief of Descanso Bay on Gabriola Island. Ink and wash drawing by José
Cardero. *Museo de America, Madrid*

View of the Vernacci Channel inside the entrance to the Strait of Juan de Fuca, by José Cardero, 1792. *Museo de America, Madrid*

efficiently the supernatural sanctions on which the *Ancien Regime* rested were taken away."[8] In addition, Charles de Brosses in 1756 wrote *Histoire des navigations aux terres australes,* a major history of Pacific exploration that urged further examination (as well as colonial settlements) by France. It was translated into English by John Callander in 1766–68 without mention of the original author and substituting England for France in making a case for English expeditions.[9]

Louis Antoine de Bougainville, a French army officer who had served against the British with Montcalm at Quebec, was given command of a voyage of exploration around the world after France's defeat in the Seven Years' War. Bougainville, who had written a treatise on calculus and established his reputation as a diplomat and a scientist, took two ships with a two hundred-man crew and sailed across the Atlantic with scientific inquiry as a major goal.[10] On board were the botanist Philibert de Commerson and the young astronomer Pierre Antoine Verón. They sailed from France on November 15, 1766, identified a flowering vine in South America that they named the bougainvillea, visited Tahiti, navigated through the Samoan and New Hebrides groups, sailed along the New Guinea coast, and rounded the Cape of Good Hope.

Bougainville completed the first French circumnavigation of the world on March 16, 1769.[11] As he arrived home, James Cook of the British Royal Navy was already in the Pacific and bound for Tahiti to observe the transit of Venus on June 3, 1769. This event, measured from different stations around the world, would help scientists calculate the distance from the earth to the sun.[12] Cook's was the first of three British voyages that would eclipse everything that had gone before, both in the scope of new discoveries and in their contributions to science.

Captain Cook, commanding the *Endeavour,* sailed from Plymouth, England, on August 26, 1768, bound for Tahiti and to search for the fabled southern continent, Terra Australis, thought to lie somewhere in the southern ocean.[13] With him were Joseph Banks, a wealthy young man with a passion for science; Daniel Carl Solander, a naturalist who had studied with Linnaeus; and Sydney Parkinson, an illustrator with a keen eye for detail. The political and geographical results of the voyage were of great importance, and the botanical results would have had at least a comparable effect had Banks and Solander been able to publish them within a few years of their return. Linnaeus believed that if the botanical plates were made available "the world would be . . . benefited by all these discoveries and the foundations of true science would be strengthened."[14]

Unfortunately, the British had problems publishing the complete results, but interested persons, thanks to Banks's generosity, were able to share in his home the descriptive text by Solander, the herbarium specimens, and the drawings by Parkinson, who died on the voyage. In November 1784 the text and the

Iris H. W.
Engstrand

30

copper plates engraved after the drawings were close to completion, and Banks wrote that "all that is left is so little that it can be completed in two months." But by that time Solander had been dead two years, and gone too were Cook and Linnaeus. International events prevented planned publication.[15]

Also in 1768, following a precedent of cooperation established with the French earlier in the century, Carlos III gave official sanction to a combined Franco-Spanish expedition of astronomers assigned to observe the transit of Venus in Baja California during June 1769. Responding to the urgings of British scientists who had sent Captain Cook to Tahiti, Spain appointed two qualified naval officers, Vicente Doz and Salvador Medina, to accompany the party of Abbé Chappe d'Auteroche from the Paris Academy of Science. Their destination was San José del Cabo, where, with the assistance of the Mexican-born astronomer Joaquín Velázquez de León, they set up their observatory, one of seventy-seven stations around the world. Despite the deaths of Chappe, Medina, and several other participants, results of the observations were successfully transmitted to Paris and coordinated with those of one hundred fifty-one other reporters. The English astronomer Thomas Hornsby in 1771 used the information to conclude the mean distance of the earth from the sun to be 93,726,900 English miles, a good estimate for the time.[16]

Captain James Cook circumnavigated the globe following his brief stay in Tahiti in 1769. He completed a second voyage around the world, sailing in the opposite direction, in 1775. On his third voyage of exploration, in 1778, the intrepid captain discovered the Hawaiian Islands and then sailed to the Pacific coast in search of a Northwest Passage. He entered Nootka Sound, anchoring in a bay he named Friendly Cove. Cook remained in the area for nearly a month, compiling a vocabulary of local words, investigating the surrounding country, and describing the Indians in some detail. He continued north along the coast of Alaska, continuing his many scientific endeavors. His survey concluded at the Arctic Ocean, where ice blocked further penetration. Failing to find a passage to the Atlantic, Cook turned his ships to the south and returned to Hawaii, where he was killed by hostile Natives at Kealakekua Bay on February 14, 1779.[17]

Spain, in the meantime, continued its pursuit of scientific interests. In 1777, the Spanish crown named the botanist Hipólito Ruiz as chief of an expedition designed to accomplish "the methodical examination and identification of the products of nature" in the viceroyalty of Peru. Accompanied by José Antonio Pavón (a fellow Spanish botanist), Joseph Dombey (a French naturalist with a doctorate in medicine), and two artists, Ruiz made an extensive examination of plant life throughout the viceroyalty and parts of Chile. Returning to Madrid in 1788, Ruiz and Pavón brought with them an impressive herbarium of dried specimens and one hundred twenty-four live plants for use in the royal botanical garden. Although plagued by financial difficulties and required to deal with Carlos IV in gaining royal support for their work, Ruiz and Pavón were able to publish three volumes of *Flora peruviana et chilensis.*[18]

In Santa Fé de Bogotá, capital of the viceroyalty of Nueva Granada, another Spanish botanist, José Celestino Mutis, received a royal sanction in 1783 to investigate the fauna and flora of that region. Having periodically requested crown support for botanical studies following his arrival as physician to the viceroy in 1760, Mutis was gratified finally to be appointed director of an official expedition. Commissioned as first botanist and astronomer, he examined the area encompassed by present-day Colombia. Probably the most significant result of Mutis's work was the remission to Madrid of almost 7,000 drawings, the majority in color, of the flora of Nueva Granada.[19]

Plans for the Royal Scientific Expedition to New Spain were formulated in 1785, just two years after the crown's sanction of Mutis's efforts. In 1787 the expedition was approved for a six-year term to establish a botanical garden in Mexico City, offer professional courses in botany, and survey the fauna and flora of New Spain. José Mariano Moziño, a Mexican-born physician, studied botany under Spanish members of the expedition and later accompanied Juan Francisco de la Bodega y Quadra to Nootka Sound in 1792. The work of the expedition was never fully appreciated because its return to Spain was plagued by the threats of the French invasion in 1808.[20]

Concurrent with the beginnings of Spain's Royal Scientific Expedition was the French around-the-world voyage commanded by Jean François Galaup, Count of Lapérouse. Departing from Brest on the first of August 1785, Lapérouse proposed to carry out his nation's objectives to increase geographical knowledge, seek the Northwest Passage, and examine the commercial and political possibilities of the North Pacific area. After successful visits to Hawaii, the Pacific coast, and Botany Bay, Lapérouse's two ships were tragically wrecked on the reef of Vanikoro, one of the Santa Cruz Islands, in 1788. The journals of the expedition, containing valuable information in terms of cartography, scientific investigation, and artistic impressions, had fortunately been forwarded to Paris for study and publication.[21]

Because Captain Cook's final voyage of 1778 to the Northwest Coast had opened the door to large profits in sea otter and other furs, considerations beyond pure science dominated the international scene. After 1789, the matter of sovereignty over the west coast of North America, and indeed over the entire Pacific basin, came to a head on the Northwest Coast when England refused to heed Spain's demand for a hasty departure. The controversy arising from the conflict at Nootka Sound needed to be solved. Although Spain had a strong claim for title based on existing European criteria, her archrival England possessed the naval strength to buttress a weaker claim.[22]

In order to bolster Spain's position, Carlos IV, acting upon the advice of the Minister of Marine Antonio Valdés, determined in 1790 that Alejandro Malaspina's expedition, currently sailing off the coast of South America, should proceed as far north as Alaska to map in detail the coastline of the Pacific Northwest. Furthermore, because of renewed speculation, they were to search again for the long-sought Northwest Passage, known in Spain as the Strait of Anian or the Strait of Ferrer Maldonado, obviously a key geopolitical location. Scientists and artists of the Malaspina expedition mapped the northern shores, drew coastal profiles, studied the Natives, investigated fauna and flora, and described mineral resources. Malaspina returned to Spain in 1794. Although he was hailed at first for his success, he then met with political disaster that resulted in his imprisonment then exile.

In 1792, a year after the Malaspina visit to the Northwest Coast, Bodega y Quadra met with the British commissioner George Vancouver to resolve the boundary questions arising out of the Nootka Sound Controversy. José Moziño, who accompanied Bodega on his mission, studied Native cultures, fauna, and flora. His ethnographic study, *Noticias de Nutka,* resulted from this effort.[23] Moziño also met with the Scottish botanist Archibald Menzies, who, as a member of Vancouver's party, also had instructions to investigate "the whole of the natural history" of the countries visited and to classify all trees, shrubs, plants, grasses, ferns, and mosses by their scientific names. Menzies and Moziño collected plants together and compared notes on local fauna.[24]

Spain's interest in supporting a costly botanical expedition to New Spain declined steadily during the reign of Carlos IV. Certain members of the court could not understand either the value of such an undertaking or the amount of time a team of scientists needed to complete a botanical survey from Nicaragua to Alaska. Certainly, they reasoned, the two-year extension of the original six-year contract was more than enough time to complete any unfinished projects. In 1802, Moziño accompanied the director, Martin Sessé, to Madrid to edit the manuscript materials and gain support for a new *Flora Mexicana* based on their collections and the approximately 3,000 paintings made by the artists employed in Mexico.[25]

Having accepted an appointment as director of the Spanish Museum of Natural History during the French occupation, Moziño was branded a traitor by returning Spanish patriots in 1812 and forced to flee with the expedition's manuscripts, drawings, and herbaria to Montpellier. After working with the Swiss botanist DeCandolle in Geneva, Moziño finally received permission to return to Spain in 1817. He died in Barcelona in May 1820.[26] Menzies, Moziño's colleague at Nootka, returned to England and published several articles in the *Transactions* of the Linnean Society of London. Although Menzies was a generous donor of the collections made during his voyages, his specimens were not described and recorded for many years. When Frederick Pursh was writing his *Flora americae septentrionalis* (1814), he concentrated his attention mainly on the collection of plants made by Lewis and Clark from 1804 to 1806.[27] Menzies, like Moziño, did not therefore receive credit for a number of species that he had seen and collected ten years before Pursh.[28]

Thus, the several unfortunate occurrences that befell the returning members of the eighteenth-century scientific expeditions resulted in some cases in the loss of materials and in others in postponed publication and credit. In England and France, despite the American War for Independence and the French Revolution, scientific inquiry went forward and the journals of Cook, Vancouver, Bougainville, and Lapérouse were duly published. In Spain, however, the political situation that brought exile for Malaspina and Moziño was not conducive to continued efforts. Not only was it impossible to assemble and edit gathered material, but, the changed circumstances in Spain's colonial empire also prevented similar subsequent efforts. Peninsular scientists would never again be given such free reign to examine and calculate the natural resources of the New World.

Today, however, a resurgent spirit of international cooperation has made possible the recovery and publication of the valuable work of both Europeans and Americans, North and South, who contributed to the wealth of knowledge during the late eighteenth century. As a result of recent scholarship, clearly formed personalities have emerged from partially obscured figures, and a new appreciation of their scientific discoveries has been gained.

NOTES

1. Linnaeus set out to organize all known plants first by their class, then by their order, genus, and species. As the basis of his classification, he took the presence and character, or the absence, of distinctive reproductive organs. In his *Systema Naturae, Genera Plantarum, Classes Plantarum* (1738), *Philosophia Botanica* (1751), and *Species Plantarum* (1753), he built up his system of classification, which, though somewhat artificially contrived, achieved almost immediate acceptance throughout Europe. Born in 1707, he was knighted by the king of Sweden in 1761 and became Carl von Linné. At his death in 1778, his widow sold his library and botanical collections were bought from his widow by James Edward Smith, who with others founded the Linnaean Society of London in 1788.

2. The travels of officials, merchants, and scientists between Europe and the Americas allowed a constant exchange of information. Despite some effort at censorship, ideas of the Enlightenment reached Spain and the Spanish colonies with almost the same speed as they entered other areas. Further, books and periodicals from the United States influenced Spanish colonial and peninsular thought. Benjamin Franklin achieved

membership in the Spanish Academy of History in Madrid, and his work was sent to Spanish America.

3. See, for example, papers resulting from the bicentennial of James Cook's visit to the Northwest Coast in Robin Fisher and Hugh Johnston, eds., *Captain James Cook and His Times* (Seattle: University of Washington Press, 1979); David Mackay, *In the Wake of Cook: Exploration, Science, and Empire, 1780-1801* (London: Croom Helm, 1985); Robin Inglis, "The Effect of Lapérouse on Spanish Thinking about the Northwest Coast," and others in *Spain and the North Pacific Coast: Essays in Recognition of the Bicentennial of the Malaspina Expedition, 1791-1792,* ed. Robin Inglis (Vancouver: Vancouver Maritime Museum, 1992); and Robin Fisher and Hugh Johnston, eds., *From Maps to Metaphors: The Pacific World of George Vancouver* (Vancouver: University of British Columbia Press, 1993). Recent Spanish publications include Carmen Sotos Serrano, *Los pintores de la expedición de Alejandro Malaspina* (Madrid: Real Academia de Historia, 1982); María de los Angeles Calatayud, *Catálogo de los expediciones y viajes científicos españoles: Siglos XVIII y XIX* (Madrid: Consejo Superior de Investigaciones Científicas, 1984); María Dolores Higueras, ed., *Northwest Coast of America: Iconographic Album of the Malaspina Expedition* (Madrid: Museo Naval, 1991); and, in Mexico, Virginia González Claverán, *La expedición científica de Malaspina en Nueva España* (Mexico: El Colegio de México, 1988). See also Iris H. W. Engstrand, *Spanish Scientists in the New World: The Eighteenth-Century Expeditions* (Seattle: University of Washington Press, 1981).

4. See Jorge Juan and Antonio de Ulloa, *A Voyage to South America,* trans. John Adams (New York: Alfred A. Knopf, 1964), pp. 3–19. Ulloa and Juan spent the years from 1735 to 1746 in South America, at times in the company of Louis Godin, Pierre Bouguer, and Charles Marie la Condamine, members of a French expedition to the northern regions of South America.

5. Francisco Javier Puerto Sarmiento, *La ilusión Quebrada: Botánica, sanidad y política científica en la España ilustrada* (Madrid: Consejo Superior de Investigaciones Científicas, 1988), pp. 11–13; Arthur Robert Steele, *Flowers for the King: The Expedition of Ruiz and Pavón and the Flora of Peru* (Durham, N.C.: Duke University Press, 1969), p. 23.

6. Pehr Kalm, another student of Linnaeus's, visited Mexico in 1781–82 and gathered a native lobelia (probably *Lobelia laxiflora angustifolia*) used in medicine and presented it to the Academy of Stockholm in 1782. His name is found in the genus *Kalmia* of evergreen shrubs of the heath family. *Kalmia latifolia* (mountain laurel) is common in North America.

7. Georges Louis Leclerc, Count of Buffon (1707–1788), a zoologist, was director of the French Royal Museum and a member of the Academy of Science.

8. David Ogg, *Europe of the Ancien Regime, 1715-1783* (New York: Harper & Row, 1965), p. 325.

9. John Dunmore, "Anglo-French Rivalry in the Pacific 1700–1800," unpublished paper presented at Vancouver Conference on Exploration and Discovery, Simon Fraser University, April 24–26, 1992, Vancouver, B.C.

10. J. C. Beaglehole, *The Exploration of the Pacific,* 3d ed. (Stanford: Stanford University Press, 1966), pp. 213–28.

11. On board was Jeanne Baret, perhaps the first European woman to circum-

navigate the globe. Disguised as a man (Jean), she signed on the expedition as an assistant to the botanist Commerson.

12. Because this rare phenomenon would not occur again until 1874 and 1882, and the results achieved in 1761 had been unsatisfactory, it was crucial that accurate measurements of the transit of Venus across the sun's disc be made. See Harry Woolf, *The Transits of Venus: A Study of Eighteenth-Century Science* (Princeton: Princeton University Press, 1959), pp. 150–97.

13. See J. C. Beaglehole, ed., *The Journals of Captain James Cook on His Voyages of Discovery*, Vol. I: *The Voyage of the Endeavour, 1768-1771* (Cambridge: Cambridge University Press, 1968).

14. Quoted in the *Bulletin of the Hunt Institute for Botanical Documentation*, Carnegie-Mellon University, Pittsburgh, Pa. Vol. 3 (Spring/Summer 1981), p. 4. See also W. Kaye Lamb, "Banks and Menzies: Evolution of a Journal," in Fisher and Johnston, *From Maps to Metaphors*, pp. 227–44.

15. Photolithographic reproduction of the prints of Australian plants, accompanied by Solander's text, revised and edited by James Britten, were published from 1900 to 1905 under the title *Illustrations of Australian Plants Collected in 1770 during Captain Cook's Voyage round the World in H.M.S. Endeavour* (London: Cassell, Petter, Galpin, and Company).

16. Iris Wilson Engstrand, *Royal Officer in Baja California, 1768-1770: Joaquín Velázquez de León* (Los Angeles: Dawson's Book Shop, 1976), pp. 68–92.

17. See J. C. Beaglehole, *The Life of Captain James Cook* (Stanford: Stanford University Press, 1974), for a complete account of Cook's life.

18. Volumes 1, 2, and 3 were published in Madrid from 1798 through 1802; volumes 4 and 5 had to wait until the late 1950s to be published by the Instituto Botánico, A. J. Cavanilles in Madrid.

19. See María Pilar de San Pío Aladrén, ed., *Mutis y la real expedición botánica del Nuevo Reyno de Granada*, 2 vols. (Madrid: Villegas Editores, 1992).

20. See Engstrand, *Spanish Scientists in the New World*, pp. 13–32.

21. M. L. A. Milet-Mureau, ed., *Voyage de La Pérouse autour du monde* (Edinburgh: J. Moir, 1798); see also Julius S. Gassner, trans., *Voyages and Adventures of La Pérouse* (Honolulu: University of Hawaii Press, 1969).

22. See Warren L. Cook, *Flood Tide of Empire: Spain and the Pacific Northwest, 1543-1819* (New Haven, Conn.: Yale University Press), and William R. Manning, "The Nootka Sound Controversy," *American Historical Association Annual Report of 1904* (Washington, D.C: U.S. Government Printing Office, 1905), pp. 279–478.

23. See José Mariano Moziño, *Noticias de Nutka: An Account of Nootka Sound in 1792*, ed. and trans. Iris H. W. Engstrand (Seattle: University of Washington Press, 1970.)

24. See C. F. Newcombe, ed., *Menzies' Journal of Vancouver's Voyage April to October 1792* (Victoria, B.C.: W. H. Cullin, 1923).

25. Engstrand, *Spanish Scientists in the New World*, pp. 173–85.

26. Iris H. W. Engstrand, "Mexico's Pioneer Naturalist and the Spanish Enlightenment," *The Historian*, Vol. 53 (Autumn 1990), pp. 29–32.

27. Born Friedrich Pursch in Saxony in 1774, the German botanist is called "the first botanist to describe plants of the Pacific Coast in a flora of North America" by

Joseph Ewan (*Dictionary of Scientific Biography,* Vol. 11, 1975, p. 218). Pursh sailed for the United States in 1799 and was later employed by Benjamin Smith Barton, who planned a flora of North America to include the discoveries of Lewis and Clark. He returned to England and completed his *Flora americae septentrionalis* (London: White, Cochrane and Company, 1814) under the patronage of Aylmer Bourke Lambert.

28. Newcombe, *Menzies' Journal,* p. xi.

GLYNDWR WILLIAMS

George Vancouver, the Admiralty, and Exploration in the Late Eighteenth Century

N
o reader of George Vancouver's journal can fail to be aware that the explorer regarded his monumental survey of the Northwest Coast as complementary to the third and last voyage of his former commander, James Cook. Vancouver saw himself as the defender of Cook, "the great and first discoverer," whose reputation had been impugned, as he complained in Cook Inlet, by "the theoretical navigators, who have followed him in their closets."[1] The two voyages, of 1776–80 and 1791–95, have been closely linked ever since. They were the century's last two major discovery expeditions fitted out by the British admiralty for the Pacific, the climax to an intensive process of oceanic exploration that began with Commodore John Byron's sailing in 1764. Yet in terms of motive, conduct, and aftermath, Vancouver's voyage differed from that of his famous mentor, and in general the Pacific discovery voyages of the period conformed less to a preordained pattern than is sometimes supposed.

Interest by the admiralty in oceanic discovery had a slow and halting growth, for until the second half of the eighteenth century exploration and the pursuit of science were not normally regarded as responsibilities of government. Edmond Halley's three voyages in the *Paramore* (1698–1701), fitted out by the admiralty at the request of the Royal Society "to improve the knowledge of the Longitude and variations of the Compasse,"[2] remained an exception. Two rare naval expeditions of discovery, commanded by William Dampier (1699–1701) and Christopher Middleton (1741–42), were controversial and set unappealing precedents. Despite exhortations from such senior figures as George Anson, First Lord of the Admiralty from 1751 to 1762, the Royal Navy failed to establish any specialist surveying service or even a hydrographic office to supervise the publication of charts.

When in the 1760s and 1770s naval expeditions left England for the Pacific, the motives behind them fluctuated as both the diplomatic situation and the personalities of those in office changed. In the first discovery expedition of George III's reign, commanded by John Byron, "trade and navigation" were paramount. Its instructions from the First Lord of the Admiralty, the Earl of Egmont, particularly regarding the Falklands, represented a return to the anti-Spanish activities of English expeditions in the South Seas from the sixteenth century onward.[3]

By the time of James Cook's first voyage in 1768, the influence of the Royal Society, supported by the monarch himself, had added a different motive to the process. The observation of the transit of Venus lay behind Cook's instructions to visit the newly discovered island of Tahiti, and the more portentous part of his instructions—to search for "a Continent or Land of great extent" south of Tahiti—was a late addition.[4] In the end, it took Cook two voyages (1768-71 and 1772-75) not to find but to eliminate the conjectural southern continent. In doing so, he became the most celebrated navigator in Europe, but the guiding hand that did much to secure his fame belonged to the Earl of Sandwich, First Lord of the Admiralty by the time Cook returned from his first voyage. The earl insisted on the second voyage going ahead, despite worries from his ministerial colleagues about Spanish reactions, and he encouraged publication of the narratives of the Pacific explorers.

As Cook had written while on his first voyage, if English priority of discovery was to be asserted against the French and Spaniards, it was essential to have accounts "published by Authority."[5] The publication of Bougainville's *Voyage autour du monde* in 1771, with an English edition the following year, emphasized the urgency of the matter. It was Sandwich who arranged that Dr. John Hawkesworth edit Cook's and Banks's journals from the *Endeavour* voyage, together with those of their immediate predecessors.[6] Hawkesworth's *Voyages* of 1773 became an immediate bestseller, despite grumbles about his busy editorial pen. In contrast, the account of Cook's second voyage was very much his own, though Dr. John Douglas was employed to lend a more elegant literary touch to the explorer's homespun writing style.

Cook was never to see the lavish two-volume account of his second voyage, for by the time it was published in 1777 he was again in the Pacific on that last voyage, which was so closely linked with Vancouver's expedition fifteen years later. With the fabulous southern continent fading from view, another chimera of past ages—a navigable Northwest Passage—was once more drawing attention, and in early 1776 Cook had been tempted to take command of a new expedition to find the Pacific entrance of the passage. At the same time Cook was looking for the Pacific entrance of the passage, other naval vessels would search Baffin Bay for the eastern entrance.

This double-pronged plan constituted the most ambitious effort yet undertaken to find the Northwest Passage and raises the question of motive. Investigation more than two centuries later is made difficult because those most closely concerned with the enterprise left no written statements of their intentions, and the formal minutes and correspondence among the admiralty records provide few clues. The viewpoint of Daines Barrington, who regarded himself as the unofficial promoter of the expedition, was characteristic of the group of enthusiasts centered on the Royal Society who prompted and prodded Sandwich in early 1774 on the subject of an expedition to the North Pacific.[7] He was indignant that the Spaniards should regard news of the forthcoming venture with suspicion, and thought they should "be convinced that the English Nation is actuated merely by desiring to know as much as possible with regard to the planet which we inhabit."[8]

This attitude was understandably difficult for the Spaniards to grasp. From Drake to Anson the English had appeared in the South Seas as predators. News of British interest in the North Pacific sent spasms of alarm through Spanish officials in Madrid and Mexico City, already on guard against possible Russian incursions from the north.

Spanish suspicions may have had some basis, for the admiralty's decision to send expeditions to search for the Northwest Passage at a time when the international situation was worsening would seem to have been influenced by motives other than its customary desire for the promotion of natural history. It was not likely to overlook the possible strategic importance of a passage, even one north of sixty-five degrees north latitude, which is where Cook was to begin his search along the Northwest Coast of America. When hostilities with Spain threatened, the ministers' thoughts invariably turned to the prospect of raiding Spanish possessions in the Pacific, but always there was the objection that raiders sailing around Cape Horn faced a difficult haul into the South Seas and gave advance warning of their intentions.

A naval expedition coming through a northern passage would give no such warning. The attempts by the government to establish a base in the Falklands had shown Britain's interest in securing an entrance into the Pacific, and it may have been more than a coincidence that the decision to send a naval expedition to look for the Northwest Passage was made in the same year (1774) as the enforced abandonment of Port Egmont in those islands. The discovery of a northern route to the Pacific might compensate for the loss of control over the longer southern one.

In the end, Cook found no passage, but his explorations during the summer of 1778 put, for the first time, the long curve of the Northwest Coast of America from Nootka Sound to Bering Strait on the maps. On his three voyages Cook had established the salient features of the Pacific. As one of his officers, James King, wrote: "The Grand bounds of the four Quarters of the Globe are known."[9] The handsome three-volume official account was entrusted once more to Dr. Douglas, who compiled it from the journals of Cook, King, and the surgeon Anderson. In his preface Douglas looked to the future as he wrote

Glyndwr
Williams

of his and the other published accounts: "Every nation that sends a ship to sea will partake of the benefit; but Great Britain herself, whose commerce is boundless, must take the lead in reaping the full advantage of her own discoveries." [10]

Within three years of the publication of Cook's final accounts such a venture was well under way. The First Fleet sailed for Botany Bay to establish the first British settlement in Australia; Bligh and the *Bounty* left for Tahiti to collect breadfruit for the Caribbean plantations; and British vessels were on the Northwest Coast of America engaged in the sea otter trade, the potential of which had been learned during Cook's third voyage. With the change from exploration to exploitation, there came a change of agency. The admiralty gave way to government departments concerned more closely with trade and colonies.

In these years the ministry most involved was the Home Office, with functions that rather incongruously included oversight of Britain's far-flung colonial empire. There was also a change of personalities, for Sandwich resigned in March 1782, and none of his immediate successors showed his interest in exploration. If there was a single guiding light in the new surge of oceanic endeavor that followed Cook it was Sir Joseph Banks, not a minister at all, but even so a man of immense influence and energy. By now he was a baronet, president of the Royal Society, adviser to cabinet ministers, and patron of the sciences on an international scale, but he never forgot that he had been Cook's sailing companion on the first voyage.

In late 1780 James King, just back with the *Resolution* and *Discovery,* wrote to him, "I look up to you as the common center of we discoverers," [11] and Banks was fully to deserve this encomium in the years that followed. In the period of national reorganization after the War of American Independence he was a central figure in renewed imperial expansion.[12]

Nowhere was this more evident than in the North Pacific, where Banks was involved in several of the expeditions that visited the Northwest Coast to collect sea otter skins. Though primarily trading ventures, these expeditions also began to throw doubt on Cook's dismissal of the inland straits reported along the coast in the old narratives attributed to Juan de Fuca (1592) and Bartholomew de Fonte (1640). The news of these coastal explorations, and of the approach to the Northwest Coast of the fur traders of the interior, drew in another figure from the period of Cook's voyages. Alexander Dalrymple, onetime exponent of the great southern continent and now hydrographer to the East India Company, argued that a strait leading from the Pacific deep into the interior of North America might yet be found. Such a route would make possible a new northern network of trade encompassing North America, China, and Japan, and dominated by a union of the East India and Hudson's Bay companies.[13]

The late 1780s saw a great stir of projects that included the Northwest Coast,

George
Vancouver,
the
Admiralty,
and
Exploration

41

but at first government was not much involved. The explorers were servants of commercial companies—on land, Peter Pond and Alexander Mackenzie of the Northwest Company, David Thompson of the Hudson's Bay Company; at sea, George Dixon, Nathaniel Portlock, James Colnett, and Charles Duncan of the King George's Sound Company established by John Cadman Etches. In Britain, Banks and Dalrymple, though working independently of each other most of the time, acted as clearinghouses for the explorers' reports and began to put pressure on ministers. Even so, it was not until 1789 that Dalrymple and Dixon submitted proposals to Evan Nepean, the busy and influential Under Secretary at the Home Office, for an overland expedition across North America to the Pacific and for the establishment of a trading base on the Northwest Coast. This post, they pointed out, could be used to attack Spanish settlements and ships in time of war.[14]

All such plans and projects came to an abrupt halt when in February 1790 news reached London of the Spanish seizure of British ships and property at Nootka Sound the previous summer. Foremost among the initial reactions of the government was a scheme drawn up by Nepean on the instructions of Grenville, the Home Secretary, for a naval expedition to the Northwest Coast. It was to investigate the events of 1789, and then establish a settlement as a challenge to the traditional Spanish claims over the whole of the coast. Approved by the cabinet on February 23, the plan underwent several changes before being shelved as the situation deteriorated during the spring to a point when it seemed that general war with Spain was imminent. In its final version before it was laid aside, the expedition, commanded by Cook's old shipmate Henry Roberts, was to call at Port Jackson, Australia, and there take on board thirty members of the New South Wales Corps and convicts to help establish a settlement on the Northwest Coast "for the assistance of his Majesty's subjects in the prosecution of the fur trade from the N.W. coast of America." [15]

In this bringing together of the far north and the far south a new manifestation of European imperialism in the Pacific can be discerned. The destination of the expedition appears to have owed much to plans sent to Banks by Etches in 1788, and by Dixon in 1789, when he lauded the advantages of the Queen Charlotte Islands as a base.[16] It was this general region, indeed, rather than the sensitive area of Nootka, that Grenville and Nepean seem to have had in mind, for one of Roberts's ships was directed to land its settlers, if possible, at Queen Charlotte Sound.[17] Banks's advice was sought in the matter of what trade goods the settlement would need, and he sent in a long list costing, he estimated, £6,800. This was a not inconsiderable sum, but in language unusual for a government minister Grenville insisted that it was "very desirable not to stint that part of the service" and warned against any "ill-judged economy." [18]

Following the Nootka Sound Convention of October 1790, the naval expedi-

Glyndwr
Williams

tion was reinstated, but with different instructions and a different commander. George Vancouver, chosen as first lieutenant on the original expedition, was appointed commander of the *Discovery,* and the *Chatham* was provided as consort. Vancouver had sailed at the age of fifteen on Cook's second voyage, and again on the third. Since the admiralty paid off the *Discovery* after his appointment, Vancouver was able to choose his own officers; he selected several who had served with him in the West Indies. But it is a significant pointer to Banks's influence that he secured the appointment of Nathaniel Portlock as commander of the *Chatham* (for health reasons Portlock had to decline).[19] The Home Office was again responsible for the direction of the expedition, and in February 1791 Grenville sent the admiralty detailed instructions to pass on to Vancouver.[20] There also seems to have been some personal contact between Vancouver and the Home Secretary, with the indispensable Nepean in attendance.[21]

Vancouver was given two tasks: to receive restitution for the land and buildings at Nootka seized by Spain in April 1789, and to explore the Northwest Coast to sixty degrees north latitude for a waterway through the continent. That it was to be a route open to ocean-going vessels is clear from the instruction not "to pursue any inlet or river further than it shall appear to be navigable by vessels of such burden as might safely navigate the Pacific Ocean."[22] Vancouver's survey would be the more important because, by the convention of October 1790, Spain had been forced to abandon its exclusive claim to the Northwest Coast. That his task of receiving restitution at Nootka was second to the need for a comprehensive survey of the coast is shown by the fact that when he left England the details of the restitution had not been settled. He was promised further instructions by the *Daedalus* storeship, but when these arrived Vancouver found they contained only a general order from Count Floridablanca, the Spanish foreign minister, to the Spanish commandant at Nootka.[23] Priorities were set out in the cover letter from Henry Dundas, Grenville's successor as Home Secretary, to the admiralty that accompanied Floridablanca's order. This was to be given to the commander of the *Daedalus,* who was instructed "on meeting with Capt. Vancouver to deliver to him the Letters above mentioned relative to the Restitutions, and to put himself under his direction for the execution of this Service, in order that Capt. Vancouver may be impeded as little as possible in the progress of his intended Survey."[24]

If Grenville and the Home Office loomed large in the direction of the expedition, Banks's association with it went well beyond the appointment of the botanist, Archibald Menzies. At Grenville's request, Banks sent detailed instructions as to how Vancouver's survey should be conducted. Drawn up with James Rennell's help, these formed "the most detailed guide for scientific and marine exploration ever set out in the eighteenth century."[25] Even in Banks's

George
Vancouver,
the
Admiralty,
and
Exploration

43

supplementary instructions to Menzies on his botanical duties there was an extra dimension. By now it had been decided that Vancouver's expedition, unlike the one planned under Roberts, would not be concerned with establishing trading settlements. Even so, Banks instructed Menzies that he was to pay particular attention to the climate, soil, and natural products, in case it should at "any time hereafter be deemed expedient to send out Settlers from England."[26]

Something rather more substantial than survey work seems, however vaguely, to be envisaged here. In many ways, especially in the diversity of his interests, Banks was exceptional. But the patron of the sciences, cosmopolitan in outlook and friendships, ready to help scholars and travelers from all nations, was also determined to promote the well-being of Britain on a global scale. And this, more than once, entailed rivalry with Britain's European foes, and above all with France. It was, perhaps not altogether by chance, to a Frenchman that Banks wrote in 1788, "I certainly wish that my Country men should make discoveries of all kinds in preference to the inhabitants of other Kingdoms."[27]

For all the obvious links between Vancouver's commission and Cook's third voyage, the former was a more workaday affair than the latter—or than the Pacific expeditions of Bougainville, Lapérouse, and Malaspina. Except for Menzies, there were no specialist scientists, astronomers, or artists on board—and it was certainly not the "full-blown scientific expedition" claimed for it in a recent book.[28] Vancouver's orders stressed that in his quest for straits or rivers navigable by ocean-going craft he was not to concern himself with "too minute and particular an examination of the detail of the different parts of the coast."[29]

Once on the coast, he saw that this policy of doing things by halves was not satisfactory. To produce charts that would settle once and for all the question of a Northwest Passage through the continent, he had to survey the whole of the mainland coast, however tortuous, even though this meant working from the ships' boats most of the time. For Vancouver and his crews, life took on an annual cycle: winter at Hawaii, summer spent in arduous longboat work along the Northwest Coast, and a call at Nootka for the promised further instructions. They never came, and Vancouver grumbled, "I was still left totally in the dark what measures to pursue."[30] While Vancouver agonized about the area of land at Nootka to be given up by Spain, in London his bulky folder describing his first laborious negotiations provoked an impatient comment from someone, probably Philip Stephens, Secretary of the admiralty: "All that We are anxious really about in this particular part of the Business is the Safety of our National honour which renders a Restitution necessary. The Extent of that Restitution is not of much moment."[31]

The great survey itself was carried on with a grim doggedness, as Vancouver and his men traced the coast regardless of whether Spanish or other surveying expeditions had already been there. There is little of the drama of Cook's season on the coast in 1778, when hopes of finding a passage to the north rose and fell almost from day to day. From the beginning, Vancouver seems to have been convinced that the reports of a great strait were groundless. His view seems to have been echoed in an early draft by Grenville of his instructions (later modified): "The discoveries of Captain Cook & of the later Navigators seem to prove that any actual Communication by Sea, such as has commonly been understood by the name of a North West passage cannot be looked for with any probability of success."[32] Triumph rather than dejection was the note struck in Vancouver's report from Nootka to his agent in London on the results of his three-year survey: "We arrived here this day month [2 October 1794] all in high health and spirits having *finally determined* the nonexistence of any water communication between this & the opposite side of America."[33]

He saw his mission, not as an attempt to find the Northwest Passage but as one to prove once and for all that it did not exist. Unlike Cook in 1778, Vancouver appears to have sought no advice from his officers as he pursued his detailed survey to the bitter end. He was not a tolerant man, and worsening health did nothing to improve his temper. It is perhaps significant that the logs of his officers reveal little of that detail and diversity of view that make the journals from Cook's third voyage of such interest. Apart from Puget's journal, the official logs that have survived are studiously brief and noncommittal. For Vancouver, his survey enabled him to contradict and humiliate those theorists who in their impatience to find a passage had belittled the achievements of James Cook.

All this was in print by August or September 1798, when the three-volume account of the voyage was published. Vancouver himself had died a few months earlier, on May 12, 1798. As was now the custom, the admiralty had made it clear to Vancouver soon after his return that it wished the events of his voyage to be made available "for Publick information," and it paid for the cost of engraving the charts and views.[34] Significantly, some of these were "in Mr. Dalrymple's Office," for in 1795 a Hydrographic Office had at last been established, with Alexander Dalrymple as the first hydrographer.[35]

Sailing twice with Cook, Vancouver had graduated in the most demanding of training schools. The insistence on exactness can be taken for granted, but there is more to his surveys than this. Several of those who had sailed with Cook inherited from him a sense of working and writing for posterity. As early as 1770 Cook, then still a little known lieutenant, had declared of his chart of the North Island of New Zealand: "I believe that this Island will never be found to differ materially from the figure I have given it."[36] Similarly, Vancouver's journal entry of August 1794, as he completed three seasons of surveys on the Northwest Coast, is weary in its finality:

George
Vancouver,
the
Admiralty,
and
Exploration

45

I trust the precision with which the survey of the coast of North West America has been carried into effect, will remove every doubt, and set aside every opinion of a north-west passage, or any water communication navigable for shipping, existing between the North Pacific, and the interior of the American continent, within the limits of our researches. The discovery that no such communication does exist has been zealously pursued, and with a degree of minuteness far exceeding the letter of my commission or instructions.

He had, Vancouver concluded, made "the history of our transactions on the north-west coast of America, *as conclusive as possible.*"[37]

The thirty-year period between Byron's voyage and that of Vancouver had seen a dramatic expansion in Europe's knowledge of the Pacific. It had brought a new dimension to the study of man and nature, revealed hitherto unknown areas for trade and settlement, and extended the boundaries of international rivalry. With hindsight, the pursuit of knowledge and all that followed seems relentless and logical. Yet to see this activity in the Pacific as part of some master plan of government would be a mistake. This is not to say that expeditions were not linked to wider national considerations, only that such considerations changed from time to time and were often not the prime motivation. Still less is it possible to identify a single government department or ministry as the directing force. Chance, and the impact of individual personality, could be as important as official government policy.

In terms of the promotion and organization of the Pacific voyages under George III, the dominant personalities were Egmont, Sandwich, and Banks. Egmont's period as First Lord of the admiralty was brief, from 1763 to 1766, but during those years he set the process of Pacific voyaging in train. From 1771 to 1782 the First Lord of the admiralty was the Earl of Sandwich, and his role was doubly important—in his promotion of Cook's second and third voyages and in his insistence on publication of those accounts. After Sandwich, the torch of Pacific enterprise passed to his Fenland neighbor and friend, Joseph Banks, not a minister but with more influence and a higher reputation than most ministers. Paradoxically, for the first time there seems to have been some overall direction of British efforts. Whatever his persuasive powers, Banks had to work through government departments, and his main collaborators were at the admiralty and the Home Office, in particular those "men of business," Philip Stephens and Evan Nepean.

But Banks was his own man and had his own interests to pursue, notably on the botanical side of the voyages. His role is sometimes shadowy, often difficult to assess in precise terms, for much of what he did went unrecorded in official documents. There is enough evidence to show his role in the chain of events that culminated in Vancouver's voyage, though his own relations with Vancouver were poor.[38] The cause of the friction—Menzies's duties as collector on the expedition—was a sign that, however large natural history loomed in Banks's world, for the hard-headed agents of imperial expansion it was not of much moment. One of the fascinating side issues of Vancouver's voyage is the realization that on the expedition's return Banks tried hard to sponsor an alternative and, one can only suggest, rival account to the admiralty-approved version written by Vancouver.[39] It is a reminder of how loosely drawn the lines of authority could be in the eighteenth-century world and a warning against supposing too rigid a division between official and unofficial, public and private.

NOTES

1. George Vancouver, *A Voyage of Discovery to the North Pacific Ocean and round the World, 1791-1795*, ed. W. Kaye Lamb, 4 vols. (London: Hakluyt Society, 1984), 4:1243 (hereafter Lamb, *Vancouver's Voyage*).

2. Norman J. Thrower, ed., *The Three Voyages of Edmond Halley in the Paramore, 1698-1701* (London: Hakluyt Society, 1981), pp. 268-69.

3. Byron's "secret instructions" are reprinted in Robert E. Gallagher, ed., *Byron's Journal of His Circumnavigation, 1764-1766* (Cambridge: Cambridge University Press, 1964), pp. 3-8 .

4. Printed in J. C. Beaglehole, ed., *The Journals of Captain James Cook on His Voyages of Discovery*, Vol. 1: *The Voyage of the Endeavour, 1768-1771* (Cambridge: Cambridge University Press, 1955), p. cclxxviii (hereafter Beaglehole, *Voyage of the Endeavour*).

5. *Ibid.*, p. 479.

6. See John L. Abbott, *John Hawkesworth: Eighteenth-century Man of Letters* (Madison: University of Wisconsin Press, 1982), pp. 143-45.

7. Council Minutes, 6:214, 216, 220, 227 (Feb. 10, 17, March 7, 12, 1774), Royal Society Archives, London; and Earl of Sandwich to Daines Barrington, March 12, 1774, Sandwich Manuscripts, National Mantine Museum, London.

8. Daines Barrington, *Miscellanies* (London: J. Nichols and J. White, 1781), p. 472.

9. J. C. Beaglehole, ed., *The Journals of Captain James Cook on His Voyages of Discovery*, Vol. 2: *The Voyage of the Resolution and Discovery, 1776-1780* (Cambridge: Cambridge University Press, 1967), p. 1436.

10. John Douglas, Introduction to *A Voyage to the Pacific Ocean . . .* by James Cook and James King (London: Fielding and Hardy, 1784), Vol. 1.

11. James King to Joseph Banks, Oct. 1780, Dawson Turner Copies, 1:304, British Museum (Natural History), London.

12. See David Mackay, *In the Wake of Cook: Exploration, Science and Empire, 1780-1801* (London: Croom Helm, 1985); H. B. Carter, *Sir Joseph Banks, 1743-1820* (London: British Museum, 1988).

13. Howard Fry, *Alexander Dalrymple (1737-1808) and the Expansion of British Trade* (Toronto: University of Toronto Press, 1970), chap. 8; Glyndwr Williams, "Myth and Reality: The Theoretical Geography of Northwest America from Cook to Vancouver," in *From Maps to Metaphors: The Pacific World of George Vancouver*, ed. Robin Fisher and Hugh Johnston (Vancouver: University of British Columbia Press, 1993), pp. 35-50.

14. See Mackay, *In the Wake of Cook,* p. 84.

15. W. W. Grenville to Governor Arthur Phillip, March 1790 (draft), *Historical Records of Australia,* Series 1, Vol. 1 (Sydney, 1914), pp. 161–64.

16. See F. W. Howay, "Four Letters from Richard Cadman Etches to Sir Joseph Banks, 1788-1792," *British Columbia Historical Quarterly,* Vol. 6 (1942), pp. 125–39; George Dixon to Joseph Banks, Oct. 20, 1789, PN 1:2, Sutro Library, San Francisco.

17. W. W. Grenville to Commodore William Cornwallis, March 31, 1790, H. O. 28161, p. 273, Public Record Office, London.

18. Grenville to Joseph Banks, April 12, 1790, H. O. 42/16, p. 18, Public Record Office. Vancouver's expedition was allocated more than £10,000 for trade goods. Lamb, *Vancouver's Voyage,* 1:39, n.l.

19. Nathaniel Portlock to Joseph Banks, Dec. 26, 1790, MS 743/1, Mitchell Library, State Library of New South Wales, Sydney, Australia.

20. These instructions are found in Lamb, *Vancouver's Voyage,* 1:283–86.

21. *Ibid.,* 4:1581.

22. *Ibid.,* 1:284.

23. *Ibid.,* 1:286–88.

24. Henry Dundas to Admiralty, July 6, 1791, Adm 1/4156, no. 50, Public Record Office.

25. Mackay, *In the Wake of Cook,* p. 100. Kaye Lamb points out that "there is no evidence that Vancouver actually received" Banks's instructions (*Vancouver's Voyage,* 1:45).

26. Joseph Banks to Archibald Menzies, Feb. 22, 1791, Add MSS. 33, 979, folio 75v, British Library, London.

27. Joseph Banks to Buache de la Neuville, March 20, 1788, Dawson Turner Copies, 6:89–90, British Museum (Natural History).

28. Lynne Withey, *Voyages of Discovery: Captain Cook and the Exploration of the Pacific* (London: Morrow Press, 1988), p. 442. The astronomer William Gooch was sent out on the *Daedalus* to join Vancouver, but he was killed in the Sandwich Islands on his way to the Northwest Coast.

29. Lamb, *Vancouver's Voyage,* 1:285.

30. *Ibid.,* 4:1580.

31. *Ibid.,* 1:108.

32. *Ibid.,* 1:41.

33. *Ibid.,* 4:1601 (emphasis in original).

34. *Ibid.,* 1:226.

35. See Fry, *Alexander Dalrymple,* pp. 249ff.

36. Beaglehole, *Voyage of the Endeavour,* pp. 275–76.

37. Lamb, *Vancouver's Voyage,* 4:1390, 1391 (emphasis in original).

38. See, for example, Banks's letter to Menzies, Aug. 10, 1791: "How Captain Vancouver will behave to you is more than I can guess unless I was to judge by his conduct towards me which was not such as I am used to receiving from Persons in his situation" (*ibid.,* 1:32).

39. See W. Kaye Lamb, "Banks and Menzies: Evolution of a Journal," in Fisher and Johnston, *From Maps to Metaphors,* pp. 227–44.

Glyndwr
Williams

ROBIN INGLIS

Lapérouse 1786:
A French Naval Visit to Alaska

I n the early evening of October 17, 1788, the twenty-two-year-old Barthelemy
de Lesseps arrived at the great royal palace at Versailles, outside Paris. He
was hurried into an audience with King Louis XVI, who soon received a
long-awaited first-hand account of the progress of the French navy's great
voyage of exploration into the Pacific and around the world, which had set out
from Brest under the command of the highly regarded Jean François de Galaup,
Count of Lapérouse, on August 1, 1785.[1]

Almost exactly one year earlier in Petropavlovsk, a tiny Pacific outpost of
the Russian empire, Lapérouse had entrusted an important package of reports,
journals, charts, and letters to de Lesseps, who had lived in St. Petersburg with
his consul general father, and had been invited to join the expedition as in-
terpreter, with the status of vice-consul in its dealings with Russians in the
North Pacific. As the visit to Kamchatka came to an end in September 1787,
and Lapérouse prepared to wrap up his extensive eighteen-month survey of
the American and Asian coasts, de Lesseps's work with the expedition was also
complete. His principal value now was as a courier, undertaking an epic year-
long journey across dangerous and little-known Siberia to deliver the expedition's precious papers to the French authorities.[2]

The dispatches that de Lesseps had safely carried home were of major importance to the government because the leading European powers had developed intense interest in the Northwest Coast. France's understanding of the
region came from the published accounts of Cook's third voyage and Antonio
Maurelle's journal from the Bodega y Quadra voyage of 1775, both of which
had been used in compiling Lapérouse's instructions, as well as the journal of
Bodega's 1779 voyage. The expedition's expertly drawn charts of the Northwest
Coast were a significant advance on the results of Cook's voyage of 1778.

There were also extensive political and commercial reports on Spanish and
Russian activities and, notably, on the prospects of a lucrative fur trade on
the coast. This strategic, geographical, and commercial information ensured
that at the end of 1788, on the eve of the Nootka crisis, Paris was probably as

View of Port de Français (Lituya Bay) drawn by Gaspar Duche de Vancy in July 1786. Lapérouse's ship *Boussole* is on the left; the *Astrolabe* on the right shows off a windmill installed as the expedition sailed toward Alaska. *Service Historique de la Marine, Vincennes*

knowledgeable about the Northwest Coast of America as was Madrid, London, or St. Petersburg.[3] This was the essential achievement of the visit of Lapérouse in the summer of 1786, which will be the focus of this paper. Although the French Revolution effectively ended France's pursuit of imperial objectives beyond Europe for a generation after 1789, her incapacity for involvement in the struggle for hegemony in the North Pacific diminishes neither the expedition's achievements nor the interest its work holds for historians, anthropologists, and geographers.

The end of France's involvement in the American Revolutionary War enabled her to launch a worldwide maritime endeavor. The principal figure was Claret de Fleurieu, Minister of Ports and Arsenals, who, as early as the summer of 1784, seemed to have formulated a series of questions about a great voyage, weighing objectives, possible routes, and costs, and compiling a set of notes on the subject. His conversations likely included the navy minister, Maréchal de Castries, the royal geographer, Jean Buache de La Neuville, the forty-three-year-old Lapérouse, and, by the end of the year, the king himself.[4]

Fleurieu was an experienced naval officer, a student of geography, and an expert in chronometers and the keeping of time at sea. He was in tune with the spirit of the enlightened times in which he lived, a spirit epitomized by the work of the *philosophes,* by the publication of the great *Encyclopédie,* and by influential learned societies where men of wealth and letters gathered to share and promote knowledge of natural history, social customs and historical development, inventions, and technology. Systematic collections that became the basis of many of the great natural history museums of Europe in the middle of the eighteenth century were created during voyages of discovery, and administrators in the French colonies were required to send specimens to the Musée d'Histoire Naturelle set up in the Jardin des Plantes in Paris.[5] Scientific knowledge was equated with progress, and the exploration of the Pacific offered a unique chance for the *academies* to put scientists into the field. Just as Joseph Banks would go with Cook, so Philibert Commerson traveled with Bougainville into the South Pacific, and the Lapérouse voyage was well stocked with scientists.

Cook's surprising success trading Nootkan furs in Canton led Fleurieu to consult secretly with a Dutch-born merchant, William Bolts, knowledgeable about English commercial matters. Bolts had been seeking a sponsor to outfit a voyage to the Northwest Coast, and Fleurieu's attention was thus directed to the North Pacific.[6] Rather than leave such an "increase in the national commerce" to private traders, French authorities determined that a commercial reconnaissance would best be carried out by the royal navy.[7] The prospect of a lucrative trade in furs, particularly attractive after the loss of France's Canadian colony some twenty years earlier, encouraged speculation about the still undiscovered Northwest Passage and the largely unexplored north China coast and the seas around Japan.

In addition, there were political concerns, especially fear of British designs on Australia and a challenge to her presence in the South Seas. Cook's achievements loomed ever large as the planners formulated an itinerary and campaign to rival his exploits and to win for France some of the glory that had flowed to England.[8] But this meant an expansion of the plans into exploration and science, so that more and more the voyage became a pursuit of knowledge.

The detailed instructions proposed to Lapérouse amounted to a veritable catalog of discoveries still to be made on the seas of the world after Cook. The numerous political and commercial tasks meant that Bolts's original concept was only one of the many objectives of the voyage.[9] Early in 1785 Louis XVI became personally involved. As a teenage student of the great cartographer Philippe Buache, the king had become passionate about hydrography, the navy, and the geography of discoveries.[10] Until the day of his death by guillotine on January 21, 1793, Louis's fervent interest in the expedition never wavered, and at Versailles he regularly charted the progress of the voyage.

By the end of the American Revolution Jean François Galaup de Lapérouse had become a genuine naval hero. As a teenage *garde de la marine* he had experienced the British navy's defeat of the French at Quiberon Bay in November 1759. During the fifteen years of peace that followed, he became a skilled navigator, experienced hydrographer, and popular commander. During the American war, he earned his reputation for leadership, bravery, and seamanship, commanding the *Astrée* against an English convoy off Cape Breton and the *Sceptre* on a raid against British forts in Hudson Bay. His achievement in Hudson Bay meant that he was an obvious candidate to command the expedition that had taken shape at the beginning of 1785.[11]

The six months of preparation for the voyage was a time of feverish activity. Cook's successful experience with solid, heavy colliers led to the refitting of two storeships for the expedition, renamed the *Boussole* and the *Astrolabe*. After the ships, the officers and scientists were crucial to a successful voyage. Lapérouse had no trouble recruiting. He chose Paul Antoine Fleuriot de Langle, who had been with him in Hudson Bay, to take charge of the *Astrolabe,* and most of the officers were men whom Lapérouse knew and with whom he and de Langle felt comfortable.

Key among the scientists were the astronomer Joseph Dagelet from the Ecole Militaire, the geologist Robert Lammanon, the highly regarded botanist Joseph Lamartinière, and the engineer Paul Monneron. On a visit to London in preparation for the voyage, the latter had received from Joseph Banks two dipping needle compasses that had been to the Pacific with Cook, which Lapérouse received "with feelings bordering on religious veneration for the memory of that great and incomparable navigator."[12] Gaspar Duche de Vancy, who had studied in Italy, was named senior artist. To assist this distinguished corps, a library of more than one hundred twenty-five books was assembled, including twenty-eight volumes on previous voyages, twenty-three on astronomy and navigation, and no fewer than sixty-four on natural history.[13]

The king's final instructions ran to more than two hundred pages in the printed journal of the voyage published in 1797. Although the route had been prepared along with a fine set of charts detailing the most up-to-date geographical information available, it was understood that Lapérouse could make his own decisions and that the instructions, exhaustive though they were, were guidelines only.[14] In fact, Lapérouse quite quickly changed the suggested itinerary. After rounding Cape Horn early in 1786, he sailed north to Maui and Alaska for a summer season in the northern hemisphere rather than west toward Tahiti and Australia.

As June 1786 progressed, the *Boussole* and the *Astrolabe* sailed through increasingly cold, damp, and foggy weather toward Alaska. Fearful of scurvy, Lapérouse reissued the heavy clothing put away after the passage round the Horn, ordered braziers lit under the halfdeck, and had quinine secretly mixed into the morning grog. On June 23, the expedition sighted the beacon of Mount St. Elias. Lapérouse wrote:

Seeing land after a long voyage usually excites feelings of delight, but this was not the effect on us. The eye wandered painfully over masses of snow covering a barren treeless land. The mountains appeared to be close to the sea which broke against the cliffs of a plateau . . . black as if burned by fire and totally devoid of any greenery.[15]

The crew's tasks were to find a safe anchorage, to get their bearings, to replenish wood and water, to trade with the Indians, and to explore, chart, and investigate for the scientific record. A promising opening was reconnoitered at what was probably the southern extremity of Yakutat Bay, but Lapérouse's officers did not find the Port Mulgrave of Dixon and Malaspina. It was not until the beginning of July, hampered by foggy weather, that, just as Cook had found Nootka Sound, the expedition discovered Lituya Bay in the shadow of Mount Fairweather. Lapérouse called it Port des Français, describing it as "perhaps the most extraordinary place in the world."[16]

The expedition stayed at Port des Français for the entire month of July, two weeks longer than planned, due primarily to a catastrophe that cost the lives of twenty-one men in a small boat accident in the very dangerous waters of the narrow entrance to the bay. When the expedition finally left, August was spent battling the elements to improve Cook's chart of the coast south to the Queen Charlotte Islands and past Vancouver Island toward California. On August 25 "a very thick fog, rising up around five in the afternoon hid the land altogether."[17]

It lasted for five days, preventing any hope of a stopover at Nootka and making a sighting of the Strait of Juan de Fuca impossible. On September 15, guided toward Monterey by a string of headlands, the expedition completed its survey of the Northwest Coast.

But this paper shall return to Port des Français and the month of July 1786. Toward the end of the eighteenth century two powers laid claim to the Northwest Coast, the Russians by decree of Catherine the Great and the Spanish by virtue of the three hundred-year-old Treaty of Tordesillas and the right of first discovery during three voyages from California in the 1770s. It is hard to imagine even a nonrevolutionary France being able to sustain a claim to the Northwest Coast, but she was a great power and could hardly be expected to be indifferent to the strategic importance of the world's last undiscovered temperate coast.

There has always been a suspicion that Lapérouse had received secret, sensitive orders from the king concerning the Northwest Coast, to be shared with no one in light of the cherished alliance with his Bourbon cousin Carlos III in Madrid. They would explain Lapérouse's journal entry concerning potential French commercial interests on arriving in Port des Français:

This port was never seen by any other navigator. It is 33 leagues northwest of Los Remedios, the extreme boundary of the Spanish voyages; about 224 leagues from Nootka; and 100 leagues from Prince William Sound. So it appears to me that, if the French government entertained any scheme to establish a factory on this part of the coast no nation could have the least pretext for opposing it.[18]

It was not by accident that Lapérouse made his major stopover at fifty-eight degrees north latitude. It was strategically positioned between what he understood to be the limits of Spanish activity to the south in Bucareli Sound and Russian activity to the north and west on Kodiak Island. In Paris, as the guarded preparations for the voyage had gathered pace, Ambassador Thomas Jefferson had reported to the American Secretary of State John Jay:

They give out that the object is merely for the improvement of our knowledge of the geography of that part of the world. Their loading however . . . appeared to me to indicate some other design, perhaps that of colonizing on the western coast of America or perhaps to establish one or more factories there for the fur trade. We are interested to know whether they are perfectly weaned from the desire to possess continental colonies in America.[19]

Jay dispatched John Paul Jones to Brest to find out more, receiving the report that conjecture suggested factories either in New Holland (Australia) or on the Northwest Coast. This opinion was echoed by a Spanish official who met with members of the expedition in Concepción in February 1786.[20]

Shortly after his arrival in Port des Français, Lapérouse performed an "act of possession" on the island in the middle of the bay. He did not do this on Maui, where the French also had reason to believe that they were the first Europeans to make a landing. Lapérouse was convinced this custom was immoral, as Europeans had no right to assume ownership of the lands of people who had lived and buried their ancestors there for many years.[21] Although skeptical of the exercise, Lapérouse went through it after he had been asked by a Native chief to purchase the island in the middle of the bay.

It is more than doubtful that the chief was the owner of any land at all; the government of these people is so democratic that the country must belong to the whole society. As many of the savages were witnesses to this bargain however, I felt it right to conclude that they gave it their approval and I accepted the offer. . . . I gave him several lengths of red cloth, some hatchets, adzes, iron bars and nails; I also gave presents to all of his entourage. The sale thus being concluded I set about taking possession of the island with the usual formalities—I buried a bottle that contained an inscription relative to this act of possession at the base of a rock, putting in with it one of the bronze medallions . . . struck in France before our departure.[22]

The political objectives for visiting the Northwest Coast involved not only a claim for possible future use but also some polite spying on Spanish and Russian activities. With respect to the California settlements, Lapérouse was to "learn the condition, strength and purpose of these establishments and to satisfy himself as to whether they were the only ones created by Spain on this coast." If he found Russian settlements in the Aleutians, he was to find out about "their administration strength and purpose; how the Russians navigate the seas; what vessels and men they employ; how their commerce is extended . . . and whether the Russians had extended . . . as far as the continent of America."[23] Information surmised from the Natives of Lituya Bay about Russian trading activities, as well as direct political observations at Monterey and in Kamchatka, allowed Lapérouse to compile an accurate report on the situation that was sent home to France with de Lesseps in 1788.

If it is hard to define precisely France's political strategy on the Northwest Coast, the importance of the commercial reconnaissance is very clear. The potential for a French fur trade between America and China remained an essential objective of the voyage, and the first phase of this endeavor took place at Port des Français. Lituya Bay is in Tlingit territory and was probably the location of summer villages for Natives from Cross Sound and Icy Strait.[24] Lapérouse estimated that about three hundred Natives were living in the bay, and he saw up to eight hundred coming and going during his visit.[25] Although Lapérouse claimed first contact with the Tlingit of Lituya, he observed that they already knew the benefits of supplying foreigners with sea otter furs.[26] The inhabitants

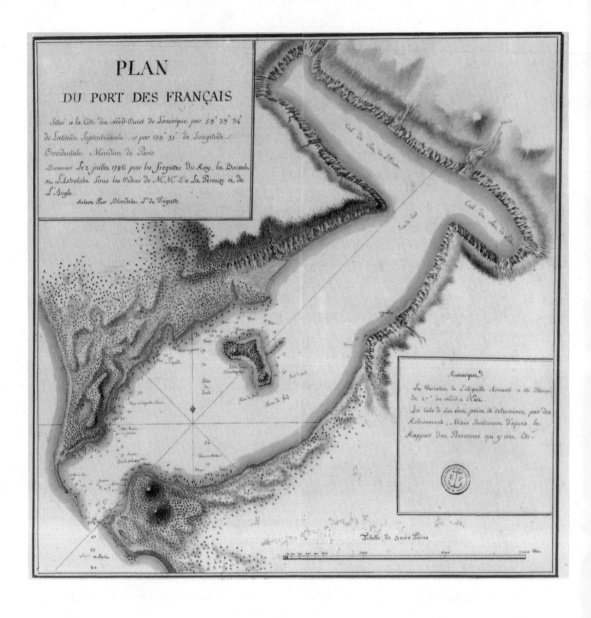

Plan of Port de Français (Lituya Bay) drawn by Lieutenant Blondela of the *Astrolabe* showing the major identifying features of the bay—the dangerous narrow entrance, "Cenotaph Is.," and the two rock- and ice-girt basins. *Archives Nationales, Paris*

of the bay are presented in the oral tradition as having initially considered the arrival of the French ships as the second coming of *Yeahlth,* the principal deity of Tlingit mythology symbolized by the Raven. The visit of a "nearly blind old warrior" to Lapérouse soon after his arrival persuaded his fellow Natives that the Frenchmen were "human strangers," or "People-who-come-from-the-Horizon." Lapérouse wrote, "The Natives, profiting from his experience, visited the ships and exchanged their furs for many strange articles."[27]

The *Boussole* and the *Astrolabe* first anchored close to the Native villages near the entrance to the bay and were "continually surrounded by the canoes of the Natives who offered us fish, sea otter skins and those of other animals and articles of their dress in return for our iron." By the time the ships had moved to a better anchorage deeper into the bay, Lapérouse reported, "the news of our arrival had quickly spread . . . [and] several canoes from beyond the bay [arrived] filled with a very considerable quantity of sea otter skins for which we traded hatchets, adzes and bars of iron."[28]

Lapérouse was to ascertain the latitude where one might begin to trap for furs, the quantity of furs available, the articles and merchandise that would be offered in trade, and the best location for a French settlement on the coast. The naturalist Dufresne was assigned to supervise the trade, with the understanding that any profits made in China would be divided among the sailors.[29] The trade in Macao proved a disappointment. Prices in China had plummeted since 1780, and sea otter skins fetched a mere ten to fifteen percent of what Cook had realized.[30] Negotiations were still continuing when the ships departed, so Dufresne was left in Macao to conclude the sales. He then sailed for France, later reporting the details of the fur trade and his commercial experiences in Asia.[31]

One of these reports expanded in great detail on Lapérouse's opinion, suggesting that Port des Français could sustain a factory:

There is, I think, no other country where the sea otter is so common as in this part of America and I should not be surprised if a factory, extending its commerce only about 40 to 50 leagues along the coast would collect 10,000 skins of that animal every year.[32]

Entitled *Thoughts on the Creation of an Establishment in the Northwest Coast of America at Port des Français,* the report suggests that eighty people could operate such a post and gives other details on potential trade in the area.[33] On his departure from Macao, Lapérouse sent home with Dufresne a packet of furs and cloth "made by the Indians of Port des Francais" as a gift to Marie Antoinette and another with eight furs and four pieces of cloth "for the cabinet of the King."[34]

The geographic-scientific goals of the expedition on the Northwest Coast were also clear. Lapérouse was to improve on the explorations and charts of the area and for "the safety of navigators . . . [was] . . . to fix with precision the latitudes and longitudes of the places . . . and verify the exactness of the description and of the charts which other navigators have made." He was to concentrate on areas not encountered in the earlier voyages and was to "observe with the greatest care, whether in those parts yet unknown, some river may not be found, some definite gulf which may by means of the interior lakes open a communication with some part of Hudson Bay," the still undiscovered Northwest Passage.[35]

When the expedition set out from France, the idea of a Great Passage was still a favorite notion of the theoretical navigators of Europe, despite Cook's opinion that Prince William Sound and Cook Inlet promised little chance of success. Cook believed any opening farther south would have been found during Samuel Hearne's trek to the mouth of the Coppermine River in the summer of 1772.[36] Fanciful maps of the coast, however, continued to be published until the results of Vancouver's conclusive survey became available. As late as 1791 Alejandro Malaspina embarked on his northern campaign primarily as a result of Buache's belief in the Strait of Maldonado, outlined to the Académie des Sciences in Paris in November 1790.

Lapérouse was skeptical of the idea of a navigable waterway across the continent. This resulted from an actual meeting with Samuel Hearne at Fort Prince of Wales during the Hudson Bay raid in August 1782. Hearne was the governor who surrendered the fort to Lapérouse, and the French navigator had taken the opportunity to discuss with him his journey to the Coppermine.[37] Despite this private opinion, however, Lapérouse led an expedition to explore the bottom of Lituya Bay, as the party "supposed that it might lead to some great river that was able to flow between two of the mountains, the source of which was one of the great lakes in northern Canada. Such was the phantom of our imagination."[38]

In fact Lituya Bay ends in a T-shaped wall of rock and ice in two basins blocked by immense glaciers. The two boats involved in the trip had to brush aside chunks of ice as they progressed. De Langle and several officers climbed onto the glacier, but "all they could see was a continuous mass of ice and snow that must have reached up to the very summit of Mount Fairweather." During this outing Lapérouse beached his boat only to have it swamped and thrown for some distance along the face of the glacier after a huge piece of ice broke off. The party soon realized the futility of further exploration and, having made suitable drawings, returned on board the ships, "finishing in a few hours our voyage into the interior of America."[39]

At Port des Français, as at every major stopover, the expedition made precise observations of longitude and latitude and checked the chronometers. Unfortunately, local Natives carried off a notebook of astronomical observations, but the loss did not prevent the creation of a fine chart of the bay. Other scientists roamed the beaches, climbed the mountainsides, and, under the protection of

armed sailors, explored the surrounding forests. On one expedition the naturalists climbed to a considerable height on the lower mountains encircling the
bay to collect some specimens. They found three unknown plants but, given
the similarity of the climate with northern Europe, much of the flora and fauna
were easily recognized. They were amazed by the abundant richness of the
vegetation, the fish and wildlife, and the awesome setting. Lapérouse summed
up their experience.

The woods were full of strawberries, raspberries and gooseberries. The rivers were full
of trout and salmon . . . . In the woods our hunters saw martens and squirrels, and . . .
the copses were full of linnets, nightingales, blackbirds and partridges. As this was the
mating season the bird songs seemed to me to be more agreeable than in Europe . . .
though the vegetable and minerals of this country very closely resemble those of other
regions, its scenery has no parallel and I do not think that the lofty mountains and deep
valleys of the Alps and Pyrennes afford so tremendous yet beautiful a spectacle.[40]

Lapérouse and his companions, however, did not find the Tlingit Natives
much to their liking. They were a gloomy, dirty, ungrateful, nomadic, thiev-
ing, and quarrelsome lot, according to the Europeans. Their language seemed
to be so much noise. Both men and women were tattooed and mutilated to
affix adornments to their bodies. The Frenchmen were particularly repulsed
by the women wearing the labret in their lower lip. Living by the hunt, the
Natives appeared to have no political structure. Even the numerous dogs were
unfriendly. Practically the only things to be admired were the canoes and
basketry, the beautifully woven hats, the twin-peaked eagle-feathered head-
dresses, and the bear crest helmets into which wooden linings were fitted. The
commander disputed western European thinking about the "Other" of North
America, explaining, "I am willing to admit that it is impossible for a society
to exist without some virtues, but am forced to state that I did not have the
wisdom to notice any."[41]

The expedition left Europe at a time when the idea of the noble savage was
well entrenched in French thought. Bougainville's voyage to the South Pacific
had reinforced Rousseau's hypothesis that man had been depraved by his development from the natural state into the false environment of an artificial
and complex society, and that it should be possible to find, in a simple society
of happy aboriginal people, a happiness that was so hard to achieve in Europe.
Lapérouse's instructions showed the influence of this idea. He was to "act with
great gentleness and humanity towards the different peoples" he would encounter. He was "not to use force except with the greatest moderation. If he
cannot obtain the goodwill of the savages by kind treatment, he should con-
strain them and should only use arms as a last resort."[42]

Lapérouse was a man of the sea, with no time for philosophers. What reason could there be for assuming that Native peoples in distant lands were intrinsically different from his own men, rogues and drunkards many of them, who were kept under control only by stern discipline?[43] The idea was dangerous, as the tragedy of Cook's murder demonstrated. At Port des Français, Lapérouse was frustrated by the persistent thievery of the Natives, who had no concept of private property and instead regarded as fair game the belongings of the strangers who took their wood and water. In the aftermath of the disastrous boat accident that had so depressed him, he lashed out at the academics with a bitter rejection of their sentimental speculations.

They write their books by their firesides while I have been voyaging for thirty years. I have witnessed the knavery and injustice of people whom they depict as good because they are so near to the state of nature; but nature is sublime only in the larger view, in detail it is less so. It is impossible to go into the woods where the hand of civilized man has not stretched to meet with the man of nature, because he is savage, deceitful and malicious.[44]

Nevertheless, his journal gives a detailed and not entirely critical view of Native life in Lituya Bay. After the boat accident he moved the ships from behind Cenotaph Island, named for the monument raised there in memory of the twenty-one drowned sailors. He anchored near the entrance to the bay in the vain hope of spotting survivors. This brought the expedition into closer contact with the Natives, who were recruited, at a substantial cost in "presents," to search for the missing Frenchmen. As Lapérouse wrote:

Our stay at the entrance to the bay afforded us a fund of information about the manners and customs of the savages, impossible to be obtained at our former anchorage. Because our ships were at anchor near their villages we visited them every day and, just as often, we had reason to feel aggrieved [by their behavior] though our conduct towards them never varied and we constantly afforded them proof of our gentleness and benevolence.[45]

Lapérouse did praise the Natives' artistic skill, noting they had ways of forging iron and molding copper. He was especially impressed with the way they spun cloth from animal hair and sewed together skins to make cloaks.

In no part of the world are straw hats and baskets more skillfully made and they adorn them with pleasing designs. They carve images of men and animals in wood and stone and decorate elegantly formed boxes with shellwork, and cut curved stone into jewels to which they give a marble-like polish.[46]

While recognizing that "the arts of life are considerably advanced," Lapérouse bemoaned the absence of agriculture, "which by making man domestic and securing him subsistence subjects him to a fear that the land he has cultivated might become exposed to ravages, and thus . . . soften[s] his manners and render[s] him fit for civilization." [47] He found the civilization of these people

in its infancy; for their manner of life . . . exposes them to be constantly agitated by fear or vengeance; since they are . . . prone to violence and . . . endlessly raising their daggers against each other. Though subject to famine in the winter, they enjoy profuse abundance in the summer for in less than an hour they can catch enough fish for the day. Thus the remainder of the time is spent in play . . . which they pursue with as much love and passion as the dissipated inhabitants of any great metropolis and, like them, make it the frequent, inexhaustible source of their quarrels.

Lapérouse somberly observed: "If to all these vices were added the baneful knowledge of some intoxicating liquor, . . . these people will hasten by rapid strides towards total oblivion." [48]

Delayed not only by the boat tragedy but also by unfavorable winds, the *Boussole* and the *Astrolabe* sailed out of Port des Français on July 30, three weeks later than expected. On August 4, the fog cleared to reveal Cross Sound and the beginning of the Alexander Archipelago. The coast was wooded and the snowcapped ranges of the continent had fallen away to the north. After Chichagof Island, the explorers saw the inlets of Baranof Island. Somewhere in this mass of islands, channels, and bays lay Port Bucareli, but Lapérouse was not able to understand Maurelle's map. Charting the region was difficult, as "three months would scarcely suffice to explore this labyrinth of navigation. I confined myself to . . . chart with precision the beginning and end of this cluster of islands, with their direction along the coast and the entrances to the principal bays." [49] From fifty-six to fifty degrees north, Lapérouse filled in the gaps on Cook's chart. His work was praised by geographers in Europe, and Bancroft later rated it "remarkable . . . quite superior to anything done before 1787." [50]

The extent of the talent and energy devoted to the exploration of the Northwest Coast by Cook, Bodega, Lapérouse, Malaspina, and Vancouver, and by traders such as Dixon, Portlock, and Marchand, was unique when compared to any other coastline in the world. But the achievements of the Lapérouse expedition were diminished by the tragedy of Vanikoro, where, after their visit to Australia, both ships were wrecked in a cyclone in June 1788. All trace of the expedition remained a mystery for forty years. We can only guess at what was lost—certainly more collections, scientific specimens and drawings, and, no doubt, private journals of the seamen on board.

Nevertheless, these bicentennial years have allowed us to embark on our own voyages of discovery to be more aware of the contributions to the earliest written history of the Northwest Coast made beyond those of the better known, and rightly praised, Cook and Vancouver. During his stopover in Maui, en route to Alaska, Lapérouse had written, "Modern navigators have no other purpose but to complete the history of man; their voyages should complete the survey of the globe and the information they endeavor to provide has no other purpose than that of improving the happiness of the people they visit and adding to their ability to sustain themselves." [51] Across the Pacific to the coast of China, on Maui, at Kamchatka and in Port des Français, Lapérouse pursued this lofty goal. In doing so he has emerged as a remarkably courageous representative of his enlightened era.

NOTES

1. John Dunmore, *Pacific Explorer: The Life of Jean-François de La Pérouse* (Annapolis, Md.: Naval Institute Press, 1985), p. 265. Written by the premier English-speaking scholar on Lapérouse, this is the most complete biography. Lapérouse always signed his name with this spelling, although there remains some debate as to whether or not officially he was "La Perouse," a usage that was standard until recently.

2. De Lesseps's journal, published in Paris in 1790, was immediately translated and published as *Travels in Kamchatka during the Years 1787 and 1788* (London, 1790).

3. George Verne Blue, "French Interest in Pacific America in the Eighteenth Century," *Pacific Historical Review,* Vol. 4 (1935), p. 261.

4. The genesis of the voyage is explored most comprehensively in Catherine Gaziello, *L'Expédition de Lapérouse, 1785-1788: Réplique française aux voyages de Cook* (Paris: Comité des Travaux Historiques et Scientifiques, 1984).

5. Dunmore, *Pacific Explorer,* pp. 190-191; Gaziello, *L'Expédition de Lapérouse,* pp. 35-38.

6. Gaziello, *L'Expédition de Lapérouse,* pp. 49-50.

7. Blue, "French Interest in Pacific America," p. 257.

8. Maurice de Brossard, "Lapérouse: Following the Path of Cook on the Northwest Coast of America," p. 2, unpublished paper presented at the Cook Conference, Simon Fraser University, Vancouver, April 24-26, 1978.

9. Gaziello, *L'Expédition de Lapérouse,* p. 55.

10. Dunmore, *Pacific Explorer,* p. 188.

11. *Ibid.,* pp. 141-71; see also Robin Inglis, *The Lost Voyage of Lapérouse* (Vancouver: Vancouver Museum and Planetarium Association, 1986), pp. 6-9.

12. John Dunmore and Maurice Brossard, eds. and trans., *Le voyage de Lapérouse: Récit et documents originaux* (Paris: Imprimerie Nationale, 1985), 1:9 (hereafter Dunmore, *Lapérouse Voyage*).

13. Dunmore, *Pacific Explorer,* p. 200.

14. Gaziello, *L'Expédition de Lapérouse,* pp. 22-23; Dunmore, *Pacific Explorer,* pp. 192-213.

15. Dunmore, *Lapérouse Voyage,* 2:109.

16. *Ibid.,* 2:123-24.

17. *Ibid.,* 2:177.

18. *Ibid.*, 2:117.

19. Jefferson quoted in Inglis, *Lost Voyage of Lapérouse,* p. 15.

20. Letter from Jose Miguel Urezberoeta to Ambrosio Benavides, Concepcion, March 24, 1786, in Archivo Historico, Estado 4289, Madrid. Urezberoeta wrote: "Notwithstanding its characterization as a [scientific] expedition . . . , the one thing we can be certain about is that its interests extend to settlement for later operations in commercial competition with the English."

21. Dunmore, *Lapérouse Voyage,* 2:99.

22. *Ibid.*, 2:125.

23. *Ibid.*, 2:31, 32.

24. For the best brief description of the Tlingit, see Frederica Laguna, "Tlingit: People of the Wolf and Raven," in *Crossroads of Continents: Cultures of Siberia and Alaska,* ed. William Fitzhugh and Aron Crowell (Washington, D.C.: Smithsonian Institution, 1988), pp. 58–63.

25. Dunmore, *Lapérouse Voyage,* 2:149.

26. Mary Jane Lenz, "Myth and Memory at Lituya Bay," in *Culturas de la Costa Noroeste de America,* ed. Jose Peset (Madrid: Sociedad Estatal Quinto Centenario and Turner Libros S.A., 1989), p. 135.

27. G. T. Emmons, "Native Account of the Meeting between La Perouse and the Tlingit," in *American Anthropologist,* Vol. 12 (American Anthropological Association, 1911), n.s. 13, pp. 294–298, and "How the White Men Came to Lituya Bay and What Happened to Yeahith-kan Who Visited Them," *Alaska Magazine,* Vol. 1 (1927), p. 151.

28. Dunmore, *Lapérouse Voyage,* 2:119, 121.

29. *Ibid.*, 1:31–32, 163.

30. Dunmore, *Pacific Explorer,* pp. 245–46.

31. These reports (Marine B4 318) are in the Archives Nationales in Paris.

32. Dunmore, *Lapérouse Voyage,* 2:121.

33. See Gaziello, *L'Expédition de Lapérouse,* pp. 210–12.

34. Letter written by Lapérouse in Macao, Jan. 26, 1787, Marine B4 386 CN 111,62, Archives Nationales.

35. Dunmore, *Lapérouse Voyage,* 1:27, 34.

36. J. C. Beaglehole, *The Journals of Captain James Cook: The Voyage of the Resolution and Discovery, 1776–1780* (Cambridge: Hakluyt Society, 1967), Part I, p. 353, n. 3, p. 368.

37. E. E. Rich, *The Fur Trade and the Northwest to 1857* (Toronto: McClelland and Stewart, 1967), p. 161.

38. Dunmore, *Lapérouse Voyage,* 2:125.

39. *Ibid.*

40. *Ibid.*, 2:142–47 and notes (qtn., 143).

41. *Ibid.*, 2:149.

42. *Ibid.* For a discussion of the concept of the noble savage, see J. F. McKenna, "The Noble Savage in the Voyage of La Perouse," in *Kentucky Foreign Language Quarterly,* Vol. 12 (1965), no. 1, pp. 45–62.

43. Dunmore, *Pacific Explorer,* p. 224.

44. Dunmore, *Lapérouse Voyage,* 2:147.

45. *Ibid.*, 2:137.

46. *Ibid.,* 2:155.

47. *Ibid.*

48. *Ibid.,* 2:147.

49. *Ibid.,* 2:167.

50. See Brossard, "Lapérouse: Following the Path of Cook" (p. 8), who quotes H. H. Bancroft, *History of the Northwest Coast* (1884).

51. Dunmore, *Lapérouse Voyage,* 2:101.

Robin Inglis

PHYLLIS S. HERDA

Ethnology in the Enlightenment: The Voyage of Alejandro Malaspina in the Pacific

The Europeans who entered the Pacific Ocean in the late eighteenth century on grand scientific expeditions came with a fervent desire to explore nature and its inhabitants. This fervor was born out of a belief, general to the Age of Enlightenment, that the world was controlled by natural laws and that by observing, comparing, and classifying these natural laws a new understanding would emerge that could, and presumably would, change the world for the better.[1] The variety of observations made on these voyages of Enlightenment was extensive and included astronomy, botany, hydrography, zoology, geography, and ethnology.[2] Although ethnology had not, as yet, been established as a formal academic discipline, there was a growing feeling in Europe that observation and scientific investigation of indigenous peoples of other lands should replace the subjective impressions of previous explorers.

The Pacific, with its seemingly geographically discrete islands, was thought to provide a perfect environment for this type of observation. Arguably before, but certainly after, the three voyages of James Cook from 1768 to 1780, inclusion of observations of a cultural nature became commonplace in the European explorer literature.[3] That this classified and empirically differentiated European images of the mysterious and exotic "Other" as future objects of European colonization was accepted without question.

The 1789–94 expedition commanded by Alejandro Malaspina and José Bustamante y Guerra represented Spain's contribution to these enlightened European voyages across the Pacific.[4] The members of the Malaspina expedition eagerly embraced the scientific earnestness of their day, and the textual and pictorial records of their voyage are full of depictions of the people they encountered.[5] A description of the indigenous people and their customs was seen from the outset of the expedition as an essential part of empirical observations.

This chapter examines the nature of the ethnological descriptions and images from the Spanish visit to the Vava'u Archipelago in the Tongan Islands, situated in the southern Pacific Ocean, and juxtaposes this construction with the Spanish imagery of other ports of call, most notably those of the Pacific Northwest, to consider the essence of ethnology in the voyages of the Enlightenment and its relation to colonization and the nascent anthropological discipline. This focus on Tonga is instructive of the process of how Europeans, in this case members of the Malaspina expedition, encountered and constructed the mysterious and exotic "Other" in the first years of ethnology as an academic discipline.

In September 1788, in a proposal to the Naval Minister Antonio Valdes, Malaspina and Bustamante y Guerra outlined for the Spanish crown a voyage that would circumnavigate the globe. True to the spirit of the Enlightenment, the would-be commanders expressed their desire to foster a scientific and philosophical understanding of the world in terms of contributions to hydrography, geography, astronomy, botany, and natural history, while also obtaining a collection of curiosities for the Real Gabinete (Royal Museum, now in the Museo de America) and specimens for the Real Jardín Botanico (Royal Botanical Gardens). Included on their list of worthwhile investigations was a desire to learn more about "Man in different climates," a topic that today would come under the anthropological umbrella of ethnology but at that time could not be divorced from the general rubric of natural history.

The history of human society has laid the foundation for more general investigations: natural history has been enriched with an almost infinite number of discoveries; and finally the preservation of Man in different climates, in extensive journeys, and among some almost incredible tasks and risks, has been the most interesting acquisition which navigation has made.[6]

Spain's belief that it was lagging behind other European nations and its commitment to the growth of scientific knowledge are recurrent themes in the literature of the Malaspina expedition. A further persistent theme emphasized the need for a detailed report of the presence of other European nations in California, Macao, and New South Wales, in addition to concern about the Russian and English presence on the Northwest Coast, an area the Spanish regarded as their exclusive domain.[7]

On July 28, 1789, two corvettes, the *Descubierta* (*Discovery*) and the *Atrevida* (*Daring*), set sail from Cádiz, Spain. After an uneventful Atlantic crossing, the ships spent one and one half years surveying the east and west coasts of "southern America," as South America was called at the time. The explorers made extensive notes on the Spanish settlements of Montevideo, Puerto Deseado, las Islas Malvinas (the Falkland Islands), San Carlos de Chiloe, Valparaíso, Callao, and Guayaquil before they arrived in Acapulco in April of 1791.

A royal decree was waiting for them in Acapulco, which directed them to amend their original itinerary, because of Spanish concessions made to the

Phyllis S.
Herda

66

British during the Nootka Sound controversy in 1790. Instead of sailing for the Hawaiian Islands, Malaspina and Bustamante were to head north and carefully reconnoiter the Northwest Coast between fifty-nine and sixty degrees latitude in order to report on the activities of the British and, more important, in the hope of locating the Strait of Maldonado (the fabled Northwest Passage), thereby reestablishing Spanish supremacy in the area. They visited Nootka Sound and Mulgrave Sound (Yakutat Bay), recording in each locale their observations and impressions of local geography, flora and fauna, and indigenous culture. The political underpinning of the expedition, however, was never far from the surface.

Following the Northwest Coast sojourn, the expedition set sail across the Pacific, sighting the Ladrones (Marianas Islands) and stopping at the Spanish settlement at Humata (Guam) before heading towards the Philippines, where the expedition remained for almost nine months. In November 1792 the explorers visited Mindanao, then traveled along the coast of New Guinea to the Solomon Islands and New Caledonia. In February 1793 they visited Dusky and Doubtful Sounds at New Zealand's South Island, then sailed to Port Jackson, where they were met by Lieutenant Governor Grose, in charge of the British penal colony. The corvettes then sailed for Vava'u, Tonga.

During their stay in the northern Tongan islands, the Spaniards kept to their expeditional tasks of recording their observations on geography, hydrography, and the local flora and fauna. James Cook had visited the southern Tonga islands in the 1770s, and the Spaniards, who had access to the Cook material, were interested in comparing their impression of Tongan culture and history with those of the British navigator. Worried about the permanent British presence in New South Wales, the expedition members ended their stay in Vava'u by burying a bottle claiming the islands for Spain.[8]

The expedition remained at Vava'u for two weeks, and on June 1 it returned to South America, where it divided, with some of the members crossing overland to the Atlantic. The land expedition rendezvoused with the two corvettes at Montevideo and, together again, they returned to Spain. After an absence of more than five years, the travelers arrived in Cádiz on September 21, 1794, loaded with botanical and zoological specimens, ethnographic artifacts, and a sizable pictorial record, as well as a mountain of notes.

The expedition was highly praised by the Spanish court on its return, and plans were made for the publication of the results of the voyage. Since Malaspina and Bustamante desired that any scientific results be made available to the scientific community and the interested public, publication was a high priority from the outset of the voyage.

However, such publication would not occur. Instead, Malaspina was placed under house arrest on April 29, 1796. The events leading to this action are shrouded in mystery, but can be aptly described as "political intrigue."[9] It is likely that Malaspina's liberal views regarding colonialism were not well received by King Carlos IV and his prime minister, the infamous Manuel Godoy. Malaspina apparently planned a separate expedition account, outlining his recommendations for more liberal treatment of the Spanish colonies. A separate report was indicated in the original voyage proposal approved by King Carlos III, but the new king did not share his father's liberalism. When Godoy learned of the report, which allegedly showed him in a bad light, he pressed Carlos IV to have Malaspina arrested.

Another version of the controversy suggests that Godoy was jealous of the royal attention shown Malaspina on his return. Godoy, whom Malaspina was fond of calling "the Sultan," feared that the explorer would replace him as Queen Maria Luisa's lover, so he plotted Malaspina's downfall. In any event, Malaspina was soon found guilty of treason and sentenced in 1796 to ten years' imprisonment. He was released in 1803, but was then exiled to Italy, where he remained until his death in April 1810.

At the time of Malaspina's arrest, Carlos IV ordered that all papers dealing with the expedition be seized and banned from publication. Manuel Godoy was reportedly so incensed by Malaspina that he made sure the decree was enforced. In an 1802 report of a minor expedition sent to the Northwest Coast, Malaspina could only be mentioned as "the commander of the expedition."[10] The majority of the appropriated material from the voyage was eventually deposited in the Hydrographic Archives then, upon the closure of that office, moved to the Museo Naval in Madrid, where it went unpublished in any form until 1885.[11]

The Malaspina expedition made two ports of call on the Northwest Coast, Nootka and Port Mulgrave (Yakutat Bay), both in 1791. For the Spaniards, the people of Nootka, compared to those of Yakutat Bay, were the more prosperous and cultured. This was evident in the depiction of the Nootkans as at first reluctant and later friendly, with an identifiable hierarchy, while those of Yakutat Bay were described in terms of uncleanliness and savage violence.[12]

Sexual promiscuity, as defined by the explorers, was another indicator of civilization for the European visitors. While in some regions, including the Tongan Islands, the Spaniards perceived casual sexual encounters as an expression of human beings living close to nature, among the people at Yakutat Bay it was labeled "prostitution." In addition, the act of labeling the encounter involved judgments associated with rank: "At first, we thought that only the more lowly class of women prostituted themselves [but] we soon realized that the least accommodating woman from the royal family would sell her favors at a low price."[13]

The theme of stratification, especially as demonstrated in political authority, sexuality, cleanliness, and violence, reappears throughout the Malaspina textual material as clear evidence of civilization. So deeply ingrained were these European cultural beliefs that the writers on the expedition, like those who sailed with Cook and Lapérouse, did not elaborate on these fundamental societal judgments.

The absolute ethnographic authority with which the members of the Malaspina expedition commented upon Tongan society and culture rested on a mere thirteen-day visit. Nevertheless, the expedition members felt confident enough in their experience in encountering the non-European "Other" on the Northwest Coast, in South America, and in the Philippines to freely form and boldly state judgments about a wide range of complex Tongan social institutions. The Pacific, and in particular what is today termed Polynesia, held a particular appeal to the explorers and chroniclers of the Enlightenment, for its geography suggested to Europeans an isolation that, in the words of the editor of Cook's third voyage, was

untrodden ground. The inhabitants, as far as could be observed, were unmixed with any different tribe, by occasional intercourse, subsequent to their original settlement there; left entirely to their own powers for every art of life; and to their own remote traditions for every political or religious custom or institution; uninformed by science; unimpaired by education; in short, a fit soil from whence a careful observer could collect facts for forming a judgment, how far unassisted human nature will be apt to degenerate; and in what respects it can ever be able to excel.[14]

Anthropologists in the second half of the twentieth century would echo those same sentiments in naming the Pacific "a laboratory for small-scale evolution."[15] What is missing in these Eurocentric delineations is the understanding that for Tongans, and many other Polynesians, their islands were not geographic or social isolates but rather positions in a marine thoroughfare that connected them to ancestral homelands as well as contemporary economic, social, political, and kin relations.

Foremost among the cultural traits delineated for description and discernment by the eighteenth-century Spaniards in Tonga and the Pacific Northwest were issues of rank and their belief that social behaviors were a direct and predictable outcome of breeding. The common Tongan people (tu'a) were described as a "luckless class," as having an "insolent curiosity," an "inconvenient restlessness" as well as an "inclination towards any sort of theft" and "destructive wiles."[16] Their designation was most clearly constructed in opposition to the "Eigui" ['eiki], or those of chiefly rank, who were perceived as "distinguished," "majestic," of "noble and true virtue," and who "conducted themselves with much decorum."[17] The coupling of breeding manifested as empirical behavior and inherent civility was, at times, pushed further with racial connotations attached to the observable. Bustamante y Guerra's description and image of a chiefly Tongan woman, "light-skinned," "Noble Dubou" [Tupoumoheofo], included the insight that

with a sweet and majestic face, [she] received us with as much pleasure as dignity. Her face, composure, *and even her colour distinguished her from the other natives,* announcing the importance of her person.[18]

The Spaniards ostensibly found European notions of civility, amenity, modesty, and decorum mirrored in the high ranking of Tonga and so subscribed this order with additional characteristics of nobility and, indeed, Europeanness. For example, the Tongan political elite are described as "the Monarch," "Prince," and "heir Prince to the Islands." [19] In another instance, the orderliness of the technologically manipulated landscape appealed to the Spanish sense of aesthetics:

The regularity of plantations, the gracious harmony of the surroundings, and the profusion of trees always coloured by flowers, all this presented itself to us in the brightest colours as marvels of Nature. . . . We admired the state of their agriculture, to which they applied themselves as the principal and most useful occupation of their society. An occupation to which they not only owed a strong physique, but also a quiet life in the bosom of plenty and pleasure.[20]

The Spaniards of course had their own interests in imaging Tongan rank in this framework. First, by constructing an image of the high ranking of Tonga as European-like, they assured themselves a place of cultural supremacy with regard to the ensuing relationship drawn between the cultures. If the highest of the Tongans displayed attributes of all Europeans, then the highest of the Europeans logically represented an indisputable elite. Second, a natural progression of cultural hierarchy can be constructed as empirically observable with an inherent superior-inferior global relationship hinted at in the portrayal. Obviously, the apparent logical progression from such a global hierarchy to naturally ordained political ascendancy and resulting European imperialism is a relatively small step. The series of deductions are alluded to in several forms in the text.

In its most clear form it appears in the comparisons that are drawn *between* cultures. So, for example, continuity is drawn between the societies of Vava'u and Nootka in North America, with a hierarchical differentiation made between these and the inhabitants of Yakutat Bay and Port Jackson. The Australians, in particular, are spoken of in exceedingly derogatory terms, with an emphasis on "their inferior size . . . absolute lack of strength . . . [and a] total lack of ideas, of activeness, of shelter, of desires, and of Luxury." [21] Once again, it is European social conventions and mores that became the measuring stick of the exotic "Other."

Perceptions of cleanliness, or the lack of it, are often invoked as clear evidence of civilization. The indigenous inhabitants of Mulgrave Sound, for example, are caricatured as having a "horrible" appearance: "They are covered with grease and filth, giving off an odour difficult to describe in all its disagreeability,"[22] while the aboriginal people of Australia are deemed "entirely naked and disgustingly dirty" and "the most miserable and least advanced nation which exists on earth."[23] Additional cultural comparisons are drawn from further afield, with an African example brought in to elucidate the cultural categorization and inferior classification of the aborigines by suggesting a similarity to the Khoikhoi of South Africa.

It is certain that, similar to the Hottentots [Khoikhoi], the young adults at times suddenly quit the house where they are being fed, and the clothing which covers them, in order to return to their own to continue their primitive wandering life, divested it would appear of all social ties.[24]

It needs to be pointed out, however, that while Tongan and Nootkan society are placed high on the classificatory scale of cultures encountered by the Spaniards (two clinching bits of Tongan evidence of "a high degree of civilization" were a ritual salutation after sneezing and a ball game similar to one played in Spain),[25] they are perceived as being socially, and arguably evolutionarily, distant from European cultures.

But among these people, whose inferior class possess nothing, where Nature is not in need of the hand of man in order to give its gifts, where the King and the most inferior plebian visit, inhabit and row, equally in a canoe, the rights of ownership are reduced indiscriminately, to the rights of the individual; that is, the preservation of himself, his wives and his children. Qualities totally typical of animal man, perhaps to a greater degree than in social man.[26]

Noble savages though the Tongans may be, but in the Spanish conception they are savages nonetheless. In the case of Tonga, the constructed image of the 'eiki Vuna (the supreme political chief) displayed contradictions that detracted notably from the perceived civility of a European style nobility of humanity. So, while generous, "noble," and of "majestic bearing," Vuna was at the same time guilty of "perpetual idleness" and of "admiring attentively and with that stupid admiration of non-civilized people, all our works and utensils."[27] Of greater gravity and significance were Vuna's lapses into violence if the common Tongan people did not obey his wishes and his "indifference . . . over the fate of his vassals."[28]

This comparing of Tongan society with feudal Europe carries with it a clear intent of denigrating Tongan society or, at the very least, devaluing its "civilized" nature. Europe in its preeminent perceived civility was seen to have passed, or at least be passing, during the Enlightenment from a feudal to a modern state. That the Tongan or Nootkan "nation" (a notion the Spaniards would not have embraced) was seen to display feudal notions to European eyes, makes it less civilized, less developed than its European counterpart. Focusing on violence as a measure of civilization is especially interesting. Greg Denning, for example, has asserted that authoritarian violence was rife on the ships of the "enlightened" British explorers.[29]

Evidence from the Malaspina voyage indicates that the Spaniards also regarded physical violence as an appropriate form of punishment. During the Vava'u visit a public whipping over a cannon was meted out to an apprehended Tongan thief, and a potential deserter was chained as a disciplinary action.[30] The Spaniards, however, chose to portray their own actions as indicators of a civilized justice, whereas Tongan judicial violence was one of "very robust executors [who] willingly pounced upon the common people."[31] The line between majesty and despot seemingly is a fine one, with civilization clearly in the eye of the beholder.

For the Spaniards, as for many Europeans who encountered Polynesia, perceived sexual promiscuity became an issue that captivated their imagination and dominated much of their writing. Although often labeling casual sexual encounters, especially of those of lower rank, as prostitution, more frequently the Spaniards imaged Tongan sexual behaviors as "free love" and as a natural expression or outcome of human beings living close to nature. In a similar voyeuristic manner, breech tattooing of Tongan men made its way into the pictorial record of the Malaspina expedition.

While Bougainville and Banks constructed their noble savage imagery in Tahiti from Greek mythology, the Tongan texts of the Malaspina expedition found their expression in Italian Renaissance pastoral poetry.

In a country where everything incites pleasure, and where no other law is known, at least with regards to the class of the common people, except the law Tasso suggested for the Golden Age: "Of the golden law, he is happy As Nature sculpts: If it is pleasurable, it is permissible."[32]

The choice of this poetry to express the nature of Tongan culture imaged by the Spaniards is revealing, for, at the end of the eighteenth century, pastoral poetry had come to symbolize not only a nostalgic yearning for a simpler time and life, free of vice and corruption, but also a yearning for a time of permissible eroticism.[33]

Phyllis S. Herda

72

It is apparent in the Malaspina texts that for the Spaniards sexual behavior operated in a powerful way as a symbol of the level of cultural advancement attained. For the most part, Tongan women are represented iconically as extreme stereotypes of their individual rank, with the accompanying behavioral manifestation almost always related to sexual intercourse or its inducement. For example, initially the Spaniards asserted that female sexually assertive behavior was prostitution, which they considered "one of the most obscene vices that infest human nature," so they banned "all women whose class and purpose was not well known" from coming aboard ship. Yet sexually assertive chiefly women were distinguished as displaying "the willingness, the modesty and adornment of countenance so their appearance changed as if from the temples of Gnido and Amantuna rather than the wretched sanctuary of some uneducated and perpetually unhappy nation."[34]

Pastoral poetry is presented to further elucidate rank in Tonga and the European hierarchy of cultures. In the poetry it is European peasantry, specifically shepherds and shepherdesses, who live the erotic life. In Tonga this positive sexuality is attributed to chiefly women, thereby subtly reinforcing a classification of European superiority through association of Tongan chiefliness with European peasantry. Despite the degradation assigned to sexual intercourse and the Spaniards' solemn declarations of preventing sexual associations in Tonga, especially involving the officers, sexual relations between the Spanish men and Tongan women occurred. Evidence is available from reading the Spanish texts and, more pertinently, from an examination of genealogies (*hohoko*) from Vava'u.[35]

While images of incidental sexual encounter between Spanish men and Tongan women were dichotomized according to the rank or class of the participants, the Tongan institution of polygamy and its institutionalization of active sexuality presented the Spaniards with a clear example of cultural degradation. On a general level, the Spaniards expressed the opinion that:

when [living conditions] are compared with the immoderate use of the women, one ought not look at [the living conditions] as but a secondary cause of the shortness of life. The Eiguis ['*eikl* or chiefs], particularly, with the liberty to extend the number of wives up to four and with the many charms with which these [wives] have been favoured by Nature . . . yield the luxury of age . . . [in order to] multiply the pleasures of marriage.[36]

More specifically, the sexual habits of Vuna, "who had no less than twelve [noble women], besides the plebians who were able to excite his fancy," was "at the . . . age of some forty-five years . . . almost blind and with evident patterns of a stupidity arising from the laxity of the fibers."[37] Once again, European limits of civility are placed on Tongan behavior and culture.

In unraveling the various descriptions made by European explorers of indigenous people around the world, it appears we learn more about the writers than about their subjects. What is perhaps more enlightening is how their subjects were imaged in the literary and pictorial records. When Europe encountered the exotic "Other" in Polynesian islands or the Pacific Northwest during the Enlightenment, it did so with a tangled web of agendas. On the one hand, there was an economic and political imperialism that engaged a significant portion of the expeditionary ethnological description. On the other hand, there was a belief in the value of "truth" as discovered through empirical observation, comparison, and, ultimately, classification of the subject—the emerging scientific method. While the classification of cultures on a grand scale would not emerge until the mid- to late nineteenth century with the schemes of evolutionary anthropology, the comparisons and hierarchies evident in the literature of the voyages of the Enlightenment certainly represent a step in that direction.

NOTES

1. Iris Engstrand, *Spanish Scientists in the New World: The Eighteenth-Century Expeditions* (Seattle: University of Washington Press, 1981), p. xi.

2. Iris Wilson, "Scientific Aspects of Spanish Exploration in New Spain during the Late Eighteenth Century" (Ph.D. thesis, University of Southern California, 1962), p. ii; P. J. Marshall and Glyndwr Williams, *The Great Map of Mankind: British Perceptions of the World in the Age of Enlightenment* (London: J. M. Dent and Sons, 1982), pp. 264–65; O. H. K. Spate, *Paradise Found and Lost* (Canberra, 1988), pp. 185–91.

3. Marshall and Williams, *Great Map of Mankind,* p. 269; Spate, *Paradise Found and Lost,* p. 196.

4. The spelling of Malaspina's first name varies in the available literature, appearing as Alejandro, Alessandro, or Alexandro, due to orthographic differences between Italian and Spanish. He apparently signed his name "Alexandro" (see, for example, J. Fernandez, *Tomas de Suria y su Viaje con Malaspina* [1939], p. 127).

5. Wilson, "Scientific Aspects of Spanish Exploration," p. xi; D. Madulid, "Malaspina, Explorer for Science," *Filipinas Journal of Science and Culture,* Vol. 1 (1981), pp. 113–21.

6. P. Novo y Colson, *Alrededor del Mundo por las Corbetas Descubierta y Atrevida . . .* (Madrid: Impr. de la vivda é hi jos de Abienzo, 1885), p. 1.

7. *Ibid.,* p. 1.

8. *Ibid.,* p. 280.

9. *Ibid.,* pp. ix–x; Donald Cutter, *Malaspina in California* (San Francisco: J. Howell, 1960), p. vii; Madulid, "Malaspina, Explorer for Science," p. 121.

10. C. Jane, ed., *A Spanish Voyage to Vancouver and the Northwest Coast of America* London: Argonaut Press, 1930.

11. Museo Naval, MS 2406, Malaspina, Alejandro, *Index and Correspondence,* Madrid.

An account of the expedition manuscripts, which accompanied Felipe Bauza y Canas when he fled Spain for exile in England, is found in Ursula Lamb, "The London Years of Felipe Bauza: Spanish Hydrogapher in Exile, 1823-34," *The Journal of Navigation,* Vol. 34 (1981), pp. 319-40.

12. Novo y Colson, *Alrededor del Mundo,* pp. 157, 223.

13. F. J. Viana, *Diario del Viage Explorador de las Corbetas Espanolas Descubierta y Atrevida en los anos de 1789 a 1794* (Madrid: Cerrito de la Victoria, 1992), p. 84.

14. Quotation from Marshall and Williams, *Great Map of Mankind,* p. 259.

15. Andrew P. Vayda and Roy A. Rappaport, "Island Cultures," in *Cultures of the Pacific: Selected Readings,* ed. Thomas G. Harding and Ben J. Wallace (London: The Free Press, 1970), p. 5; William Howells, *The Pacific Islanders* (London: Weidenfeld and Nicholson, 1973), p. 5.

16. Novo y Colson, *Alrededor del Mundo,* pp. 261, 263, 275, 380.

17. *Ibid.,* pp. 260, 261, 263, 277.

18. *Ibid.,* p. 276 (emphasis added).

19. *Ibid.,* pp. 263, 268, 277.

20. *Ibid.,* pp. 277-78.

21. Alejandro Malaspina, "Examen Politico de las Colonias Inglesas en el Mar Pacifico, Islas del Mar del Sur," I, MS 318, Museo Naval, Madrid.

22. Novo y Colson, *Alrededor del Mundo,* p. 157.

23. Malaspina, "Examen politico."

24. *Ibid.*

25. *Ibid.*

26. Novo y Colson, *Alrededor del Mundo,* p. 378.

27. *Ibid.,* pp. 267, 277.

28. *Ibid.,* p. 268.

29. Greg Dening, *Mr. Bligh's Bad Language: Passion, Power, and Theatre on the Bounty* (Cambridge: Cambridge University Press, 1992), pp. 62-63, 114.

30. Novo y Colson, *Alrededor del Mundo,* pp. 261, 269.

31. *Ibid.,* p. 265.

32. *Ibid.,* p. 268; see also p. 385, but note that although one passage is attributed to Battista Guarini's *Il Pastor Fido,* it comes from Torquato Tasso's *Aminita,* Act I chorus.

33. Laurence Lerner, *The Uses of Nostalgia: Studies in Pastoral Poetry* (London: Chatto and Windus, 1972), p. 81; Nicholas Perella, *The Critical Fortune of Battista Guarini's "Il Pastor Fido"* (Florence: Biblioteca dell' Archivum Romanicum, 1973), p. 16; Renato Poggioli, *The Oaten Flute: Essays on Pastoral Poetry and the Pastoral Ideal* (Cambridge: Harvard University Press, 1975), p. 12.

34. Novo y Colson, *Alrededor del Mundo,* pp. 261-62, 272.

35. *Ibid.,* pp. 261, 280.

36. *Ibid.,* p. 384.

37. *Ibid.*

Part 2 Science and Technology

JOHN M. NAISH

The Health of Mariners: Vancouver's Achievement

We are faced with the difficulty of imagining what it would be like to be a sick man or a healer two hundred years ago. People then were full of prejudices, erroneous theories, and absurd expectations, as future generations, no doubt, will say of us. But we must try to picture a world without the germ theory of infection, a world that attributed infections to miasmas, fogs, and bad smells, or to the working of one's bilious humors.

In the eighteenth century the miasmatic or climatorial theory of infectious disease held sway. As an example, overripe cheese was thought to be dangerous because of its smell, and fever in jails and institutions was put down to their stink, rather than to germs carried by lice, fleas, and polluted water. The microbial nature of infectious disease was generally unsuspected. But, especially for the seafarer, the world was changing fast. Not only had navigational advances made long voyages possible, but food technology and methods of storage were changing. The move from cask to concentrates was speeding up. Scurvy was the one overwhelming threat to the exploitation of the Pacific by sealers, whalers, and fur traders. This was a dragon that Vancouver helped to slay.

But there were other problems of health afloat. For the sailor at anchor in either a crowded seaport or in some delectable bay in the Caribbean, there were many dangers besides scurvy. All the evils of overcrowding, vermin, parasites, and what we now call *cross-infection* threatened the sailor in just the same way they threatened the slumdweller. The eighteenth century intelligentsia attributed such scourges as jail fever (now known as typhus), plague, diphtheria, and scarlet fever to the bad smells and unhealthy mists that drifted around seaports. As for such tropical killers as malaria (caused by a parasite in the blood cells) or yellow fever (a mosquito-borne virus that blasts holes in the liver), they thought heat and humidity caused them. Without even suspecting night-biting mosquitoes, people nevertheless thought correctly that the evening air was the most dangerous. Since ships had to anchor on the downwind side of tropical islands, sailors got both the land smells and the mosquitoes. Hence, the shipboard mortality from these insect-borne diseases in the Caribbean was horrific: at least five percent of a ship's crew died each year served there.

On top of a heavy burden of ill health brought from the land there were the special risks of a sailor's life, including badly set broken bones, hernia, hypothermia, exposure-pneumonia, frostbite, and seawater sores. Madness appears to have affected a high proportion of officers, and suicide, often disguised as "man overboard," was common in all ranks. The practices of sweetening wine with lead acetate and storing wine in pewter vessels undoubtedly resulted in lead poisoning among officers, and this may have accounted for some of the mental problems.[1] Is it any wonder that the eighteenth-century embodiment of wit and intelligence, Dr. Samuel Johnson, should have said of a nautical vocation, "No man will be a sailor who has contrivance enough to get himself into a jail; for being in a ship is being in a jail, with the chance of being drowned.[2]

There were positive features, however, to seafaring, especially for a sailor in a British ship. As a basis for life, the navy man had a better diet than he could expect ashore. It may have been of necessity monotonous, but most young men of that era valued a full belly above everything else. In terms of daily caloric intake, protein content, and the presence of essential minerals, the victuals provided were adequate, and certainly more regular and better than the poor working-man could expect ashore.[3] The sailor was of course subject to the exigencies of long voyages and the activities of dishonest victualling officers and pursers. In the absence of refrigeration and modern storage techniques, a ship on a long voyage soon ran out of fresh food. But the British authorities were aware of the problems and took steps to mitigate them. The French explorers, in contrast, were endangered by corruption ashore.[4]

The sailor wore light, healthy clothing that enabled him to work among the rigging, where he was exposed to plenty of clean air. Diseases carried by lice and other bugs disappeared as soon as a ship got to sea, because sailors' clothing was frequently washed and dried in the sun. Simple cross-infections also burnt themselves out in a closed community.

Good nutrition at sea was important, not only because of its effect on recruitment and crew morale, but because the authorities had long realized the relationship between diet and health. They would have been very stupid if they had not deduced that scurvy was related to the lack of fresh food, for desperately ill scorbutic sailors recovered miraculously on land, though some poignantly died in the boats rowing them ashore. Everyone knew that it was fresh greens and fruit that cured scurvy, although they did not know why. It so happened that the eighteenth century was a great turning point in the history of dietetic medicine. Before the invention of the ship's wheel, the sextant, and the chronometer, long voyages had in general been coastwise, and explorers such as da Gama and Díaz usually lived off the land as they crept along the shores of Africa. Even so, da Gama's men were affected by scurvy as they made their way north up the east coast of Africa. The timely meeting with two Moorish boats laden with oranges gave them providential relief.[5] This reported incident is the first record of the curative powers of oranges, though John Woodall, the surgeon general of the British East India Company, was the first to publish in the *Surgeons Mate* of 1617 the advice that ships should be provisioned with oranges and lemons. He then tarnished his wisdom by adding, "If citrus is not available, use sulphuric acid."[6]

It was the voyage of George Anson in 1740 that taught seafarers that, however large the flotilla and well-found the ships, men would die like flies if deprived of fresh food on long voyages.[7] Anson started out with eight ships and 1,955 men. He came home with one ship and only 540 of his original complement. Most of them (995) died of scurvy, but shipwreck also occurred, caused by scorbutic weakness and debility of the crew. Thirty years later Cook returned from his first voyage with no losses from scurvy. Portable soup blocks, invented by Dubois in 1757, were a good way to get the men to eat green food gathered near the shore. The two most popular shore greens were scurvy grass (*Cochlearia curiosa*) and orache (*Chenopodium bonus-henricus*), but Cook used different shore greens in the southern hemisphere. The experiments and conclusions of Dr. James Lind in the 1750s had, by the time of Cook's return from his first voyage, percolated through to the most intelligent British naval officers.

Meanwhile the Spanish, who had the fullest experience of long Pacific voyages, had been going their own way. The lessons learned on those voyages were rarely published, but recent historical research by Dr. J. De Zulueta and others has shown that Spaniards were aware of the value of citrus fruit juices as far back as the sixteenth century.[8] But it was no part of official policy to victual their ships with antiscorbutics, hence the appalling health record of the explorations of the Northwest Coast from San Blas in the 1780s. The French explorers Bougainville, Lapérouse, and D'Entrecasteaux all suffered in different degrees from the shipping of low-quality provisions and the consequent decay of stores during their voyages. This had an unexpected and beneficial consequence. The ships became infested with rats living off the rotting food, and both officers and men appreciated the gastronomic virtues of roast rat. What they did not realize was that rat meat, like all fresh meat, contained significant quantities of ascorbic acid. So it was the rats, cooked in the inimitable Gallic fashion, that saved many of Bougainville's men from death.[9]

It is important to consider the causes and symptoms of scurvy, using today's knowledge to explain how the disease arises. This should be done in consideration of the fog of ignorance in which eighteenth-century minds were struggling. There are two important dates in the history of scurvy. The first was 1753, when James Lind published his *Treatise of the Scurvy,* which was followed very much later by the discovery by A. Holst, the Norwegian scientist, that the guinea pig could be used to determine the antiscorbutic properties of food.[10] The second critical date was 1912, when Gowland Hopkins and Casimir Funk both published their papers on vitamins, establishing that certain essential substances were in food, substances that were necessary to prevent illness.[11]

James Lind, a humble naval surgeon, had employed a true experimental scientific method when he had charge of the health of a 60-gun ship, the *Salisbury,* of the Channel Fleet. He gave different groups of scorbutic seamen different dietary supplements, even such unlikely aids as seawater and diluted sulphuric acid, and he watched for improvement. Only the seamen who were given lemons got better.

Lind used unforgettable language in describing the manifestations of scurvy. Large discolored spots, or hemorrhages, were dispersed over the whole body. The legs swelled and the gums became puffy and painful. The sufferers had a tendency to swoon and suffered both from shivering and terrors. Scars of wounds that had been healed for many years broke out afresh, and sores that appeared on the legs would not heal, showing "a luxuriancy of fungous flesh." Men being taken ashore to recuperate might swoon and die instantly.[12]

In his more complete 1797 publication, *The Health of Seamen,* Lind was full of practical suggestions for commanders to follow in order to avoid scurvy. For example, officers were advised to grow cress on wet flannel or lettuce in earth boxes on the quarterdeck. Lemon juice could be preserved in pint bottles under a thin layer of olive oil with the cork fully waxed over. Every sailor was advised to have his own personal supply of onions. This was very good advice. In his classic, *Two Years before the Mast* (1840), Dana described how the cook rescued a man almost dead from scurvy by squeezing onion juice through his swollen lips. The admiralty took no bold action on any of Lind's eminently practical suggestions, except that shipboard surgeons were provided with supplies of rob of orange or lemon for treatment of the scorbutic. Rob was an Arab recipe for a heat-evaporated citrus syrup. Although its ascorbic acid content was much reduced by heat and storage, it was still of some value in the treatment of scurvy.

Ascorbic acid, or vitamin C, is a fairly simple chemical compound that is an essential component of all growing tissues. In mammals, it is necessary to prevent hemorrhage from bruised blood vessels and to promote the healing process. Because the human body cannot manufacture ascorbic acid, it must be taken in the diet to maintain the body's stores. The recommended daily requirement is about thirty milligrams per day, although much less will suffice to keep scurvy at bay.

John M. Naish

82

Portions Needed to Supply Daily Ascorbic Acid

Foodstuff	Ounces
Blackcurrants	0.5
Rose-hip syrup	0.5
Citrus fruits	2.0–3.0
Brussel sprouts	2.5
Boiled cabbage	6.0
Potatoes	5.0–18.0
Peas	20.0
Milk	80.0 (4 pints)
Fruit Juices:	
Lemon	2.0
Orange	2.0
Grapefruit	3.0
Tangerine	4.0
Lime	6.0

Depending on the body's limited storage capacity, early symptoms of scurvy will begin to show two to three months after leaving land. Deprivation experiments with human volunteers during the Second World War showed that, however well-fed the volunteer was beforehand, the ascorbic acid levels in the blood became unmeasurable after only six weeks, but overt symptoms of scurvy often did not appear until after three months. Ships' provisions were mainly cereal, in the form of wheat biscuit and oatmeal, and meat, in the form of brine-pickled beef or pork. Because scurvy was so closely associated with the consumption of salted food, many erroneously thought that scurvy was caused by the salt or even the fat skimmings on top of the salt stew. The manifestations of scurvy—weakness, fatigue, easy bruising, bleeding from the gums, and failure to heal small injuries—were not only life-threatening themselves but also rendered the sailor incapable of carrying out his duties. Many a shipwreck was caused by crew disoriented by scurvy.

When he set out in 1791 with about one hundred forty-five very young and fit men, Vancouver knew a great deal more about scurvy than most men of that time. He was a faithful disciple of Cook, whose ideas were an amalgam of common sense and acquired knowledge. The emphasis was on cleanliness, ventilation of quarters, vermin control, firing, and frequent recreation ashore. Vancouver always tried to find a secure anchorage every six weeks or so, so that his men could go ashore and gather green food, berries, and nuts. Both Cook and Vancouver recognized the importance of fresh meat, as opposed to salted meat, and the restorative value of fresh plant food. Further, they did everything in their power to provide such food for their sailors. Toward the end of Cook's life, he learned the value of brewing beer flavored by fresh spruce needles instead of kiln-dried hops. This advance in nutritional thinking was the key to Vancouver's great success in preserving crew health.

In his immense task of charting the Northwest Coast, Vancouver had to halt his ships from time to time and from place to place in secure anchorages where he could take ashore his astronomical instruments and determine his exact position. The carpenters, blacksmiths, and sailmakers also needed to work ashore, and, most important, so did the brewers. Instead of using malt as a substrate for the brewing of alcohol, Vancouver used molasses, stored in barrels and obtained cheaply from the West Indies. When the mixture of molasses and water had been brought to the boil in huge vats, the mixture was allowed to cool, and then yeast and spruce needles were added. Often the needles of the western hemlock were used instead of spruce. The resulting spruce beer was run into casks, which could be stored on board. It was palatable, and the sailors were allowed as much as one-half gallon per day. During the period October 1791 to January 1795, while he was mainly away from settled lands, Vancouver found anchorages suitable for brewing on thirty-six different occasions.[13] Brewing is mentioned specifically in his journal on eight of these occasions. Menzies mentions three more examples in Alaska.[14]

It is almost certain that Vancouver had spruce beer brewed about once each month during his Alaskan and British Columbian explorations and perhaps less frequently when the ships were in California and Hawaiian waters, where the crew had access to fresh fruit, vegetables, and meat. Elwyn Hughes has shown by careful analyses that many aqueous extracts of antiscorbutic plants lose most of their ascorbic acid in the course of preparation, and fermentation might cause further oxidation.[15] However, the daily consumption of spruce beer was about one-half gallon (approximately two liters), so even one milligram of ascorbic acid per one hundred milliliters would ensure the required daily intake of thirty milligrams.

There were two episodes of scurvy on the voyage, both at the end of long passages at sea. The first was in October 1792, as the *Discovery* was nearing San Francisco after a tediously long passage from Friendly Cove, Nootka Sound. It is notable that the crew of the *Chatham,* which had separated to explore the Columbia River, found fresh victuals ashore and so did not get scurvy. The second and more serious outbreak of scurvy was in March 1795, after an exceptionally long voyage from the Cocos Islands, which had been visited in January.

During the summers of 1793 and 1794, when Vancouver spent many months in Alaska, he was acutely aware of the dangers of scurvy, as he had read of

Meares's disaster in Prince William Sound in 1787.[16] Menzies sent out parties to gather raspberries, blueberries, orache, and salicornia greens.[17] The methods employed by Vancouver and Menzies were generally successful, and their overall record in preventive medicine is outstanding. In Vancouver's lengthy expedition, only five men were lost out of one hundred eighty men at risk in the period between the time the ships left Falmouth in April 1791 until they returned to Ireland in October 1795. Three of these deaths were from accidents. The total mortality of one death in every eleven months among an average population of about one hundred sixty represents an annual mortality rate of 0.65 percent. Compare this with the expected annual mortality of six percent for ships trading in the Caribbean and Vancouver's achievement is shown to be very remarkable.

However much the admiralty and the British government were distracted in 1795 by the war with France, and despite the cold shoulder they gave George Vancouver upon his return, they must have learned valuable lessons from his record in preventive medicine afloat. Three years later, in 1798, they at last accepted Sir Gilbert Blane's advice to make citrus fruit juices part of the daily victuals. Penny-pinching as usual, they later used West Indian limes for their stores, a relatively poor source of ascorbic acid, but it was a measure that undoubtedly saved thousands of lives in the years that followed. It attracted the scorn of the American sailors who were then invading the Pacific in gallant cohorts of free enterprise. British sailors, thought to be namby-pambys for drinking lime juice instead of whisky, were christened "Limeys." Spruce beer had been a godsend in its day, but it was superseded by the much more convenient citrus juice.

Another surefire way of preventing scurvy was used only intermittently and was never promoted by the medical profession. Sprouting peas and beans contain plenty of ascorbic acid, and the dried seeds store well. Thus, the best answer to scurvy at sea in the days of scientific ignorance, the repeated germination of peas and beans and the consumption of their sprouts, was never tried on a large scale. Instead, the doctors spent more than four hundred years theorizing about the cause of scurvy, using whatever was the fashionable or politically correct jargon of the time. To name but a few of these in order of appearance, consider: splenetic humor, bad air, damp skin, potassium deficiency, alkalinity of the blood, putrefaction, and ptomaine poisoning.

Today we not only know a great deal about vitamin deficiency in general, and scurvy in particular, but we can always look to the seamen and the arctic explorers as experimental animals. Only forty years ago Surgeon Commander Cleeve of the Royal Navy was able to use the port and starboard watches of a battleship to conduct a dietary experiment that showed the great importance of a high fiber diet. He reached conclusions from his studies afloat that initiated whole programs of research and great advances in understanding.[18] So, like Vancouver's men, sailors and explorers in the wilderness can help the rest of us. Vancouver, by his tender care of his crew, was a true pioneer of health promotion.

NOTES

The author is most grateful to Kenneth Carpenter, Professor Emeritus in the Department of Nutritional Sciences, University of California, Berkeley, for his helpful suggestions and criticism during the preparation of this paper. The author also thanks Anne Savours (Mrs. Shirley) for her indication of useful sources.

1. A. Heywood, "The Treatment of Lead Poisoning," *Medical History* (Wellcome Institute for the History of Medicine, 1990), Supp. 10, pp. 82–101; J. Eisinger, "Lead and Wine," *Medical History* (Wellcome Institute for the History of Medicine, 1982), Supp. 26, pp. 279–302.

2. Boswell, *Life of Johnson,* ed. L. F. Powell of G. B. Hill's edition (Oxford: Clarendon Press, 1934), Vol. 1, March 16, 1759, p. 348.

3. N. A. M. Rodger, *The Wooden World* (London: Collins, 1986), pp. 82–86.

4. A. Carre, "Eighteenth Century French Voyages of Exploration," in *Starving Sailors* (London: National Maritime Museum, 1981) (hereafter Carre, *Starving Sailors*).

5. K. J. Carpenter, *The History of Scurvy and Vitamin C* (Cambridge: Cambridge University Press), pp. 1–2.

6. J. Woodall, *The Surgeons Mate* (London: 1617; Kirkup, 1978).

7. Carpenter, *History of Scurvy,* pp. 46–51, quoting R. Walter, *A Voyage round the World by George Anson, Esq.,* 4th ed. (London, 1748); B. Somerville, *Commodore Anson's Voyage into the South Seas and around the World* (London: Heinemann and Watt); and Carre, *Starving Sailors,* pp. 51–59.

8. J. De Zulueta and L. Higueras, "Health and Navigation in the South Seas: The Spanish Experience," in Carre, *Starving Sailors,* pp. 51–59.

9. Carre, *Starving Sailors,* p. 82.

10. J. Lind, *A Treatise of the Scurvy* (Edinburgh: Millar, 1753; reprint, Steward and Guthrie, 1953); A. Holst and T. Frohlich, "Experimental Studies Relating to 'Ship Beriberi' and Scurvy," Ch. 1., Introduction, "The Etiology of Scurvy," *Journal of Hygiene,* (Cambridge: Cambridge University Press, 1907), pp. 619–33, 634–71.

11. H. G. Hopkins, "Feeding Experiments Illustrating the Importance of Accessory Factors in Normal Dietaries," *Journal of Physiology,* Vol. 44 (1912), pp. 425–60; C. Funk, "The Etiology of Deficiency Diseases," *Journal of State Medicine* (1912), pp. 20341–68.

12. Lind, *Treatise of Scurvy.*

13. George Vancouver, *A Voyage of Discovery to the North Pacific Ocean and round the World, 1791-1795,* ed. W. Kaye Lamb, 4 vols. (London: Hakluyt Society, 1984) (hereafter Lamb, *Vancouver's Voyage*).

14. Archibald Menzies Journal, 1791–94, Add MS 32641 and 1794–95, British Library, London; National Library of Australia MS 255; W. M. Olson, *The Alaska Travel Journal of Archibald Menzies, 1793-1794* (Fairbanks: University of Alaska Press, 1993) (hereafter Olson, *Menzies's Journal*).

John M.
Naish

86

15. R. E. Hughes, "The Rise and Fall of the 'Antiscorbutics,' " *Medical History,* Vol. 34 (1990), pp. 3452–64, quoting F. W. Fox and W. Stone, "The Antiscorbutic Value of Kaffir Beer," *South Africa Journal of Medicine and Science,* Vol. 3 (1938), pp. 7–14.

16. Lamb, *Vancouver's Voyage.*

17. Olson, *Menzies's Journal.*

18. T. L. Cleeve, *The Saccharine Diseases* (Bristol: John Wright, 1958).

The Health
of Mariners:
Vancouver's
Achievement

JOHN KENDRICK

The Evolution of Shipbuilding in the Eighteenth Century

W*ith a favourable wind on Friday the 7th [1791], we sailed, and anchored in Long Reach about five in the evening. Although this trial of the ship may appear very insignificant, yet as she had never been under sail, it was not made without some anxiety.* *The construction of her upper works, for the sake of adding to the comfort of the accommodations, differing materially from the general fashion, produced an unsightly appearance, and gave rise to various opinions unfavourable to her qualities as a sea-boat; for which reason it was natural to pay the minutest attention to her steering and other properties when in motion; and we obtained in the course of this short trip, the pleasing prospect of her proving handy, and in all other respects a very comfortable vessel.*

GEORGE VANCOUVER, *A Voyage of Discovery . . . 1791–1795*

During the eighteenth century, the perfection of the chronometer and the publication of ephemerides such as the *Nautical Almanac* revolutionized navigation. In contrast, the evolution of shipbuilding and ship design was slow and fairly steady for a long time, and improvements during the eighteenth century were part of a process that was well under way by 1700, and continued after 1800. The application of science was the one quantum change to the design of the hulls of deep-sea vessels that is specific to the eighteenth century. Other than this, it was a time of improvement rather than invention in the design of the rig as well as the hull.[1] As much as anything, the improvements depended on seamen who, like George Vancouver, did not reject a vessel just because it differed from the general fashion.

By 1700, ships had crossed all the world's oceans, and regular trade routes had been established from Europe to the Atlantic coasts of the Americas, to Africa, and to India and the Spice Islands. The Manila fleet made regular annual voyages from Acapulco to the Philippines and back. The navies of European countries had ships built especially for their service, rather than relying on converted merchantmen, while merchant ships were designed for special

88

occupations, such as fishing or timber transport, or for special needs, such as adaptability to the shallow waters of the Baltic or the shoals off Holland. Masts, rigging, and sails had been developed to the point that most long voyages were completed, and most of the completed voyages achieved at least some of their objectives.

Shipbuilding in 1700 was based on the practices and prejudices of builders who guarded their knowledge from those not admitted to the craft. That knowledge was based on the slow accretion of experience. If something worked, it was repeated. If it did not work, there might be no one alive to tell what went wrong. Under these circumstances, the acceptance of new ideas was understandably slow and grudging, both on the part of builders and of the mariners whose lives depended on the soundness of their ships.

This paper will discuss ships used for exploration, treating features common to most European ships and omitting the subtle differences of ship design and shipbuilding among the major maritime nations. Although it is true that shipbuilding in 1700 was an arcane art, there had been some attempts to record the process. The *Album de Colbert* was compiled prior to 1677, although the exact date is not known.[2] The earliest text on shipbuilding known to this author was published in 1587 in Mexico.[3] It starts with the premise that all matter is composed of the four elements, earth, air, fire, and water. From earth and fire come metals, while trees are made of earth, water, and air. The book offers useful advice (one can hardly say rules) on the building and rigging of ships and contains the earliest drawing of the form of a ship's hull. There is even reason to believe that a ship built on the basis of this book could sail successfully. Only a few other early books on the topic are known. In Spain, Antonio Garrote published a book in 1673 that is known chiefly for its lists of ships and their dimensions.[4] In Britain, Daniel Newhouse's effort of 1701 offers a dictionary of nautical terms.[5] Dassié's *Architecture navale* was published in France in 1677, the only known text on the topic in that country until the eighteenth century.

These works of the seventeenth century or earlier indicate how little information about shipbuilding was published at the time. Drawings hardly existed. For a new ship, the master shipwright would carve a half model of the hull. When the lines looked right to his practiced eye, the shape of the frames was taken off the model and enlarged in the molding loft. When the ship was under construction, the lines might be further corrected if they looked wrong.

In 1700, some but not all vessels in European navies were built and rigged in naval dockyards. The yard built the hull and turned it over to the owner, who would rig it with whatever masts and sails he thought suitable. Since ships might have many different owners and different uses during their lifetimes, they might also have a number of different rigs. Thus, although there was some agreement on hull design, there was almost none for the rig. In general, the

Figure 1. Typical ship of ca. 1700. A third sail on each mast, called the topgallant, was coming into use at this time. *Courtesy of Don Rafael Berenguer*

rig of a deep-sea vessel of the seventeenth century might look like that shown in the first figure. Except for the large and unwieldy mizzen, it carried only square sails, each hung from a yard attached to a mast. Even the bowsprit had its square sails. Sometimes a spritsail topsail on a short mast was mounted on the bowsprit.

A ship rigged like this could make little if any progress against the wind, and it was awkward to tack. On long voyages, one had to follow the prevailing winds, which never seemed to prevail in the desired direction when needed. Navigators established preferred routes according to the season on the basis of experience, their own or by word of mouth, and pilot charts were printed as late as 1940 to depict the preferred routes.

The size of the sails was limited by the strength of the crew. This in turn limited the size of ships, since dividing a sail horizontally into upper and lower members brought complications and extra weight in the masts and rigging. When steel masts and steel wire rigging came into use, a ship might have six or even seven sails on one mast, but that was not possible with wooden masts in the eighteenth century.

The application of science to ship design can be traced back to the early eighteenth century, although it is possible that it goes back further. The first scientific theories were concerned with the stability of the hull, to determine what keeps a ship upright. Mathematical procedures were developed that are still in use today. In 1720, a Spanish text on the subject appeared, Antonio Gaztañeta's *Proporciones de las medidas más esempciales para la fabricación de navios.* It is broadly similar to a modern text on the stability of a hull form.

Gaztañeta's book attracted little attention outside Spain. The Paris Académie des Sciences offered a prize for the development of a theory of stability in the year that Gaztañeta's book was published. It was left for Fredrik Henrik Chapman to set out the theory and gain the reputation of being the father of naval architecture. His *Architectura navalis mercator* was published in 1765. Born in Sweden in 1721, Chapman was born to English parents, but his father had joined the Swedish navy in 1716.[6] Chapman used stability theory to analyze the performance of ships before they were built. His design calculations use the same analytical procedures as those adopted by present-day naval architects.

The theoretical mathematics of stability was well understood in the eighteenth century, and an accurate calculation of the stability of a hull design could be made. This was not mere academic cheeseparing. It is probable that the *Wasa* capsized and sank in Stockholm harbor in 1628 because of an unstable loading condition. The *Mary Rose* may have gone down off Portsmouth in 1545 for the same reason. In both cases, the monarch was watching.

The dynamics of a hull form, however, were not well understood in the eighteenth century. No one could calculate why one hull would move through the water faster than another under identical conditions. The best shape of a hull was still a matter of experience and judgment, even though Euler's *Scientia navalis* in 1749 set out some theoretical principles of hull resistance. These were of no use in the absence of any measurements of the resistance of actual hulls. Chapman did some tank towing experiments, but used only simple geometric forms, including various parabolas, an arrowhead shape, and a triangular block. His equipment was so crude that not much was learned, except that the triangular block, towed flat side first, took a long time to cross the tank. Hull resistance was not thoroughly studied until the days of high-speed steel naval vessels, and finally racing yachts. Australia won the America's Cup in 1983 because of a keel design incorporating stubby "wings" at the lower edge, which no one had previously considered. The wings suppress the turbulence at the bottom of the keel, preventing the unnecessary consumption of energy.

The most comprehensive nineteenth-century text on shipbuilding was in the marine volumes of the *Encyclopédie* of Diderot and d'Alembert. These two French *philosophes* attempted to compile a complete record of human knowledge. Their political writings were probably the cause of the French Revolution and had considerable influence among the promoters of the American Revolution. However, it is the scientific work on marine subjects that is relevant to the subject of this paper. As revised for the 1783 edition by the Paris publisher Pancoucke, it contains 2,400 pages of text and just over 1,500 figures. It includes the principles of navigation and a description of the naval and merchant marine administrations, but most of it is related to the design, construction, and rigging of ships. The mathematical theory of stability is fully explained, but the *Encyclopédie* also includes practical matters, such as the shape of trees and branches required to make the many angled or curved pieces for a ship.

It did not follow that the theories were applied to the design of all ships. On the contrary, it is likely that many of the world's shipwrights had never heard of them. If they had, they probably would have continued to base their designs on tradition. The British admiralty was particularly rigid. New designs were not officially permitted, although shipyards often bent the rules.[7] Vancouver's ship the *Discovery* escaped conformity to the establishment because it was designed and built as a merchant ship, then purchased by the navy while it was still on the stocks and converted for long-distance sailing. In spite of Vancouver's initial optimism, the *Discovery* gave him a good deal of trouble on the voyage. The structure at the forward end was weak, and the workmanship no better. He was not long at sea before suffering damage that had to be put right in Capetown. The problems were never completely overcome. Vancouver's consort, a former naval tender named the *Chatham,* performed better.[8]

Even although it was smaller and presumed to be slower, it sometimes arrived before the *Discovery* at their various rendezvous points.

Most of the explorers' ships were used vessels that had not initially been built for long voyages. James Cook used four different ships on his three voyages, the *Endeavour* on his first, the *Resolution* and the *Adventure* on his second, and the *Resolution* (again) and the *Discovery* on his third (this was not Vancouver's flagship). All of Cook's ships were converted Whitby colliers, ships built for carrying coal along the east coast of England. They were roomy, flat-bottomed vessels with the capacity for all the stores and equipment needed for a long voyage.

The French explorer Lapérouse was given two transports, converted and renamed the *Astrolabe* and the *Boussole*. Neither ship gave the expedition any problems until they were wrecked, presumably in a hurricane. Alejandro Malaspina, the Italian in the Spanish service, was able to have his *Descubierta* and *Atrevida* specially built to his own specifications, not to a naval standard. He had already circumnavigated the world, had made at least one other extensive Pacific voyage, and knew what he wanted. His main requirements were a simple rig, ample space for stores and for the accommodation of the crew, and only enough guns to deal with possible hostilities from Natives without firearms. His ships performed well, surviving winds that probably reached hurricane force while he was on his way from Australia to Tonga. With the possible exception of Malaspina's ships, none of these explorers' vessels had the benefit of any scientific theory of hull design.

A book published in 1794 shows the gap between theory and practice.[9] The author, William Hutchinson, was not a builder or a trained scientist but a master mariner. Evidently he understood something of physics and of hydrostatic theory. He knew that the volume of water coming through "plug holes of equal bigness" varied as the square root of the depth below the surface, but he could not articulate his theory very well. He wrote: "That hole at four feet deep would leak or let in as much water again as that at one foot, . . . and that at sixteen feet four times as much."[10]

Hutchinson understood the relationship between the center of gravity, the center of "cavity" (buoyancy), and the stability of a ship. He correctly stated that, if the ship were too stable, it could have a violent rolling motion, which in one of his ships became "so laboursome as to roll away two topmasts." The lower the center of gravity of a loaded ship, the more powerful is the righting force when it heels. This reduces the period of roll, and the ship will roll violently from side to side. To avoid this, modern ships built to transport steel are designed to carry part of the cargo on deck. With all this, Hutchinson expressed an understanding of the theory but could apply it only qualitatively to

Figure 2. Typical ship of the late eighteenth century. The square sail on the bowsprit was then going out of use. *Courtesy of Don Rafael Berenguer*

design. A vessel should not be "over-sharp" in the bows, but neither should it be "over-full bowed." He could not say how sharp was "over-sharp," and could only express the condition of "over-full" with the colorful language of a seaman. The principle was understood from the middle of the eighteenth century.

Although there was a limited knowledge of hull dynamics by the end of the eighteenth century, knowledge of the forces of the wind on sails was a complete blank. When Lieutenant William Bligh inspected the *Bounty* in 1787 before his voyage to Tahiti, he ordered the masts to be cut down "as I thought them too much for her, considering the nature of the voyage." There was no scientific calculation. It was done only because he thought the ship was overpowered. He also thought there was too much ballast, so he reduced the iron in the hold to nineteen tons from forty-five, "for I am of the opinion, that many of the misfortunes which attend ships in heavy storms of wind, are occasioned by too much dead weight in their bottoms." [11]

Again, opinion rather than science, ruled, although the science of naval architecture now confirms that he was right. The ship suffered no important "misfortunes" until the crew mutinied, although Bligh was unable to round Cape Horn in a prolonged storm and had to retreat to the Cape of Good Hope and sail eastward from there. With a taller rig and more ballast she might have been successful in rounding Cape Horn, but who can tell, and who can dispute his decision? No one can offer any proof that the cut down rig was the reason he had to retreat.

Ignorance of wind forces continued, even late in the nineteenth century. As late as 1882, W. H. White wrote, "Up to the present time, accurate knowledge is almost entirely wanting respecting the laws which govern wind pressures on large sails." [12] In spite of the lack of theory, there was great progress in sail configuration, as shown by the second figure. The large lateen mizzen sail of the seventeenth century was replaced by the spanker, which was a fore and aft sail on the aftermost mast. This was not only much easier to handle but also more effective for maneuvering the ship. The square sails on the bowsprit had almost gone out of use, being replaced by fore and aft headsails, which were simple sails mounted high above the turbulence caused by the ship's hull and rigging. The eighteenth-century mariner probably thought turbulence was something that happened among the crew when the cook ruined the dinner. He would have said the headsails were clear of dirty air.

Most of the vessels that explored the Northwest Coast were rigged similarly to the accompanying figure but were smaller vessels, with only one square sail on the mizzen mast. Other than this, they differed from the figure as shown in the table on p. 96.

SHIP	COMMANDER	Differences from Figure 2
Discovery	Vancouver	Two headsails
Endeavour	Cook	Two headsails, two spritsails
Adventure	Cook	Two headsails
Resolution	Cook	Two headsails
Discovery	Cook	Two headsails
Bounty	Bligh	None, one sail on mizzen
Descubierta	Malaspina	Two headsails
Astrolabe	Lapérouse	No data [13]

The improvements to rigs in the eighteenth century, based on experience and a willingness to experiment with sails not of the general fashion, were the most important advance in ship design during the century. There were still some misconceptions, such as the idea that sails should always be hauled as taut as possible. But an empirical science grew up, which led to better setting of sails by means of lines attached to them to control their shape.

Rigs grew taller, with three or even four sails on each mast, and various fair-weather sails were added for use in light winds. With all this, by 1800 the deep-sea ship was an efficient machine to use for long voyages. This led to the exploration during the eighteenth century of all the oceans of the world.

A mixture of science and pseudoscience was used for the design of rigs. If the masts were stepped too far forward, a ship would tend to turn away from the wind; if the masts were too far back, the ship would turn into the wind. This was the pure science part of rig design. Applied science told the designer that a ship was easy to control if the masts were placed so the ship would tend to turn up into the wind, balanced by equally slight turning of the rudder. Under these conditions, a ship was said to "carry weather helm," a phrase going back to the days of tiller steering, when the helm or tiller was held slightly to the weather side of the ship.

It was not only the placement of the masts that controlled this balance, but the shape of the underwater body of the hull. When a ship is on an even keel, the wetted surface is symmetrical. But when it heels over in response to the wind pressure, the water line takes an odd shape, and most hulls, if driven straight ahead by an external force when heeled, will turn away from the low side. A seaman would say that the hull is "ardent." To offset this, the masts are moved forward a bit, an estimate based on the mariner's best experience.

There was no mathematical equation to explain the answer at the time, but the laws of a pseudophysics were invoked to give a clue. First, it was assumed that all sails were perfectly flat and that they were all turned exactly to the longitudinal axis of the ship. Sail plans were drawn with the sails in this impossible position. It was further assumed that the wind pressure was exerted at the exact center of each sail. Then it was taken that all the forces of wind on sails were countered by the lateral resistance of the hull, exerted through the center of the profile of the immersed hull. The leverage of each sail could then be calculated and combined at a "center of effort," which was placed forward of the center of lateral resistance by about four percent of the length of the ship, to counteract the ardency of the hull. Such a calculation could be performed either by pages of calculations or graphically, as shown on a number of sail plans.

In the clear light of modern naval architecture, it appears none of these assumptions is true. Yet at the time, they provided a basis for comparing successful designs, thus reducing the number of ships of new design. When there were complaints of badly performing ships, the masts were moved forward or aft to correct bad sailing qualities.

The total sail area was based on rules of thumb. It was not possible for the shipbuilder to simply increase or decrease all dimensions of a sail plan proportionate to the size of the ship. A sail plan successful for one hull would be inadequate for a larger similar vessel if it were just scaled up, and a smaller one would be overpowered if it were just scaled down.

Both the location of shipyards and the methods of construction were governed by the limits of muscle power. Although Newcomen invented an atmospheric steam engine in 1705, it was of little use. James Watt discovered the principle of the condensing steam engine in 1769, but it was not applied to industrial uses until close to the end of the century. Until then, the only forms of motive power in a shipyard were the muscles of men and animals. Water power was rarely used in shipyards, although often used to turn waterwheels for grinding corn or pumping water. In England, forests, like everything else in the country, were close to the sea, so shipbuilding could be concentrated in relatively large yards. In Spain, with oak forests in the interior near rivers, shipyards were located at the mouths of many rivers, where timber could be floated to the sea. During the eighteenth century, the Spanish concentrated shipbuilding in a few places, such as El Ferrol, Cádiz, Cartagena, and Havana, although ships were still built in small yards at the mouths of rivers throughout the nineteenth century. To reduce the volume of wood to be transported, and then pulled out of the river manually, logs were squared with an adze, and curved pieces might even be hewn to approximately their final shape.

In the seventeenth century, one of the major French shipyards was in the dockyard at Toulon. In the Service Historique de la Marine in the Château de Vincennes there is a set of drawings showing the process from start to finish. It is known as the *Album de Colbert.* Jean Baptiste Colbert (1619–83) was a promi-

Figure 3. The naval dockyard of Toulon, late seventeenth century. *Musée de la Marine, Paris*

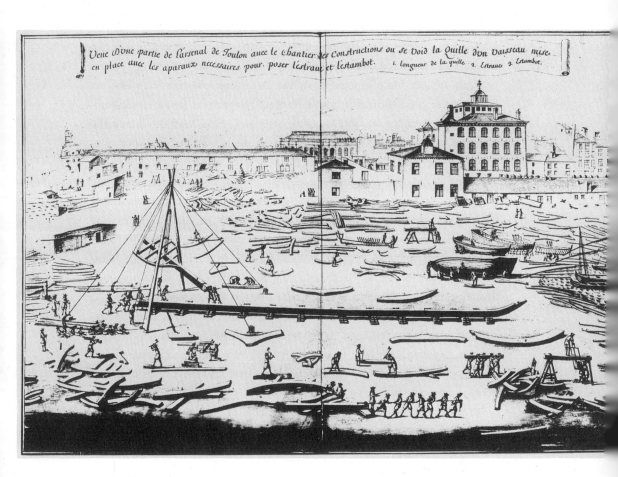

nent minister under Louis XIV, who established the French Academy of Science and the Paris Observatory. The king either commissioned the drawings or acquired them, presumably because of their scientific interest. The first drawing in the Colbert album shows the shipyard, with the stern frame of a ship just being hoisted into place. A ship of the size shown would have had scaffolding erected on each side of the hull during construction. Presumably the artist omitted this to give a clear view of the process. It takes eighteen men to erect the frame, nine hauling on the hoist and nine guiding it into place. There are also three men with staves supervising the operation. Others are moving timbers in the yard or hewing or sawing them to size and shape. This was a major shipyard; most ships of the time were built in much simpler facilities. The fifty plates in the Colbert album follow each step of the work to the finished vessel.

A much more extensive album commissioned by the Marqués de la Victoria in Spain shows the building and fitting out of a vessel of 1736. It includes construction, rigging, sailmaking, a ropewalk, and other details. Similarly, the Royal Dockyards on the Thames were extensive, with storehouses for the myriad articles required to fit out and equip a ship, but without much more in the way of shipbuilding tools than in a small shipyard.

Until more recent times, when ships began to be built in pieces and welded together, the launching of a ship was a critical operation, as well as a ceremonial occasion. The weight of the ship was transferred from the stocks to a launching frame lashed to an anchorage inshore from the bow of the ship. A wooden anchor stock might be tied to a line leading from the bow of the ship, so that when it has slid into the water there would be something to take hold of to tow it to its berth. When all was ready, the master carpenter took an axe and a mallet and cut the lashings. At that instant, the ship was cut off from the land and became forever a part of the sea. The ceremony persists to this day—at a ship's launching in Europe the sponsor cuts a ribbon with a miniature mallet and axe or chisel.

By the end of the eighteenth century, the deep-sea ship had become about as efficient as it could be, until iron and steel came into use. It had assumed an appearance that did not change radically to the end of the days of sail. The usefulness of fore and aft sails was recognized, even though it was not understood, and steering was greatly improved by the belated invention of the steering wheel, which replaced a lever called a whipstaff used until the end of the seventeenth century. The lateen mizzen was abandoned in favor of the more effective and manageable spanker. There was still a maze of rigging lines made of thick hemp rope, which caught the wind and blew the ship downwind, not simplified until steel wire came into use. If the wind failed there was no auxiliary power except for the ship's crew, who would get into a boat and tow the ship. This was essential at times for getting in and out of harbor, but impractical for moving a ship any distance.

To sum up, the eighteenth century saw the introduction of science to ship design and a willingness to try out new designs, partly because ship owners and mariners gained confidence in scientific ideas. Little was known of the dynamics of a ship moving through the water or of the action of waves on the hull. This remained for nineteenth-century naval architects to work out, and even they had only the most rudimentary ideas of the action of wind on sails. Long before this was understood, someone thought of putting a steam engine in a ship. Square riggers then survived only on long runs, particularly in the Pacific, where there were no coaling stations.

On the Northwest Coast, the ships used in the major expeditions were usually converted from an earlier, more simple purpose. Science was rarely applied to the most important sailing ventures of the era. And, as this era passed into the age of the steamship, the Northwest Coast was prominent again, as San Francisco was often the final port of call for these wooden ships. San Francisco Bay had been crowded with laid up square-riggers during the gold rush, when crews deserted en masse. It later became crowded with square-riggers again when the trade deserted them. Indeed, San Francisco's first industry was shipbreaking, or dismantling old vessels. The revival of this industry in the 1930s marked the end of the wooden sailing vessel that had been so patiently developed over several centuries.

NOTES

1. Rig: The configuration of masts and sails on a vessel. This and other nautical terms are defined in the glossary at the end of this paper.

2. Hubert Berti, *Album de Colbert* (Nice: Omega, 1988).

3. Diego García Palacio, comp., *Instrucion [sic] Nauthica, y regimento de las Naos . . .* (Mexico City, 1587; rpt. Madrid: Ediciones Cultura Hispanica, 1944).

4. Antonio Garrote, *Recopilación para la nueva fábrica de vaxeles españoles* (Madrid: Consejo Científicos, 1691).

5. Daniel Newhouse, *The Whole Art of Navigation* (London: T. Nelson, 1701).

6. Daniel G. Harris, *F. H. Chapman: The First Naval Architect and His Work* (London: Conway Maritime Press, 1989), p. 9.

7. Howard I. Chappelle, *The History of the American Sailing Navy* (New York: Bonanza, 1949), p. 9. In this passage, Chapelle was writing of ships built in British yards prior to the American Revolution.

8. The *Chatham* was a brig, a two-masted vessel with square sails on both masts.

9. William Hutchinson, *Treatise on Naval Architecture* (London, 1794, rpt. Greenwich: Conway Maritime Press).

10. *Ibid.,* p. 10.

11. William Bligh, *A Voyage to the Southern Seas . . .* (London: George Nicol, 1792), pp. 2, 3.

12. W. H. White, *A Manual of Naval Architecture,* 2d ed. (London: John Murray, 1882), p. 484.

13. Taken from secondary sources. Not all of them are in agreement. We have no information on Lapérouse's *Astrolabe* and *Boussole,* except that before their conversion they were *flûtes,* a term used loosely to mean some form of cargo-carrying vessel.

GLOSSARY

Bowsprit. A pole mounted in the bow of a ship, pointing forward.

Fore and aft sail. A sail attached at its forward edge to a mast or stay, which can be angled to the wind as desired without interference from the rigging.

Frames. The usually curved members rising from the keel to the deck to which the outer planking is attached. When all the frames are in place or laid out on a drawing, they define the lines of a ship.

Gaff. A form of yard, with the forward end flexibly attached to a mast, and the after end supported by a line led from higher up on the mast.

Headsails. A general term for the fore and aft sails forward of the foremast.

Heel. The tilt of a hull from the upright position under a lateral force such as the wind in the sails. The greater the stability, the less the heel under a given force.

Helm. An alternative name for a *tiller.*

Hull. A general term for the structure and shell of a ship below the deck level.

Lateen. A triangular sail suspended from a yard, secured to the mast at or near the center of the long edge. The forward end of the yard is held down at deck level. The aftermost sail in a 1700 ship was a lateen.

Lines. A general term for the shape of a ship's hull.

Mizzen. The aftermost mast in a vessel with more than two masts.

Rig. The configuration of masts and sails on a ship. In Britain, various rigs were given names, such as snow, barque, brig, schooner, and so on, but these terms were used with different meanings, sometimes more to describe the size of a ship rather than the sails it carried. Nomenclature was equally confused in France and Spain.

Ship. Strictly speaking, a vessel with at least three masts carrying square sails on all masts, not to be confused with the vessels described under *Rig,* none of which is technically a ship. The word is also used generically to mean any seagoing craft.

Shroud. A line giving support to a mast in the lateral direction.

Spanker. A fore and aft sail, with the leading edge attached to the mizzen mast, and the upper edge supported by a gaff. A most useful sail, since it could be angled to push the head of the ship towards the wind to facilitate tacking.

Spritsail. A square sail hung from a yard suspended below the bowsprit.

Square sail. Usually not square in shape, but swung square to the wind when it is blowing from behind the ship.

Stability. Used as a metaphor for the technical term *metacentric height.* The metacenter is a point related to the buoyant forces on the immersed part of the hull. The higher it is above the center of gravity of the ship and all its loads, the greater the stability.

Stay. A line giving support to a mast in the longitudinal direction.

Step. A socket on the keel or on a strong deck beam, in which the foot of a mast is inserted. As a verb, it means the placement of a step.

Stock (singular). The crosspiece at the top of an anchor. Nothing to do with *stocks* (plural).

Stocks (plural). The blocks in a shipyard on which the keel is laid. A ship under construction was said to be "on the stocks."

Tack. To tack a ship is to turn it into the wind, then continue the turn until the wind is blowing from the other side.

Tiller. A horizontal arm attached to the rudder post, by which the rudder is turned.

Wear. The opposite of *tack,* to turn away from the wind until it blows from the other side. An easier maneuver for a square-rigged ship than tacking, but one that drives the ship downwind.

Yard. A wooden beam attached near its midpoint to a mast, from which a square sail is hung.

ALUN C. DAVIES

Testing a New Technology: Captain George Vancouver's Survey and Navigation in Alaskan Waters, 1794

The instruments and methods for determining longitudes developed during the second half of the eighteenth century, the new navigational technology, were so superior to previous methods that their impact may be appropriately described as revolutionary. This can be seen when the crude maps of the North Pacific drawn in the mid-eighteenth century are compared with Vancouver's Great Chart.[1]

Earlier maps created by Spanish, Russian, and British explorers and traders were of poor quality. The imprecisions of their roughly drawn coastlines induced European governments to mount expensive scientific and surveying expeditions during the last quarter of the century. Consequently, by the early nineteenth century accurate maps of Pacific coastlines were available thanks to the voyages of Cook, Lapérouse, Malaspina, and especially George Vancouver. This paper examines the problems Vancouver encountered in his application of the new technology, specifically in his use of chronometers to determine longitudes during the third survey season. It also notes some of the consequences of Vancouver's experiences for both the chronometer manufacturing industry and for later expeditions.

Vancouver's objective at the outset of his expedition was to determine accurately latitudes and longitudes and to acquire any other useful navigational information. He had sailed with Cook on his second and third voyages, and he emulated the great navigator's well-established routines of taking water temperatures; recording barometric pressures; measuring tides, shoals, and currents; and sketching coastlines. To accumulate data, Vancouver was supplied with the latest products of London's scientific instrument makers.[2] The most complex were the chronometers.

Chronometers embodied the supreme accomplishments of contemporary mechanical technology. They were highly accurate timekeepers that carried Greenwich time (or that of some other base meridian). This enabled mariners to deduce longitude relatively quickly, simply, and to a degree of accuracy acceptable for navigational purposes. The invention and development of the cross-staff, back staff, quadrant, and, in the mid-eighteenth century, the sextant, meant that the determination of latitudes was not difficult. But until the era of Captain Cook, longitudes could only be estimated by dead-reckoning, that is, by plotting a ship's course after guessing allowances to be made for speed, tides, currents, and direction, a method so crude that small islands in open seas were best approached by heading for latitude far to the east or west and then running that latitude to the destination, sometimes with wild errors that caused expensive delays and losses.[3]

In the 1760s two very different developments enabled longitudes to be determined reasonably accurately. One, developed by Nevil Maskelyne, the British royal astronomer, was the lunar method.[4] After a complicated and lengthy process of observation and computation, involving tables of lunar distances, longitudes could be calculated (with a good pocket watch to time observations) to within about thirty miles' error with a sextant.[5] The second method of determining longitude was to compare time in one place (local time, easily established from the noon sun) and time in some other place of known longitude.

The solution was simple. The problem arose in constructing a timepiece of such high quality that it would retain its original time throughout a long voyage, despite changes in temperature and the perpetual instability of a ship (which ruled out using a clock with weights and a pendulum). That a chronometer gained or lost on Greenwich time did not matter *if the daily rate of that gain or loss could be established* and factored into the calculations. Once the "going rate," as it was called, was known, a chronometer permitted longitudes to be calculated far more rapidly than by the ponderous, weather-dependent exercises needed to obtain good celestial measurements. Establishing longitude by chronometer compared with longitude by lunars was the navigational equivalent of factory textile production compared with hand-loom weaving.[6]

Vancouver's expedition was equipped with chronometers made by the greatest horological craftsmen of the day. They included Larcum Kendall's third instrument (called K3), with which Vancouver was familiar from his earlier voyages with Cook.[7] The expedition also had three box chronometers made by John Arnold (now known as A14, A82, and A176), and a watch chronometer made by Thomas Earnshaw (E1514). Vancouver was also supplied with a portable tent observatory for which other state-of-the-art instruments were provided. They included a regulator, also made by Thomas Earnshaw.[8]

Regulators were weight-powered pendulum clocks of very superior quality and were among the finest products of contemporary high technology. By measuring the movement of the Moon or Jupiter against other celestial bodies with a telescope, in effect using the sky as a clock face, a regulator could be used to measure the accuracy of the spring-driven chronometers. If necessary a new going rate would be admitted for the latter. The chronometer itself would not be adjusted but allowances made in the subsequent mathematical calculations. The new going rate would hold until another appropriate occasion offered itself for further verification. Ideally, an expedition's portable observatory would be set up on shore for at least a week and preferably longer, because of the time it took to "settle" the regulator. A sustained spell of clear nights was also necessary to make useful observations. These were some of the central features of the new navigational technology pioneered by Cook and employed by Vancouver.

Every solution produces its own problem. With chronometers the difficulty was monitoring their behavior. It was necessary to know their daily gaining or losing rate. On long sea expeditions, weeks or months might elapse between opportunities to take celestial readings with the full paraphernalia of astronomical instruments in the optimum conditions of a shore-based observatory. Deck observations were never as satisfactory. It was precisely this challenge, determining the true going rates of his chronometers, that dogged Vancouver's third surveying season in Alaskan waters.

Fluctuations in the rates of chronometers arose from human and mechanical imperfections. Each instrument was an empiricism, handcrafted over about a two-year period by a score or more of workers and subcontractors acting under the direction of a master craftsman. Not even chronometers made in a batch performed identically. Each component was finished separately and was therefore unique. The accuracy of the performance of each mechanism depended partly upon the skill of the master craftsman in the final stages of assembly. It also depended upon a set of variables outside the maker's control (at least during this period of the instrument's development). They included changes in temperature, humidity, barometric pressures, metal fatigue, and the quality of the lubricating oil.[9]

Whenever possible, Vancouver set up his observatory where previous observations had been taken so that comparisons could be made. On his outward journey he called at places where Cook and others had earlier defined longitudes after extensive observations, such as the Cape of Good Hope, and Dusky Sound in New Zealand. Vancouver added other calling places, such as King George Sound in Australia. He also stopped at Tahiti and Kealakekua Bay, Hawaii, not merely for water, refurbishment, rest, and recreation, but also to check his position and verify his chronometers' rates. On the home run the expedition visited Monterey, diverted to Valparaíso to establish its longitude, and went on to St. Helena. On the Northwest Coast, the most important location for George Vancouver was Nootka Sound.

Nootka was crucial not just because of its status on the diplomatic agenda. It was the base point for the expedition's survey. Its position became in effect a secondary meridian, a regional equivalent of Greenwich. Vancouver set up his tent observatory there four times: at the end of the first surveying season in October 1792; at the opening and close of the second in May and October 1793; and lastly in October 1794 at the end of the third season.

During the first two surveying seasons, Vancouver worked his way up the coast northwest from Nootka. But the third season's survey started at Cook Inlet and headed south.[10] This presented Vancouver with problems, somewhat analogous to those experienced by land surveyors building railroad lines towards each other from opposite ends. The lines did not invariably meet, and at the last moment adjustments had to be made. Not able to rate his chronometers at Nootka at the beginning of the third survey season, Vancouver "carried" rates set in Kealakekua Bay, Hawaii, in January 1794. They were later adjusted four times during the survey season, at Cook Inlet, Port Chalmers, Cross Sound, and Port Conclusion.[11] But at none of these places were the chronometers rated under optimum conditions, that is, on shore by the portable observatory. Only when he returned to Nootka in October, after the conclusion of the survey, was the observatory at last erected "for the purpose of ascertaining the rate and error of our chronometers, in order to correct our survey from cape Douglas to cape Decision."[12]

Why did Vancouver not set up his observatory during his survey of Alaskan waters? There were several explanations. First, in Cook Inlet, at the beginning of the last season, the weather was simply too cold to spend a week or more in a canvas encampment.[13] To take the chronometers ashore would mean moving them to an icy, wet, windy place from the shelter of a warm cabin, with probably disastrous consequences for accuracy of the mechanisms. As Vancouver subsequently learned, even at the best of times chronometers had to be moved with extraordinary care: when one (A176) *was* taken ashore at Port Conclusion to assist observations, its subsequent going rate became very erratic.[14]

To obviate moving the instruments, time could be "carried" from the box chronometers in the captain's cabin to observers on the deck or on shore by means of a chronometer watch, that is, a pocket watch with an especially high quality movement that would run sufficiently accurately for the relatively short duration of the exercise. The expedition had been supplied with such a watch, made by Thomas Earnshaw. For a time its consistent rate outperformed the box chronometers, but it had unfortunately broken down during the second survey season.[15] Although not mentioned in his journal, Vancouver and his fellow officers undoubtedly had ordinary pocket watches that must have been pressed into use as deck watches on such occasions.

Without the assistance of the portable observatory, Vancouver satisfied himself with observations on the deck of the *Discovery* at anchor and, sometimes, briefly on shore. For a time this procedure appeared adequate. Thus in May 1794 he noted:

Alun C. Davies

Although circumstances did not permit us to make such astronomical observations on the spot as I considered to be necessary for determining the longitude of our station at the head of Cook's Inlet, yet we were fortunate in obtaining those that very satisfactorily shewed the rates of our chronometers, from which authority we were able to ascertain the longitudinal mensuration of our survey, and to deduce from subsequent observations what I considered as its *true* longitude.[16]

Using as a starting point the longitudes indicated by the chronometers calculated according to the Kealakekua rate, Vancouver arrived at what he described as a "true longitude," calculated from the mean of his chronometers' rates in conjunction with those arrived at by lunar observations.

At the end of May 1794, near Port Chalmers, the weather improved. While the boat parties were away on running surveys, Vancouver again contemplated setting up the observatory on land. Once more he decided against it, for "the shores did not afford any convenient situation."[17] He still believed that his deck observations yielded information adequate to monitor the chronometers' rates. And for a few days, at least, pleasant summer weather enabled him, on the *Discovery*'s deck, to

procure some good lunar distances, and to add other astronomical observations to those we had already made for ascertaining the rate of the chronometers. I did not now much regret that a proper place had not been found for the reception of the observatory, as the inclemency of the weather hitherto would have rendered it an useless object of our attention, and the instruments might have received some damage had they been landed.[18]

Vancouver's calculation of the longitude of Port Chalmers was therefore based on chronometer rates set in Kealakekua Bay in January and adjusted at Cook Inlet in April. He considered the positions reasonably correct. But one assumption was now dangerously pyramided upon another.

When he next rated the chronometers in early June (after making "repeated good observations" over two weeks) at the end of the exercise K3 stopped. It was restarted "by applying a gentle horizontal motion."[19] Vancouver was now uneasy. He concluded that as soon as possible the observatory ought to be set up and the chronometers properly rated. The next appropriate place where this might be done was Cross Sound, while the *Discovery* and *Chatham* were anchored off Port Althorp. But the weather turned poor and Vancouver himself was unwell.[20] The best that could be managed was twenty sets of observations. They suggested that, although the rates of A14 and A176 seemed steady, K3's had decreased slightly. He made yet another minor adjustment and pressed on to Port Conclusion with every intention of erecting the observatory there, to do the job properly.

Port Conclusion proved no more suitable than Cross Sound. Poor weather, "boisterous, unsettled, and rainy," once more prevented assembling the observatory on shore. He noted:

As a convenient situation could not be found near the ship, . . . I was not particularly anxious to land the instruments; and under the circumstances of the weather, I had not much regret that they had remained unremoved.[21]

The weather was too poor even to take lunars, and Vancouver once again made a provisional calculation of longitudes by chronometers, the rates of gaining or losing of which he was now uncertain. Sure enough, when eventually he managed to take eighteen sets of observations on shore he discovered further changes in their daily rates. A14 and K3 had increased, but A176 was slowing a little.[22]

Vancouver's worries were confirmed. The changes in rates might be tiny, but inexorably they cumulated and errors compounded. The assumed precision of much of the recent survey work was now questionable, at least in relation to the positions (calibrated to Nootka) that Vancouver had established during the first two seasons. But six months had now elapsed since the chronometers had last been properly rated by the portable observatory. It became imperative to press on to Nootka so that the extent of error might be ascertained and adjustments made. Until then, all longitudinal positions in the survey must be regarded as provisional. Vancouver's unease intensified during the last run southward to Nootka. As he returned along the route surveyed in earlier seasons, where positions "of several conspicuous situations [had been] fixed by former observations," he found that whilst his observed lunars conformed to earlier findings, longitudes by chronometers did not.[23] The chronometer rates were clearly awry.

On September 2, 1794, the *Discovery* anchored again in Friendly Cove, Nootka Sound. Vancouver's "essentially important" priority was to set up the observatory to check the chronometers' rates, in order "to correct our survey from Cape Douglas to Cape Decision." For twenty-nine days, over a six-week period, Vancouver made meticulous observations. With relief, he discovered that they revealed that his latitude and longitude for Nootka were still "the same as on our first visit to this place in the year 1792."[24] He therefore recalculated his estimations of the changes in the chronometers' rates for the latter part of the final season's survey so that all positions were now calibrated to Nootka.

A last task remained before commencing the long journey home. Vancouver had sailed twice with James Cook and was infected by the great navigator's passion for accuracy. On four separate occasions, over two years, Nootka's longitude had been set and confirmed by Vancouver, but with the same in-

Alun C. Davies

struments and using the same methods. Vancouver's position for Nootka itself now needed calibrating to other key places in the North Pacific. It was in the spirit of the new scientific navigation that Vancouver therefore determined to check, with the same instruments, the position of some other place where

longitude had been settled by professed astronomers, by which means the accuracy of our calculations would be confirmed, or the error they might have been liable to become apparent; leaving it at the discretion of geographers, or of those who might hereafter follow us, to adopt or reject such corrections as their own judgement might direct.[25]

Consequently he headed for Cabo San Lucas, at the tip of the California peninsula, where the transit of Venus had been observed in 1769 and its longitude thereafter accepted as definitive.[26]

En route from Monterey, Vancouver diverted to the island of Guadeloupe (which he was relieved to find exactly where he had expected it to be!).[27] As this area of the Pacific had been extensively navigated by the Spanish, he also checked his positions against those on copies of Spanish charts. They agreed. With "much gratification" he concluded that "from St. Lucas in California to Cape Douglas in Cook's Inlet . . . the position of the western coast of America . . . would be found *tolerably correct*."[28] At last, no doubt to the great relief of his crew, he headed for home.

Even on the home run Vancouver did not relax. The ghost of Cook stood at his shoulder, and he used the return journey to record the positions of as many islands as he could find. Confident of the reliability of assigning longitudes by a combination of chronometers and lunars, using each as a check on the other, he repeatedly demonstrated the superiority of the new navigational technology over the old by recording the positions suggested by the old, crude dead reckoning method, alongside those indicated by lunars and chronometers.[29]

Because Vancouver died before completing his journal for publication, its concluding section was edited by his brother John. Information about the final stages of the expedition in general and the chronometers and their rates in particular is regrettably sparse.[30] Had Vancouver lived longer, he would no doubt have offered a much more detailed assessment of the merits, and problems, of the new navigational technology. As his experience in the third survey season revealed, longitudes arrived at by chronometer were uncertain without the benefit of an observatory to check the instruments' rates. Given the still-developing state of chronometer technology, good celestial observations remained necessary to rate the instruments, as well as to provide a ponderous, but reliable, alternative method of determining longitudes. Several subsequent generations of midshipmen therefore continued to be trained to find longitude by both methods.

The return of the expedition and the publication of Vancouver's account of the voyage were enthusiastically received by London's chronometer manufacturers.[31] Vancouver's experiences reaffirmed Cook's positive verdict on the merits of chronometers for navigation and surveying. The expedition's fifty-four months' duration, through extreme weather conditions, constituted the longest trial of the instruments so far. Promotional pamphlets from the houses of Arnold and Earnshaw, the chronometer makers who had supplied Vancouver's instruments, resounded with favorable testimonials culled from the records of the expedition, extolling the new technology in general and their products in particular.[32] Over the next thirty years the annual production and stock of chronometers steadily increased; their quality improved, their price fell, and their use for ocean navigation became commonplace.[33]

Until 1815, preoccupation with the Napoleonic Wars disrupted the Board of Longitude's use of chronometers on other surveying expeditions, with the important exception of Flinders's voyage to Australia in 1803 (well away from the theaters of naval warfare).[34] The systematic survey of hitherto uncharted coastlines and the compilation of an enormous inventory of navigational information resumed only when the wars ended. Thereafter, Vancouver's great survey set the standard. Between 1816 and 1826, several thousand miles of Africa's coastline were surveyed and charted using the methods initiated by Cook and developed by Vancouver: lunars and chronometric methods were used as checks on each other to establish the positions of hundreds of coastal promontories.[35] With the increase in the number and improvements in the quality of chronometers, so the chronometric method prevailed, and in the 1820s and 1830s leading firms of chronometer manufacturers, eager to publicize the merits of their products, loaned large numbers of their instruments to the numerous expeditions that sailed to determine the positions of key places on the globe.[36]

The problems that Vancouver had encountered in calibrating his longitudinal positions in the third survey season foreshadowed those that would confront Lieutenant Henry Raper, R.N., half a century later. Raper had systematically collected longitudes of more than two hundred maritime positions across the five continents.[37] He argued that eighteen key places should have their longitudes thoroughly determined by observatories and the results accepted by all navigators: this would create a grid linking fundamental points where the rates of chronometers might be checked.[38] In practice, he concluded, "the absolute longitudes of . . . points [were] of secondary importance, since it is an obvious principle that consistency among the several places is of far more consequence than their absolute positions."[39] Vancouver, after his efforts to calibrate his Alaskan survey to the longitude of Nootka, would have understood and approved. It was similar to the strategy he had applied in his great survey of the North Pacific half a century earlier.

How accurate were Vancouver's positions in terms of modern values? His latitudes were respectably reliable, but his longitudes were somewhat off. He was generally too far east by about fifteen minutes of arc (sometimes up to nineteen minutes), or about ten to twelve miles. (The Spanish were about fifteen and one half minutes too far west.) Given that the North Pacific was half a world and many months' sailing away from most explorers' base meridians, these were "extremely good results, . . . [for] an observational error of one minute [in time] gave a longitudinal error of thirty minutes [of arc]."[40]

Why did the errors occur? Some general explanations may be offered. First, celestial observations were just that. These readings were not infallible measurements. At sea, instruments were hand held, sometimes by inexperienced officers, often in poor weather on a moving deck. When good conditions prevailed, Vancouver was keen to take as many sets of observations as possible, sometimes hundreds, with the dozen sextants at his service. They were then averaged on the assumption that the arithmetical mean of a large sample would produce an acceptable result. Sometimes it did. But if large numbers of observations reiterated the same errors, the mean of the findings was skewed.

Other reasons for imperfect celestial observations include the need to correct for the Moon's apparent position by allowing for *refraction* (the distorting effects of the earth's atmosphere along the line of sight) and *parallax* (because of the relatively close position of the Moon to the Earth, compared with other heavenly bodies). Modern astronomers understand much more than did their eighteenth-century predecessors about the gravitational effects of other heavenly bodies on the movement of the Moon, and of the consequences of the Earth's imperfect shape. Astronomers today use satellite observations and computers; in the eighteenth century they used telescopes and algebra. Celestial observations could give *respectable* findings, even away from a major observatory, but they were at best adequate, and not precise. The main drawback of navigation by lunars was that it was time-consuming. It was the very slowness of the lunar method that made the chronometric method so attractive. As Cook had concluded, with a reliable chronometer, calculations "are rendered short beyond conception and easy to the meanest capacity."[41]

Crucial to the application of new navigational technology were the *Nautical Almanac* and *Tables Requisite*. Cook and Vancouver had faith in the veracity of tables to which they routinely referred in the course of lengthy mathematical calculations. But we now know that there were some errors in the early *Nautical Almanacs* that might have infected their calculations. Like a modern computer virus, the errors were self-perpetuating.[42] Other errors arose from "compass mis-calibrations . . . and distortions [that were] almost certainly the result of some appallingly bad arithmetic."[43]

One must not forget the untimely death of William Gooch, who was sent to join the expedition. His loss robbed the expedition of the services of a specialist astronomer. He had been intended, like Charles Green, William Wales, and William Bayly on Cook's great expeditions, to devote himself to making expert observations, to working and reworking, and checking and rechecking the thousands of complicated, longhand, arithmetical and algebraic calculations. George Vancouver was an outstanding navigator but essentially a part-time astronomer. He was preoccupied with the day-to-day management of two ships, one hundred and fifty men, and a diplomatic mission, and he was afflicted with ill health. It is a measure of his high qualities as a man and of the superb training he received from Cook that he achieved so much. And it is an indication of the improvements yielded by the new technology that Vancouver's Great Chart was used by navigators throughout the nineteenth century.

APPENDIX

"The Going Rates": Daily Rates of the Chronometers during the Third Survey Season, 1794, and the Home Run, 1794–95

			Seconds gained daily		
			K3	A14	A176
The third survey season					
1794	February	Kealakekua, Hawaii (Observatory) (Alaskan Waters)	15.16	21.12	48.28
	May	Cook Inlet	26.22	22.90	52.37
	June	Port Chalmers	26.50	23.00	51.40
	July	Cross Sound	25.80	23.00	51.40
	August	Port Conclusion	26.11	24.00	49.37
	September	Nootka	28.30	23.40	41.57
	October	Nootka (Observatory)	28.29	23.60	41.57
The home run					
1794	November	Monterey	30.53	24.10	50.25
	December	At sea	21.35	20.00	41.50

Alun C. Davies

112

'94-5	Dec/Jan	Cocos Islands	21.35	20.20	41.50
1795	May	Valparaíso	29.34	25.10	58.57
	July	St. Helena	28.22	24.50	57.00

Source: George Vancouver, *A Voyage of Discovery to the North Pacific Ocean and round the World,* ed. W. Kane Lamb, 4 vols. (London: Hakluyt Society, (1984) 4:1664-65.

NOTES

For helpful comments on an earlier draft, I wish to record thanks to my colleague Kenneth Brown (Queen's University, Belfast); to the late Professor Mansel Davies (Criccieth, North Wales); and to Nicholas Doe, of White Rock, British Columbia, Canada. Above all I am grateful to Dr. Glenn F. Massay, University of Alaska, Anchorage, at Palmer for initiating my interest in Alaska's history. Needless to say, the conventional disclaimer applies, and remaining errors are mine.

1. See illustrations in Glyndwr Williams, "Alaska Revealed: Cook's Explorations in 1778," in *Exploration in Alaska: Captain Cook Commemorative Lectures,* ed. Antoinette Shalkop (Anchorage: Cook Inlet Historical Society, 1980), pp. 69, 71-73.

2. Andrew David, "Vancouver's Survey Methods and Surveys," in *From Maps to Metaphors: The Pacific World of George Vancouver,* ed. Robin Fisher and Hugh Johnston, (Vancouver: University of British Columbia Press, 1993), pp. 51-69, 291-97.

3. David W. Waters, "Navigational Problems in Captain Cook's Day," in Shalkop, *Exploration in Alaska,* pp. 40-58; and Waters, "Early Time and Distance Measurement at Sea," *Journal of the Institute of Navigation,* Vol. 8 (1955), pp. 153-73; Eva G. R. Taylor, "Five Centuries of Dead Reckoning," *Journal of the Institute of Navigation,* Vol. 3 (1950), pp. 280-85; Charles H. Cotter, "Early Dead Reckoning Navigation," *Journal of the Institute of Navigation,* Vol. 31 (1978), pp. 20-27.

4. Derek Howse, *Nevil Maskelyne: The Seaman's Astronomer* (Cambridge: Cambridge University Press, 1989), pp. 85-96; Eric G. Forbes, "The Foundation and Early Development of the Nautical Almanac," *Journal of the Institute of Navigation,* Vol. 18 (1965), p. 393.

5. D. H. Sadler, *Man Is Not Lost: A Record of 200 Years of Astronomical Navigation with the Nautical Almanac, 1767-1967* (London: HMSO, 1968); Alan Stimpson and Christopher Daniel, *The Cross Staff: Historical Development and Modern Use* (London: HMSO, 1967).

6. William Wales, *The Method of Finding the Longitude at Sea by Timekeepers to Which Are Added Tables of Equations, Altitudes, More Extensive Than Any Hitherto Published* (London, 1794; 2d ed., 1810).

7. A. C. Davies, "Horology and Navigation: Vancouver's Expedition, 1791-95," *Antiquarian Horology,* Vol. 21 (1994), pp. 244-55.

8. A. C. Davies, "Vancouver's Chronometers," in Fisher and Johnston, *From Maps to Metaphors,* pp. 70-84. The Earnshaw regulator survives. It had been in private hands for the sixty years before reappearing in December 1993 and selling at auction to an

Australian museum for £27,600 (approx. $40,000) (Sotheby's, *Sale of Clocks, Watches, Wrist-watches and Barometers* [London: Dec. 16, 1993], p. 288).

9. A. C. Davies, "The Life and Death of a Scientific Instrument: The Marine Chronometer, 1770–1920," *Annals of Science,* Vol. 35 (1978), pp. 509–25.

10. Robin Fisher, *Vancouver's Voyage: Charting the Northwest Coast* (Vancouver and Seattle: Douglas and McIntyre and University of Washington Press, 1992), pp. 85–112.

11. See appendix on pp. 112–13.

12. George Vancouver, *A Voyage of Discovery to the North Pacific Ocean and round the World, 1791–1795,* ed. W. Kaye Lamb, 4 vols. (London: Hakluyt Society, 1984), 4:1398 (hereafter Lamb, *Vancouver's Voyage*).

13. *Ibid.,* 3:1208ff, 1227. The air temperature in Alaskan waters in April started at twenty-six degrees and twenty-seven degrees, rose to thirty-five degrees at Kodiak, then to forty degrees to forty-five degrees; although colder—thirty-six degrees—at Turnagain Island, "The weather was serene, the air comparatively mild" (p. 1227).

14. *Ibid.,* 4:1395. On August 24, 1794, en route to Nootka for the last time, Vancouver checked the chronometer rates and noted their changes, particularly that of A176, "which it is necessary to remark, had been there [Port Conclusion] taken on shore for the purposes of observation." The other chronometers, K3 and A14, remained in Vancouver's cabin.

15. Davies, "Vancouver's Chronometers," p. 76.

16. Lamb, *Vancouver's Voyage,* 4:1262–63.

17. Whidbey, master of the *Discovery*, was Vancouver's chief assistant for astronomical and navigational matters. He later described the procedures applied by Vancouver in the survey of "3000 leagues of the N. W. shore of America" in Joseph Whidbey, "Remarks on Timekeepers," in *The Naval Chronicle,* Vol. 2 (1799), pp. 505–12.

18. Lamb, *Vancouver's Voyage,* 4:1272, 1274.

19. *Ibid.,* 4:1298.

20. *Ibid.,* 4:1362–63.

21. *Ibid.,* 4:1369.

22. *Ibid.,* 4:1391.

23. *Ibid.,* 4:1394–95. At Scot's Islands, Vancouver concluded that the chronometers "had varied since our last observations by them in Port Conclusion."

24. *Ibid.,* 4:1409–10.

25. *Ibid.,* 4:1427–29.

26. Doyce B. Nunis, Jr. (ed.), *The 1769 Transit of Venus: The Baja California Observations of Jean-Baptiste Chappe d'Auteroche, et al.* (Los Angeles: Natural History of Los Angeles, 1982). D'Auteroche noted that "a few well-made observations are worth infinitely more than a greater number of suspect ones, and consequent uncertainty" (p. 99).

27. Lamb, *Vancouver's Voyage,* 4:1425–26, 1428.

28. *Ibid.,* 4:1432 (emphasis added).

29. Vancouver adjusted his chronometers' rates four more times—at sea, off the Cocos Islands, at Valparaíso (after determining its longitude), and lastly at St. Helena. *Ibid.,* 4:1439–40, 1447, 1454–57, 1484, 1522–23, 1536–37.

30. *Ibid.,* 1:292.

31. Davies, "Vancouver's Chronometers," p. 82.

32. Thomas Earnshaw, *Longitude: An Appeal to the Public* (London, 1808; reprinted St. Helens, 1986, with an introduction by R. John Griffiths), has numerous references to the performance of E1514 on the Vancouver expedition.

33. Davies, "Life and Death of a Scientific Instrument," pp. 509–25.

34. Lewis and Clark were provided with an Arnold chronometer with which, in conjunction with lunars, they determined longitudes. Silvio Bedini, *Thinkers and Tinkers: Early American Men of Science* (New York: Scribner, 1975), pp. 330–31; and Bedini, "The Scientific Instruments of the Lewis and Clark Expedition," *Great Plains Quarterly*, Vol. 4 (1984), pp. 54–69.

35. Richard Owen, *Tables of Latitudes and Longitudes by Chronometer of Places in the Atlantic and Indian Oceans; Principally on the West and East Coast of Africa; To Which Is Prefixed an Essay of the Management and Use of Chronometers* (n.d.). Also see David Harries, "The Chronometer Pioneer (Commander Richard Owen)," *Horological Journal*, Vol. 122 (1979), pp. 37–43, who notes that Owen's work on chronometers was published as *Essay on the Management and Use of Chronometers* (n.d.).

36. Manufacturers sent fourteen chronometers with Captain Sabine, the astronomer on Parry's expedition, and twenty-two with FitzRoy on the *Beagle*.

37. Henry Raper, *The Practice of Navigation and Nautical Astronomy* (J. D. Potter, 1840; 10th ed., 1880). The two hundred longitudes were published in installments in issues of *The Nautical Magazine and Naval Chronicle* from 1839 onwards and eventually consolidated in Raper's *Table of Maritime Positions*. See also, Charles H. Cotter, "A Brief Historical Survey of British Navigation Manuals," *Journal of Navigation*, Vol. 36 (1983), p. 245.

38. Raper, *The Practice of Navigation*, pp.viii–ix.

39. Henry Raper, "On the Necessity of Adopting Secondary Meridians," *The Nautical Magazine and Naval Chronicle for 1839* (London: J. D. Potter, 1839), p. 461.

40. M. W. Emmott, "Captain Vancouver and the Lunar Distance," *Journal of Navigation*, Vol. 27 (1974), pp. 490–95 (qtn., p. 493). Henry R. Wagner, *The Cartography of the Northwest Coast of America to the Year 1800*, 2 vols. (Berkeley: University of California Press, 1937), 1:243. For differences in the longitudes established by Spanish explorers and by Cook and Vancouver, see Lamb, *Vancouver's Voyage*, vols. 2–3, pp. 685, 744–45, 1004.

41. J. C. Beaglehole, ed., *The Journals of Captain James Cook on his Voyages of Discovery*, Vol. 2: *The Voyage of the Resolution and Adventure, 1772–1775* (Cambridge: Cambridge University Press, 1955–74), pp. 78–79.

42. Nicholas Doe (letter to author, May 20, 1994) suggests that the errors lie in the original equations themselves, rather in navigators' computations: "They were not arithmetic errors, but algebraic errors." Also see Nicholas Doe, "Vancouver's Longitude Errors, 1792" (unpublished paper), p. 26.

43. Nicholas Doe, letter, March 29, 1994.

ANDREW DAVID

From Cook to Vancouver:
The British Contribution
to the Cartography of Alaska

lthough various Russian expeditions had explored the coast of Alaska
since the voyage of Bering and Chirikov in 1741, it was not until the
publication of the official account of Captain James Cook's third
voyage in 1784 that the first reasonably accurate chart of Alaska
appeared. From the time of Cook's exploration in 1778 until Vancouver's detailed survey sixteen years later, the British voyages to the Northwest Coast
were instrumental in efforts to expand knowledge of the cartography of Alaska.
Although Cook did little more than provide a general outline of the coast, his
trade in sea otter furs and his failure to find the Northwest Passage encouraged
a wave of British seamen to return to the region. In large measure, their significant efforts and the advancing technology of the day yielded the first accurate
charts of the coastline as it is known today.

Cook was directed by their Lords Commissioners of the admiralty to attempt to "find out a Northern passage by Sea from the Pacific to the Atlantic
Ocean."[1] To carry out this assignment, he made landfall on the Northwest
Coast at Drake's New Albion in March 1778 in the *Resolution* and, accompanied
by the *Discovery,* he then began a running survey along the coast to the northernmost reach of the Arctic, always looking for inlets or rivers that might lead
to Hudson or Baffin Bay and beyond, to Europe.

Cook carried two maps depicting Russian discoveries in the North Pacific.
The first map, by Gerhard Friedrich Müller, was published by the British geographer Thomas Jeffreys in 1761.[2] Although this map depicts with reasonable
accuracy the tracks of Bering and Chirikov, it also shows the Northwest Coast
of America bulging out toward Kamchatka, leaving a channel about 500 miles
wide, leading northeast towards Bering Strait. If this map had been accepted
during the planning of Cook's voyage, the explorer would have assumed that
the only way to the Arctic Ocean was through Bering Strait and that the obvious route to follow was across the Pacific to Kamchatka and then through the
channel shown on Müller's map.[3]

The second map held by Cook was by Jacob von Stählin, published in

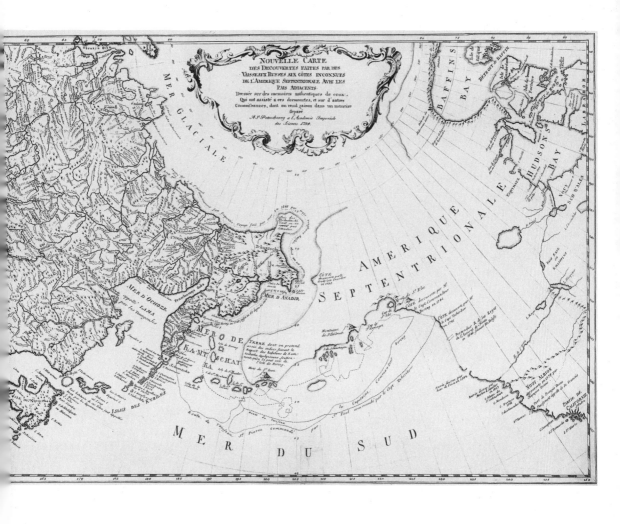

Map 1. G. F. Müller, "Nouvelle carte des découvertes faites par des vaisseaux russes,"
1754. *James Ford Bell Library, University of Minnesota*

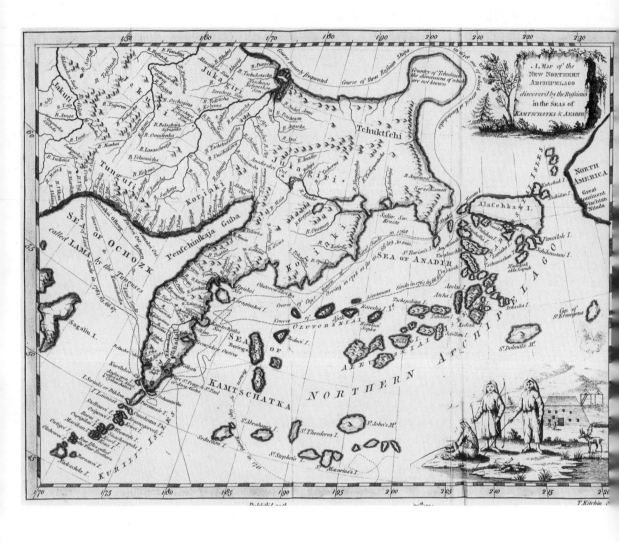

Map 2. Map from J. Von Stählin, *An Account of the new Northern Archipelago . . .*,
London, 1774. This map among its many inaccuracies shows Alaska as an island.
James Ford Bell Library, University of Minnesota

England in 1774.[4] This map, based on the travels of the Russian explorer Lieu-tenant Ivan Sindt, shows a break in the North American continent at about sixty-five degrees north latitude and one hundred forty degrees west longitude. Referring to the map, the admiralty instructed Cook to begin his search for the Northwest Passage from the American rather than the Russian coast.

On March 29, 1778, Cook anchored in Nootka Sound, on the Northwest Coast of Vancouver Island. Bad weather had kept him off the coast for several days, causing him to regret "passing the place where Geographers have placed the pretended Strait of Admiral de Fonte."[5] Leaving Nootka, he did not sight land again until May 1, in the vicinity of Cape Ommaney, near modern-day Sitka. Here Cook began a running survey of the coast of Alaska guided by the Müller and Stählin maps. On May 12 he was off the mouth of a substantial inlet. To this point, Cook had followed the coast as it ran in an east-west direction, but beyond the inlet it "seemed to incline well to the Southward, a direction so contrary to the Modern Charts, founded upon the late Russian discoveries, that we had reason to expect that by the inlet before us we should find a pas-sage to the North."[6]

The weather was so threatening that Cook sought an anchorage, first in English Bay, then in Snug Corner Cove. In a matter of days, a detail survey re-vealed that the inlet was a large bay, which Cook named Sandwich Sound in honor of his patron. But it was named Prince William Sound in the published versions of his charts.

Upon leaving Prince William Sound, Cook followed the coast in a south-westerly direction, attempting to reconcile what he saw with Müller's and Stäh-lin's maps. Eventually the coastline turned to the northwest, where Stählin's map showed a channel leading to the north. Cook altered course and on May 26 entered another large inlet, working slowly to the north against the tides, reaching the head of the inlet five days later. Here he sent William Bligh, the Resolution's master, to examine a channel leading to the northeast. Bligh reported that the "inlet [Knik Arm] or rather river contracted to the breadth of one league by low land on each side, through which it took a northerly direc-tion."[7] The following day Lieutenant James King examined a channel leading to the east, which he assumed was the mouth of a large river. The tide turned before King got halfway there, running so strongly that the boats retreated. So Cook called this unexamined feature River Turnagain.

Cook could not spare the time to make a detailed survey of the inlet, which was later named Cook's River in his honor, and still later, Cook Inlet by geog-raphers. Instead, he returned to the open sea, where he followed the Alaska Peninsula in a southwesterly direction. After two weeks he found a channel leading north, which led to a bay on the north coast of Unalaska Island. The Native Aleuts called the bay Samgoonoodha, a name Cook adopted for his charts. From there, he worked his way along the northern side of the Alaska Peninsula and then northwest and west around Bristol Bay.

In July he sighted Saint Matthew Island and another island he named Anderson's Island, which he supposed were among the many islands laid down on Stählin's map.[8] Soon he was off Cape Prince of Wales in Bering Strait, then, entering the Chukchi Sea, he followed the coast to the northeast until he met an impenetrable wall of ice, where he abandoned his search for the Northwest Passage after being nearly trapped on a lee shore by the main body of ice.

His last Alaskan port was at Unalaska, where he was entertained by the Russian Gerasim Grigorovich Izmailov, who allowed Cook to copy two Russian manuscript charts.[9] One depicted the coastline of the Sea of Okhotsk and part of Kamchatka, and the other showed Russian discoveries farther east. In return, Cook presented Izmailov with an outline chart of his voyage, which Izmailov used to plot Cook's track on to one of his own charts, and then sent to Petropavlovsk.[10]

After Cook's death in Hawaii, Charles Clerke took command of the expedition and in 1779 set off from Petropavlovsk on another attempt to return to England through Bering Strait. Once again, the party met impenetrable ice, and so Clerke returned to Petropavlovsk, where he died within sight of the coast of Kamchatka on August 22, 1779. Clerke's gallant attempt took him well into the Chukchi Sea and almost as far north as Cook had reached the previous year, but he was unable to add materially to Cook's discoveries.

Cook's exploration of Alaska was based on a technique known to hydrographic surveyors as a running survey, a method he had perfected during his exploration of New Zealand and Australia during his first voyage, when he obtained his longitude by means of lunar distances.[11] For his second voyage, Cook had been supplied with two chronometers, which he successfully tested, resulting in even greater accuracy in his determination of longitude. For his third voyage, he was once more supplied with two chronometers.

At Nootka Sound a portable observatory was set up ashore to enable Cook and William Bayly, the expedition's astronomer, to establish the sound's geographical position and to obtain rates for the chronometers. The observatory was set up again on the expedition's second visit to Unalaska. Between these two observation points, sets of lunar distances were obtained at sea on twenty-nine different days. Longitude was also obtained on board the ships by chronometer.[12] It was the expertise of the observers and the advent of these two new methods of obtaining longitude, coupled with the publication of the *Nautical Almanac,* that enabled Cook and his officers to fix the position of the coasts and islands they encountered with greater accuracy than had the Russians who preceded them.

More than thirty manuscript charts have survived from the two visits by

Andrew
David

Cook and Clerke to Alaskan waters.[13] The only one that can be attributed to Cook is a chart that Izmailov forwarded to the British admiralty from Unalaska. Some years after the voyage, Bligh was adamant that, apart from Cook, he was "the only person that surveyed & laid the Coast down, in the *Resolution.*"[14] His massive survey from Nootka Sound to Kamchatka is held in the British Hydrographic Office, although the northern part is missing.[15] That part may have been among the "surveys, drawings, and remarks for fifteen years past, which were numerous," that he was forced to leave on board the *Bounty* at the time of the mutiny.[16] Henry Roberts, who served as master's mate on board the *Resolution,* drew two large charts of the North Pacific, probably based on surveys by Cook or Bligh.[17] He also included plans of Prince William Sound and Cook Inlet, English Bay and Norton Sound in his journal.[18] Roberts also drew a plan of Prince William Sound and Cook Inlet for John Gore's journal.[19]

On board the *Discovery,* Bayly and four of the officers drew charts depicting the coast of Alaska. Bayly drew five charts,[20] Thomas Edgar, the *Discovery*'s master, prepared plans of Prince William Sound, Cook Inlet, Providence Bay, and English Bay,[21] and James Burney, the senior lieutenant, included nine charts and two plans relating to Alaska in his journal.[22] The midshipman Edward Riou drew three charts, including a massive chart of the North Pacific, which compares favorably with that drawn by Bligh.[23] Most important, a chart of Alaska was drawn by George Vancouver, another *Discovery* midshipman, who later returned under his own command to complete the full coastal survey.[24]

A small-scale chart of the North Pacific, a chart of Cook's River and Prince William Sound, a chart of Bering Strait and Norton Sound, and a plan of English Bay were eventually engraved from these many surveys and published in 1784 in the official account of Cook's third voyage. In the same year, William Faden published an almost identical chart of the North Pacific drawn by Henry Roberts.[25] These charts not only illustrate the achievements of Cook and his officers in drawing accurate maps of Alaska in just five months but also demonstrate Cook's ability to pass on his skills to his junior officers.

In such a running survey there were bound to be errors and omissions, since, in the time available, it was not possible for Cook to examine the coast in detail. He was unable to establish the insularity of Kodiak Island, but he was able to overcome some gaps by using Izmailov's chart, which appears to have been based on the Krenitsyn/Levashev voyage to the Fox Islands in 1768–69.[26] Subsequently, Henry Roberts acknowledged the use of these charts when detailing the authorities for his engraved world map.[27]

Over the years, Cook's work was superseded by the more detailed surveys of his successors, but many of the names he gave to features along the coast survive. The names Mount Edgecumbe, Cross Sound, Fairweather Mountain, Montague Island, Bristol Bay, Norton Sound, Cape Prince of Wales, and

Icy Cape are perpetual reminders of Cook's cartography. Cook also retained Russian names, such as Bering's Mount St. Elias and Shumagin Islands. The nomenclature used by Cook's officers, however, differed from that adopted by their captain and from one another, particularly in the vicinity of Cook Inlet. Thus Bayly's name for Knik Arm was Seduction River, while Gore's name, on the chart Roberts drew for him was Queen Charlotte's River. Bligh's name on the other hand was Bligh's River—a touch of vanity, perhaps, but at least he was the person who explored this inlet. Gore differed from everyone else by adopting the name Eastern Channel for Turnagain Arm. He also named Cook Inlet on his chart as the Gulf of Good Hope, while Edgar titled his chart of the inlet "A Plan of Cook's River." In the entrance to Cook Inlet, Bligh named the Barren Islands as the Romantick Isles, although Bligh himself was hardly a romantic!

The publication of accounts of Cook's third voyage drew attention to the lucrative market for sea otter skins in the Chinese port of Canton, and the British were the first to exploit this trade. James Strange reached Nootka Sound on July 6, 1786, with two ships, the *Captain Cook* and the *Experiment*. After collecting what skins were available at Nootka, Strange made for Prince William Sound, anchoring in Snug Corner Cove. Here he was joined by the *Sea Otter*, which had sailed from Bengal. A sketch plan of the cove, published by Dalrymple in 1789, is the principal cartographic record of Strange's visit to Alaska.[28]

Three other British vessels reached the Northwest Coast in 1786. The *Nootka*, commanded by John Meares, reached Unalaska in August and was welcomed by the Russians. Meares worked his way up the coast, passing between Kodiak Island and the mainland, arriving at Snug Corner Cove. He had expected to rendezvous with the *Sea Otter* there, but when there was no sign of her he made the disastrous decision to winter in Prince William Sound.

The other two ships that year were the *King George*, commanded by Nathaniel Portlock, and the *Queen Charlotte*, commanded by George Dixon and sent out from England by the newly formed King George's Sound Company. Both Portlock and Dixon had sailed with Cook during his third voyage, but neither had drawn any charts of Alaskan waters on that voyage. They reached Prince William Sound in April 1787, where they found Meares in great distress, twenty-three of his crew having died of scurvy during the harsh Alaskan winter. All three vessels soon parted company. Portlock and Dixon stayed in Alaska to collect furs, but Meares retreated to Hawaii after only a brief foray in southeastern Alaska. Meares returned in 1788, but he confined his activities to the area south of Nootka Sound.

Like other merchants in the sea otter trade, Meares, Portlock, and Dixon were primarily concerned with commerce, so exploration and charting took a secondary role. Nevertheless, all three included charts and plans in the pub-

Andrew

David

lished accounts of their voyages. From a cartographic point of view, Portlock's voyage was the most significant. The frontispiece in his *Voyage* is a small-scale chart of the Northwest Coast from Cape Edgecumbe to Cook Inlet, based mainly on Cook's surveys but also showing the tracks of the ships in 1786 and 1787. In his text, Portlock included plans of Port Graham and Coal Cove, McCloud Harbor, the west side of Montague Island, Port Etches, and Portlock's and Goulding's Harbor.[29]

Dixon also included a small-scale chart of the Northwest Coast from Nootka Sound to the Shumagin Islands as a frontispiece to his *Voyage*. His visit to the Northwest Coast is commemorated on his chart by the name of Dixon's Straits (Dixon Entrance) between the Queen Charlotte Islands and the mainland. As well as showing the tracks of the two ships in company, the chart also shows the track of the *Queen Charlotte* after the two ships parted in May 1787, when Dixon made significant discoveries. These included Port Mulgrave, Port Banks, and Norfolk Sound (Sitka Sound), which were reproduced in Dixon's *Voyage*. Port Mulgrave lies on the southeastern side of Yakutat Bay, which Dixon named Admiralty Bay on his chart.

Meares included three small-scale charts in his *Voyages*. One covers the whole of the North Pacific, the second depicts the track of his companion vessel, and the third is a mostly imagined map of North America, demonstrating the supposed inland navigation from Hudson Bay to the West Coast. On this chart a river is depicted flowing westward from the (Great?) Slave Lake, with three imagined outlets, one into the head of Prince William Sound and the other two entering Cook Inlet through Turnagain River (Arm) and Cooks River (Knik Arm). Halfway between the lake and the three outlets, Meares boldly inserted the legend, "Falls said to be the Largest in the known World."

Another legend on all three of Meares's charts read, "Sketch of the Track of the American Sloop Washington in the Autumn of 1789," which runs from Dixon Entrance to the Strait of Juan de Fuca. This report had unexpected consequences when Captain Vancouver encountered Captain Robert Gray and his American sloop *Columbia* south of the entrance to the Strait of Juan de Fuca on April 29, 1792. Gray, who had been in command of the *Washington* in 1789, denied having made a voyage to southern Alaska, saying that he had only penetrated fifty miles into the Strait of Juan de Fuca.[30]

In 1787 James Colnett arrived on the Northwest Coast in the *Prince of Wales,* accompanied by Charles Duncan in the *Princess Royal*. In their first season Colnett and Duncan traded in British Columbian waters. After wintering in Hawaii, the two ships separated. Duncan continued to work in British Columbian waters and in the Strait of Juan de Fuca. Colnett, however, made for Prince William Sound, anchoring first in Macleod Harbor before working his way south via Port Etches, Port Mulgrave, Sitka Sound, and Dixon Entrance.

Although Colnett returned to the Northwest Coast in 1789 in the *Argonaut,* he did not revisit Alaskan waters. A number of surveys of Alaskan waters are contained in Colnett's journal, including surveys of Macleod Harbor, Port Etches, and Port Mulgrave.[31] His journal also contains three small-scale coastal charts, covering the Northwest Coast from Cook Inlet to the Queen Charlotte Islands.[32] Most of the detail was probably taken from Cook, but the southern-most area, not seen by Cook, is clearly Colnett's own survey. When Faden published a second edition of his chart of the North Pacific on January 1, 1794, he made use of the published charts and accounts from the voyages of Portlock, Dixon, Meares, and Colnett.

The fur traders were apparently well supplied with navigational instruments, since the accounts of their voyages indicate they obtained their longitude by means of lunar distances. They possessed sextants, copies of the *Nautical Almanac* for several years in advance, and the *Tables Requisite.* Dixon also possessed a pocket chronometer, which would have given even greater accuracy in determining longitude.[33] But the fur traders gave little indication of the survey methods they used, though Dixon and Colnett state in the titles of their harbor plans that they were "by compass." Such plans were probably sketch surveys, with bearings taken by compass, distances probably by estimation, and detail drawn in by eye. It is likely that the other fur traders carried out their surveys in a similar manner.

The extent and intricacy of the Northwest Coast was such that neither Cook's running survey nor the various surveys carried out by the fur traders conclusively disproved the existence of a navigable channel leading into the interior of the continent and possibly to Hudson Bay. Meares thought that such a channel existed and included in his *Voyages* an article about known observations of that passage.[34] The opportunity to make a comprehensive search for such a channel came with the signing of the Nootka Convention in 1790. To implement this convention, the British sent Captain George Vancouver to the Northwest Coast in the *Discovery,* accompanied by the *Chatham,* to negotiate with the Spanish commissioner at Nootka Sound on the restoration of land seized by Estéban José Martínez from Meares in 1789. Vancouver was also instructed to examine the Northwest Coast of North America in detail to acquire

accurate information with respect to the nature and extent of any water-communication which may tend, in any considerable degree, to facilitate an intercourse for the purpose of commerce, between the north-west coast, and the country upon the opposite side of the continent.[35]

If Vancouver found any inlets or large rivers communicating with the interior of the continent, he was to ascertain their direction and extent but not

Andrew
David

to follow them farther than they would appear to be navigable by any vessel likely to enter the Pacific Ocean. One of the places where it was thought a navigable channel might exist was at the head of Cook Inlet. Vancouver was further instructed that the survey was to be carried out "without too minute and particular an examination of the detail of the different parts of the coast."[36]

Vancouver was well supplied with surveying instruments, including two chronometers, two sextants, an astronomical quadrant, a theodolite, a chain and lines (presumably for measuring a base), a case of quicksilver for an artificial horizon, two station pointers, and a portable observatory.[37] In addition to the sextants supplied by the navy, many of the officers on board Vancouver's ship had their own, probably totaling twelve in all.[38] A supply ship brought additional instruments to Vancouver at Nootka Sound in August 1792, including three chronometers issued to the expedition astronomer, who was killed in Hawaii on his way to join the group.[39]

In his survey of the Northwest Coast, Vancouver relied on a number of observation points, generally situated several hundred miles apart, to provide a rigid framework for his survey. He obtained their latitudes by a series of meridian altitudes of the sun and their longitudes by a series of lunar distances. Between each point he obtained further meridian altitudes of the sun, whenever possible, to establish the latitudes of prominent headlands. At each point he also determined the rates of his chronometers by observing equal altitudes of the sun, to enable him to carry forward his longitude by chronometer. Each section of his survey then was adjusted to fit the established positions of his observation points and any values for latitude and longitude obtained between them.[40]

Although Vancouver began his survey of the Northwest Coast in 1792, it was not until the following year that he reached Alaskan waters. After spending the winter of 1792–93 in Hawaii, Vancouver returned to Friendly Cove in Nootka Sound on May 20, 1793, where he had obtained an accurate geographical position the previous year. During the next four months, boat parties surveyed the maze of islands and inlets that encumber this part of the coast, while the ships kept pace by moving from one anchorage to another. Observation points were established in Restoration Bay at the seaward end of Burke Inlet and at Salmon Cove toward the head of Observatory Inlet some two hundred miles farther up the coast. At both these anchorages the observatory was set up ashore to obtain fresh rates for the chronometers and to obtain longitudes by lunar distances.

In accordance with his instructions, Vancouver concentrated his survey on the continental shore, searching for possible channels leading to the lakes in the interior of the continent. On reaching Salmon Cove on July 23, Vancouver left the two ships at anchor and set off on an extensive boat expedition in the yawl, accompanied by Lieutenant Peter Puget in the launch. At the same time,

James Johnstone, master of the *Chatham,* was sent to explore the coast to the south. Vancouver first explored Observatory Inlet and then Portland Canal, obtaining the latitude of its northern end by use of an artificial horizon. He then continued north into Alaskan waters through Behm Canal, which he named in honor of the former Russian commandant at Petropavlovsk. In this channel Vancouver came across a remarkable rock that he called the New Eddystone for its resemblance to the well-known lighthouse off the south coast of England. After rounding the northern end of Revillagigedo Island, Vancouver landed on its western side to take a round of angles. When some Tlingit Indians crowded round him, he reembarked, but his boat was soon surrounded by their canoes. Puget was too far off to offer assistance, and so Vancouver was forced to open fire, killing perhaps eight or ten Indians.

With two of his seamen wounded in the attack and his provisions almost exhausted, Vancouver retreated. He had circumnavigated Revillagigedo Island in twenty-three days, although he carried provisions for just fourteen. He worked down Observatory Inlet, then north through Clarence Strait, anchoring first in Port Stewart and later in Port Protection at the northern end of Prince of Wales Island. From here, Joseph Whidbey, master of the *Discovery,* and Johnstone were sent way on the final boat expeditions of the season. In Sumner Strait, Whidbey encountered a long rolling swell that indicated he was close to the open sea. Vancouver named a nearby promontory Cape Decision, as he was now certain there were no navigable channels leading into the interior of the continent.[41]

Vancouver wintered once again in Hawaii. Instead of resuming his survey of the south coast of Alaska at Cape Decision, he proceeded instead to Cook Inlet to complete his survey of the coast from west to east. On April 3, 1794, he sighted an island off the southern tip of Kodiak Island, which he identified as Bering's Foggy Island, naming it Chirikov Island for Bering's companion. He spent the next few days carrying out a running survey of the east coast of Kodiak Island, noting that Ugak Island, which had been seen by the *Discovery*'s officers during Cook's third voyage, was not shown on Cook's chart.

The smoking volcanic peak of Mount Augustine was a useful landmark during Vancouver's passage up Cook's River, which was made difficult by numerous shoals and strong tidal streams. The presence of a great deal of ice was an additional hazard before he found a secure anchorage near the mouth of Eagle River. Here, fresh rates were obtained for the chronometers while latitude was obtained on shore by a meridian altitude of the sun using an artificial horizon.[42] Boat parties were sent away to survey the two arms of the inlet. Vancouver, accompanied by Archibald Menzies, the *Discovery*'s surgeon, set off in the pinnace to examine the head of Knik Arm. Coming abreast of a small hillock, they landed and climbed to its summit from where they

Andrew

David

126

had a good view of the Banks & sandy shoals which seemd to extend across the inlet about 3 or 4 miles above the ship, & backd one another to the very head of the arm: Our station at this time was little more than a league above where Capt Cooks boats returnd, & had they come up thus far what a satisfactory view they would have had of the termination of this great inlet, where they could behold the impossibility of navigating it higher up, & consequently preventing the indulging of those chimerical speculations concerning its spacious & unbounded extent.[43]

Having proved that this inlet was not the estuary of a river, he adopted the name Cook Inlet on his chart instead of Cook's River.

Meanwhile Puget, now in command of the *Chatham,* having become separated from Vancouver on the way north from Hawaii, surveyed the mouth of the inlet, and then carried out a running survey of its western side before joining Vancouver in Knik Arm. The two then worked their way down the eastern side of the inlet to complete the survey.

On sailing from Cook Inlet, Vancouver made directly for Prince William Sound, leaving gaps in his survey of the intermediate coast. On May 26 he anchored on the northwestern side of Montague Island. From here two boat parties, under Whidbey and Johnstone, were sent away to carry out a detailed survey of Prince William Sound. The former started his survey at its western entrance, while Johnstone surveyed its eastern side. Although the weather was too unsettled to land the observatory, Vancouver obtained some observations to rate the chronometers; some lunar distances were also observed.[44]

While he was in the sound, Vancouver was visited by a party of local Russians, who allowed him to copy one of their charts covering the area from Kamchatka to Cross Sound.[45] Vancouver noted that the chart "in many particulars varies very materially from that published by Mr. Meares." [46] However, it did confirm the insularity of Kodiak Island, enabling Vancouver to incorporate this detail on his chart. Meanwhile, Puget was sent to continue the survey to the east of the sound. On the return of Whidbey and Johnstone, Vancouver sailed to rejoin Puget, spending a day visiting the Russian trading post at Port Etches en route. Vancouver was unable to rejoin Puget in Yakutat Bay, and so he continued to Cross Sound, some sixty-five miles southeast, finding sheltered anchorage in Port Althorp, where he was joined by Puget. On receiving Puget's survey of Yakutat Bay, Vancouver discarded Dixon's name Admiralty Bay in favor of Bherings Bay, as he incorrectly concluded that this must be the bay where Bering had first anchored.[47]

While Vancouver remained at anchor, Whidbey began a survey eastward from the entrance to Cross Sound. At first he was hampered by ice calving from Brady Glacier, which in those days extended to the entrance to Glacier Bay. This is in marked contrast to today's conditions: Brady Glacier has retreated an astonishing sixty miles, with the result that Icy Strait, leading east from Cross Sound, is ice-free throughout the year. After examining Lynn Canal, leading north from Icy Strait, Whidbey proceeded down Chatham Strait, passing between Baranov and Admiralty Islands, until he had a clear view of the ocean west of Cape Decision. He then returned to Vancouver's anchorage, having traveled six hundred miles in sixteen days!

In Whidbey's absence, Vancouver surveyed the entrance to Cross Sound. In spite of inclement weather, he obtained fresh rates for his chronometers and the latitude of his observation spot, but he was unable to obtain any lunar distances to obtain longitude. On Whidbey's return, Vancouver sought an anchorage farther south, carrying out a running survey of the west coast of Baranov Island en route. On rounding the southern end of this island, he found a sheltered anchorage for the last time in Alaskan waters, at the western entrance to Chatham Sound, which he aptly named Port Conclusion.

From here, Whidbey and Johnstone were sent away to complete the survey. When the two met, the examination of the Northwest Coast was done, dispelling any remaining doubts that a navigable passage existed between the North Pacific and the interior of the American continent. Vancouver soon started south, anchoring in Friendly Cove to obtain fresh rates for his chronometers before sailing on October 16 for Monterey and ultimately for England.

Only five manuscript surveys have survived from Vancouver's two visits to Alaskan waters, all of harbors in southeastern Alaska.[48] The principal cartographic record of Vancouver's survey is the atlas of engraved charts and coastal views published with the first edition of his *Voyage* in 1798. In this atlas the coast of Alaska is covered by a small-scale chart of the whole Northwest Coast and four coastal sheets covering the coast from Queen Charlotte Islands to Kodiak Island on which are inset plans of Port Stewart, Port Chatham, Port Chalmers, and the entrance to Cross Sound, including Port Althorp, Port Protection, and Port Conclusion. The printing plates for these charts were stolen shortly after the atlas was printed, and so, when the second edition of Vancouver's *Voyage* was published in 1801, it included a new chart of the Northwest Coast without any plans of the Alaska anchorages.[49] Vancouver's survey is included in Arrowsmith's Chart of the Pacific Ocean published in 1798, with further editions in 1810 and 1814.

Vancouver's survey was not fully superseded for many years. Although it had its limitations, due primarily to the limited time available to survey the entire coastline, Vancouver's latitudes are very close to modern values, but his longitudes are not. In his first visit to Alaskan waters in 1793, his lunar distances placed Salmon Cove just seven and one half minutes too far to the east, and most of his other longitudes for this season were also in error by simi-

Andrew David

128

lar amounts.[50] In 1794, Vancouver was able to observe lunar distances only in Prince William Sound due to bad weather conditions. Since the rates of his chronometers had become erratic, his longitudes placed Cook Inlet and Prince William Sound up to forty minutes and Cross Sound and Port Conclusion up to twenty minutes too far east.[51] These errors may seem large by modern standards but they fully met the requirements of navigation in the early years of the nineteenth century.

No survey lasts forever, and more modern survey methods evolved as the demands of trade and safety required more detail. So, as Vancouver's survey superseded those of Cook and the fur traders, his survey was superseded in turn by those carried out by the U.S. Coast Survey more than a century later. Even so, it is surprising that Vancouver's survey lasted for so long, remaining the only reliable authority for navigating remote waters of Alaska for most of the nineteenth century. His charts were also consulted for determining the Alaskan/Canadian boundary in the Anglo-Russian Convention of 1825. Vancouver's detailed survey also gave him much more scope for bestowing names than his predecessors. Indeed, with the passage of time it is the names that Cook, the fur traders, and Vancouver bestowed on the Alaskan coast that are a lasting memorial to their vast achievements.

NOTES

1. J. C. Beaglehole, ed., *The Journals of Captain James Cook on His Voyages of Discovery,* Vol. 3: *The Voyage of the Resolution and Discovery, 1776-1780* (Cambridge: Cambridge University Press, 1967), p. ccxx (hereafter Beaglehole, *The Voyage of the Resolution and Discovery*).

2. Gerhard Friedrich Müller, *Voyages from Asia to America, for Completing the Discoveries of the North West Coast of America* (London: T. Jeffreys, 1761), frontispiece. See also Beaglehole, *The Voyage of the Resolution and Discovery,* plate 2.

3. Glyndwr Williams, *The British Search for the Northwest Passage in the Eighteenth Century* (London: Royal Commonwealth Society, 1962), p. 173.

4. Beaglehole, *The Voyage of the Resolution and Discovery,* plate 3.

5. *Ibid.,* p. 335.

6. *Ibid.,* p. 343.

7. *Ibid.,* p. 366.

8. *Ibid.,* pp. 405, 406.

9. *Ibid.,* pp. 452–56.

10. Document number 58 in the compendium of documents published in Russia in 1989 pertaining to the North Pacific. Both a letter to the admiralty and chart prepared by Cook eventually reached England. Cook letter, Oct. 20, 1778, and MPI 83, Adm 1/1612, Public Record Office, London.

11. For a description of a running survey, see Andrew C. F. David, ed., *The Charts*

and Coastal Views of Captain Cook's Voyages, Vol. 1: *The Voyage of the Endeavour, 1767–1770* (London: The Hakluyt Society, 1988), pp. xxix–xxxi, and Vol. 2: *The Voyage of the Resolution and Adventure, 1772–1775* (1992), pp. xxxi–xxxii.

12. William Bayly, *The Original Astronomical Observations Made in the Course of a Voyage to the Northern Pacific Ocean* (London: William Richardson, 1782), pp. 45–53, 93–123, 229–71.

13. All these charts will be illustrated and described in Andrew C. F. David, ed., *The Charts and Coastal Views of Captain Cook's Voyages*, Vol. 3: *The Voyage of the Resolution and Discovery, 1776–1780*, forthcoming from the Hakluyt Society.

14. Rupert T. Gould, "Bligh's Notes on Cook's Last Voyage," *The Mariner's Mirror*, Vol. 14 (1928), p. 371.

15. A317, Hydrographic Office, Ministry of Defence, Taunton; the chart measures 830 by 2786 millimeters.

16. William Bligh, *A Voyage to the South Sea* . . . (London, 1792), p. 157.

17. C302 and A356, Hydrographic Office.

18. MS.F2, p. 2, MS.Q152, p. 2 and MS.Q151, p. 249, Dixson Library, State Library of New South Wales, Sydney, Australia.

19. MPI 82 (extracted from Adm 55/120), Public Record Office.

20. Vancouver Maritime Museum, Vancouver, B.C..

21. Adm 55/21, ff. 158, 163v, 172 and 172v, Public Record Office.

22. Safe 1/64, pp. 136, 147, 158, 169, 180, 181, 186, 193, 200, 209, 223, Mitchell Library, Sydney.

23. 524/2, 524/4, and E48, Hydrographic Office.

24. 810 A-1778, American Geographical Society Collection, Milwaukee Library, University of Wisconsin.

25. Tony Campbell, "A Cook Mystery Solved," *The Map Collector*, No. 32 (1985), pp. 36–37.

26. William Coxe, *Account of the Russian Discoveries between Asia and America*, 2d ed. (London: J. Nichols and T. Cadell, 1780), pp. 251–66.

27. James Cook and James King, *A Voyage to the Pacific Ocean . . . for making Discoveries in the Northern Hemisphere*, 4 vols., 2d ed. (London: J. Nichols and T. Cadell, 1785), 1:lxxxii.

28. A chart by S. Wedgbrough depicting the track of the *Experiment* from Bombay to Prince William Sound is reproduced in James Strange, *James Strange's Journal and Narrative* (Madras: Government Press, 1928).

29. Manuscript versions of these charts are held in the British Hydrographic Office in an atlas that once belonged to George Rose, a British statesman, who was associated with the planning of the voyage. Rose Atlas, items 14–20, HO.

30. George Vancouver, *A Voyage of Discovery to the North Pacific Ocean and round the World, 1791–1795*, ed. W. Kaye Lamb, 4 vols. (London: The Hakluyt Society, 1984), 2: 501–502 (hereafter Lamb, *Vancouver's Voyage*).

31. Adm 55/146, ff. 199v, 201, 211, Public Record Office.

32. *Ibid.*, ff. 236, 204, and 225.

33. George Dixon, *A Voyage round the World* . . . (London: G. Goulding, 1789),

appendix 2, p. 47; and Nathaniel Portlock, *A Voyage round the World* . . . (London: G. Goulding, 1789), p. 203.

34. John Meares, *Voyages Made in the Years 1788 and 1789, from China to the North West Coast of America* (London, 1790), pp. xli–lxvi and accompanying chart.

35. Lamb, *Vancouver's Voyage,* 1:283–84.

36. *Ibid.,* 1:285.

37. Roberts to Philip Stephens, Jan. 4, 14, 1790, Adm 1/2395, Public Record Office.

38. For a full list of instruments supplied to Vancouver, see Andrew C. F. David, "Vancouver's Survey Methods and Surveys," in *From Maps to Metaphors: The Pacific World of George Vancouver,* ed. Robin Fisher and Hugh Johnston (Vancouver: University of British Columbia Press, 1993), pp. 54–55, 291–92.

39. For a full list of instruments supplied to William Gooch, who was appointed astronomer of the expedition, see David, "Vancouver's Survey Methods," pp. 56, 292–93.

40. For a detailed discussion of Vancouver's survey methods, see David, "Vancouver's Survey Methods."

41. Lamb, *Vancouver's Voyage,* 3:1064.

42. Wallace M. Olson, *The Alaska Travel Journal of Archibald Menzies, 1793–1794* (Fairbanks: University of Alaska Press, 1993), p. 94 (hereafter Olson, *Menzies's Journal*).

43. *Ibid.,* p. 100.

44. Lamb, *Vancouver's Voyage,* 4:1274–75.

45. Olson, *Menzies's Journal,* p. 132.

46. Lamb, *Vancouver's Voyage,* 4:1287.

47. For further information on Vancouver's choice of name see Lamb, *Vancouver's Voyage,* pp. 1321–32, and Beaglehole, *The Voyage of the Resolution and Discovery,* pp. 338–39, n. 5.

48. These are harbor plans of Port Stewart and Port Conclusion by Puget, 558 and 561, Hydrographic Office; Port Protection and Port Stewart by the master's mate John Sherriff, PRO, Adm 53/334, ff. 107 and 110, Public Record Office; and a third harbor plan of Port Stewart by the master's mate John Stewart, Adm 55/28, f. 207, Public Record Office.

49. Lamb, *Vancouver's Voyage,* 1:245.

50. *Ibid.,* 1:52–54, 3:1028, n.l..

51. David gives possible causes for Vancouver's errors in longitude, noting that in the first line on p. 66, "feet" should read "minutes" in two places ("Vancouver's Survey Methods," pp. 65–66).

CAROL URNESS

Russian Mapping
of the North Pacific to 1792

From the beginning of their exploration of Siberia and the North Pacific, Russians made maps of their findings. The mapmakers were usually *pro-myshlenniki* (fur traders), who had no formal training in surveying or mapmaking.[1] Most of these early maps were unknown outside of Russia and were largely unknown even within it until recently. However, they document the Russian contribution to the developing body of knowledge about the North Pacific in the eighteenth century.

Russian mapmaking was neither informal nor haphazard. During the rule of Peter the Great it became more organized and technically more professional. The School of Navigation, established in 1701, trained *geodesists* (land surveyors) as well as navigators in the skills needed to make maps.[2] Peter inaugurated a systematic effort to map all of Russia, and he named Ivan K. Kirilov to oversee the work of the *geodesists* and to make new maps based on their findings.[3] In 1719 he ordered the *geodesists* Ivan M. Evreinov and Fedor F. Luzhin to travel to the Russian Far East to explore and map the southern part of Kamchatka and the Kurile Islands. Following this expedition, in May of 1722 Evreinov presented Peter with a new map and a report of their findings. At Peter's order these and other maps of northeastern Siberia were engraved by the German mapmaker Johann Baptist Homann. One of these maps accompanied the instructions for the naval expedition that became known as the First Kamchatka Expedition.[4]

During the First Kamchatka Expedition, 1725–30, Russian navy personnel led by Vitus Bering mapped the overland route from St. Petersburg to the Sea of Okhotsk. They sailed to Kamchatka, built another ship there, and sailed it from the Kamchatka River northward along the coast, mapping as they went. The maps that the expedition produced were the first to show the northeast part of Siberia accurately. They also offered new information on the mainland as well, finally recognizing the eastern limit of Siberia at what we know today as Bering Strait.[5]

During the Second Kamchatka Expedition, from 1733 to 1743, the Russian navy had major responsibilities for mapping. One assignment was to map the Arctic coast from Archangel to Kamchatka. Another assignment, given to Martin Spanberg, was to discover and map a route from Russia to Japan. But the most critical project was left to Vitus Bering and Aleksei Chirikov, who were ordered to explore and map the coast of America. Their two ships sailed together in 1741 but were quickly separated in a storm. Both reached America. Chirikov returned the same year, but Bering was shipwrecked in the Commander Islands, where he died. The survivors, including Sven Waxell, the commander after Bering's death, and the naturalist/physician Georg Wilhelm Steller, returned to Kamchatka in 1742. The mapping done during these two voyages included a portion of the American coast, observed through the rain and fog, and several Aleutian Islands encountered on the return to Kamchatka.[6]

Mapping was one thing; compiling the results for publication was quite another. The maps drawn by the *promyshlenniki* were often sketch maps. Maps done by *geodesists* were of small areas, and they had to be put together like a giant jigsaw puzzle. The available instruments made the calculation of longitude very difficult, rendering the results problematic. Ivan Kirilov incorporated the map made by the First Kamchatka Expedition in his 1732 general map of Russia. The expedition map also appeared in France in a book by Jean Baptiste Du Halde in 1735 and was widely copied thereafter. There is no indication that the Russian government felt any need to keep the results of this expedition secret. Manuscript copies of the map were presented to several European rulers.[7]

Western European mapmakers in general were mixed in their acceptance of this new configuration of northeastern Siberia. A major objection to it came from the Swiss geographer Samuel Engel, who charged that the Russians did not have the skill to make the needed astronomical observations to ascertain longitude. Therefore, Engel claimed, the Russians had extended Siberia thirty degrees to the east in order to make it appear that the Northeast Passage along the arctic coast of Russia was difficult. According to Engel, the Russians had already discovered a northeast passage, were using it, and were hiding it from other Europeans for commercial reasons.[8]

Publicizing the mapping of the Second Kamchatka Expedition was more controversial, and more complicated. Gerhard Friedrich Müller, a historian from the Academy of Sciences, had traveled in Siberia from 1733 to 1743 with the expedition, at times with Bering. When Müller saw the maps being prepared for the atlas to be published by the Academy of Sciences, he offered suggestions for improving them. Müller was rebuffed, probably because of the length of time that had already been expended on the atlas, which was published in 1745.[9]

Müller started to develop his own maps, including a general map of Siberia. However, in 1746 an order came from the Empress Elizabeth that all materials relating to the Second Kamchatka Expedition were to be turned in to the government, perhaps because of unauthorized distribution. A map with informa-tion about the American voyages had been published in Paris in 1744; similar maps appeared in Paris and Berlin in 1746.[10] These maps were not authorized by either the Academy of Sciences or the government. Garbled accounts of the voyages had been published also, some of them in connection with the mys-terious death of Steller on his return journey from Siberia. Members of the Academy of Sciences, most of whom were of foreign origin, were the logical sources of these publications.

For several years no new information was released. In April 1750, Joseph Nicolas Delisle gave a presentation to the Académie des Sciences in Paris, dis-cussing the state of Russian exploration in the North Pacific. Delisle had been a member of the Russian Academy of Sciences for over twenty years, so his presentation seemed authoritative. In fact, Delisle had very little information about the voyages to America, was in trouble with the Academy, and had re-turned to France because his contract was not renewed.[11] To the great annoy-ance of the Russians, Delisle published his 1750 memoir and an accompanying map in 1752 (Map 1). According to this map, Bering never reached America but had only sailed eastward to the island where he died. Also, Chirikov's name was joined to that of Delisle de la Croyère, J. N. Delisle's brother, on the route to America, as if the two shared equal responsibility for the voyage. This infuri-ated the Russians. In addition, Delisle had connected the Russian discoveries to the voyage of Admiral de Fonte, who supposedly sailed across North America in 1640.[12]

Most geographers at the time correctly considered the de Fonte voyage a fake. The Russians responded by assigning Müller to refute Delisle's map. As a rebuttal, Müller wrote an anonymous work titled *Lettre d'un Officier de la Marine Russienne . . . 1753*, which contradicted Delisle in many points and which, to obtain the broadest readership, was published in German, English, and French. Müller also prepared a map to accompany this account of the discoveries. The map, which is titled *Nouvelle carte des découvertes faites par des vaisseaux russes aux côtes inconnues de l'Amérique avec les pais adiacentes*, was published by the Academy of Sciences in 1754. (See map, p. 117.) The same map was reissued in 1758, this time accompanying Müller's fuller account of the Russian dis-coveries.[13]

Müller had the map made by the First Kamchatka Expedition in 1725–30, which gives an accurate portrayal of the extent of Siberia and a clear image of the size and shape of Kamchatka and of the coast north of it to sixty-seven degrees. With respect to America, Müller followed the map of the Bering and Chirikov voyages made by Sergeant Aleksei Pushkarev sometime between 1741 and 1743. The Pushkarev manuscript map is called a summary map of the Bering and Chirikov voyages and is reproduced in the Efimov *Atlas*.[14] The map's

Carol
Urness

134

Map 1. J. N. Delisle, "Carte des nouvelles découvertes," 1752. *James Ford Bell Library, University of Minnesota*

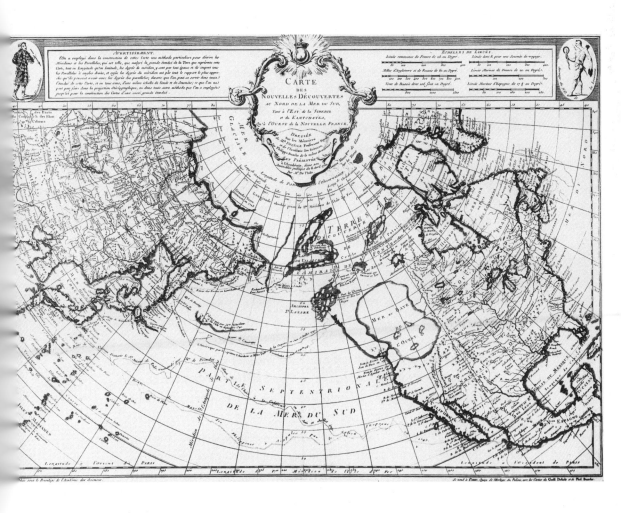

most arresting feature is the huge peninsula jutting westward from the North American coast toward Kamchatka. This is the feature that got Müller into trouble, for he put it on his map of 1754.

In his commentary, Müller specified the principles he used in making the map. About using dotted lines to indicate the presumed coastlines, Müller wrote, "My work in this [part of the map] has been no more than to connect together by dots, according to probability, the coast seen at various places."[15] The big land mass jutting westward from North America was indicated by dotted lines. Müller followed the example of another mapmaker, John Green, who used dotted lines in several areas of his map of North and South America, which was published by Thomas Jefferys in 1753. About the coastlines of North America, Green had written, "I have continued the Coast Northward, by a pricked Line, in the Direction, which I judge it may trend, in order to inclose Baffin's-Bay, as exhibited in the Second Sheet [of the map.]."[16] Müller noted that he had just received this map by John Green at the time he was preparing his own map.

The "turtle's head" on Müller's map evoked strong criticism, though time proved him correct. This massive land protuberance made either a northeast or a northwest passage almost impossible, for ships would have to sail far around the peninsula in order to reach China, Japan, and the East Indies. Müller took the same liberties in his maps as Delisle: "I have deemed it proper, following the examples of Messrs. Delisle and Buache, to connect the Russian discoveries with the American regions already known."[17] But on his map, unlike the Delisle and Buache maps, no passages are shown in the interior of North America. Müller indicates on the American coast the "Pretendue R. de los Reyes de l'Amiral de Fonte en 1640 suivant Mr. Delisle," but it does not extend into the interior.

The discoveries attributed to the de Fonte voyage were believed by Arthur Dobbs, a strong proponent of continued searching for the Northwest Passage. Dobbs maintained that the Russians had never reached the American mainland and that their sightings were all of islands.[18] Müller countered Dobbs with: "I should wish that Mr. Dobbs were right; Russia would lose nothing by that. It would get its future possessions even more incontestably, because no European could boast of ever having had knowledge of this great island."[19] By placing the dotted coastlines on his map, Müller unwittingly joined the controversy about northern sea passages from Europe to the East, and across North America. His map was criticized harshly, in spite of the logic of his explanation for the coasts shown on it.

Once again the strongest critic of Müller's map was Samuel Engel. The huge land mass protruding from America would make northern passages more difficult. Engel denied the existence of this land, insisting on an easy Northeast

Carol
Urness

Passage from Europe to the East. He wrote that Müller was forced to conceal the truth about the Russian voyages in the North Pacific, and even accused Müller of intentionally suppressing the information.[20]

In the period immediately following the Bering and Chirikov voyages to America until 1764, Russian exploration in the North Pacific was left to fur traders, who kept moving eastward. The sea otters in the Commander Islands were soon hunted out. In 1745 Russian hunters reached Agattu in the Near Islands; in 1748 they were hunting at Kiska in the Rat Islands. In the mid-1750s hunters were active in the Andreanof Islands, and shortly thereafter they began hunting in the Fox Islands.[21] Fur traders made maps. In his article, "After Bering, Mapping the North Pacific," Stuart R. Tompkins presents a chronological list of voyages, citing many instances of mapmaking by fur traders.[22] In 1751, for example, Mikhail Nevodchikov made a map of Attu, Agattu, and Semichi that was sent to the Russian senate. A 1762 map made by the Cossack Ponomarev was presented to Catherine II and was forwarded to the admiralty. The merchant Semen Krasil'nikov presented a map of the Aleutians east to Umnak to Catherine in 1766. Rewards given to these mapmakers, including exemption from taxes, are indicated. Most of the original maps have not survived, and it is difficult to know how much influence these crude maps had on the Russian charting of the North Pacific.

In the 1760s, the government resumed an active role in exploring the North Pacific. In 1764, the navy lieutenant Ivan Sindt was put in charge of an expedition with responsibilities for "1. close monitoring of the seaborne fur trade. 2. careful surveying of all islands lying between Kamchatka and America, and a scrupulous determination of their resources."[23] Sindt sailed east of Chukchi Peninsula. His map from the voyage is decorated with nonexistent northern islands that undoubtedly originated with maps made by fur traders. In 1773 the Sindt map was incorporated into a revised version of Müller's 1754/58 map, made at the Academy of Sciences.[24] The maker of this map is not known. The base map is the 1754/58 Müller map, and the islands are Sindt's (Map 2).[25]

The map was made public when Jacob von Stählin, another member of the Academy, published it and an account of Russian voyages in a historical and geographical almanac for 1774. The government immediately denounced the publication and ordered the destruction of all copies of it. This made the publication and map seem more authentic and desirable. German and English translations appeared the same year.[26] The map in general is Müller's, but it is attributed to Stählin because of these publications. In the accompanying text, Stählin provides background on Russian explorations, and then lists many islands and provides descriptions of them. Stählin writes of a fictional lieutenant, "Mr. Syndo," who made the discoveries, and his route to these northern islands is on the map.

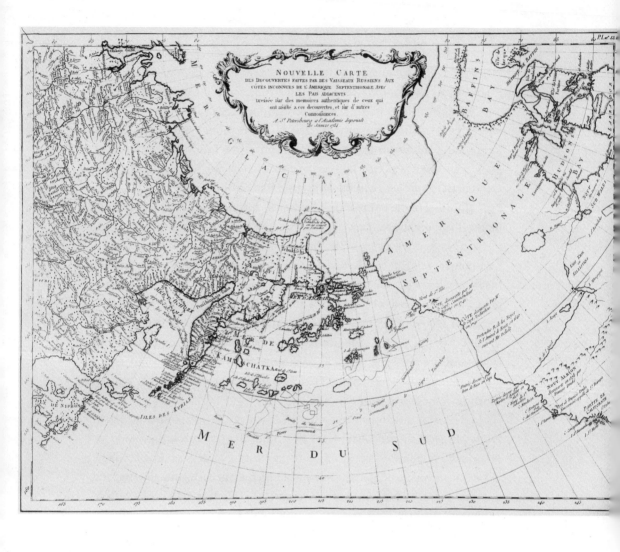

Map 2. Müller/Stählin map "Nouvelle carte," 1784. *James Ford Bell Library, University of Minnesota*

About Stählin's work Peter Simon Pallas, a member of the Academy who was active in its geographical work, wrote to his colleague in England, "Staehlin's Cart & account were made up from the very first & rude accounts & Sketches, wherefore it is full of lyes, and faults committed by the Editor: the Isles in the Cart are all placed in a wrong situation, to the northward, where they form two chains to the east, one between Kamtshatka & America, the other between the Tshuktshi country & America."[27] The Müller/Stählin map shows how right Pallas was. Another famous member of the Academy who was involved in geographical work, Mikhail Lomonosov, felt that the error in the placement of the islands too far north was because the fur traders did not understand the magnetic declination of the compass.[28] This is the map that so annoyed Cook during his voyage to the North Pacific.[29]

In the late 1700s the question of territory in the North Pacific became crucial. As a matter of policy, Catherine II was not enthusiastic about claiming lands so far away. She wrote: "Much expansion in the Pacific Ocean will not bring concrete benefits. To trade is one thing, to take possession quite another."[30] Still, Russians were occupying the islands to a greater extent than ever before, and the trade was valuable. Maps were one means to confirm Russian territorial claims. In 1780, Pallas published a map of the North Pacific, together with his account of the Aleutian Islands, in the *Neue nordische Beyträge* (Map 3). The map included information from Cook's voyage. Pallas had concerns about the accuracy of this map and asked Mikhail Tatarinov, a mapmaker at the navigation school in Irkutsk, to look at it. The resulting manuscript map, dated 1781, has an improved configuration of the western Aleutian Islands. The notes on it concerning the explorations of Captain James Cook in the North Pacific are by Pallas (Map 4).[31]

When the accounts of the Cook explorations in the North Pacific were published, the revelation of the rich fur trade with China brought the threat of encroachment on "Russian" territory in the North Pacific. The Russian rights of prior discovery did not always go unquestioned in the eighteenth century. For example, Alexander Walker, after his visit to the North Pacific in 1785–86, wrote:

The Russians have possessed themselves of their Country without conquering it; but merely on that presumptuous and most unjust of all pleas—the right of discovery. Nothing can be more iniquitous than the rule which Civilized Governments have established, of taking Possession of the Countries of every People, who may be more rude and barbarous than themselves.[32]

On the Northwest Coast, Russian territorial claims were subject to challenge by Spain and, in the late eighteenth century, to encroachment by American, British, French, and other traders who might visit the region.

An Englishman who had been a midshipman with Captain Cook, Captain

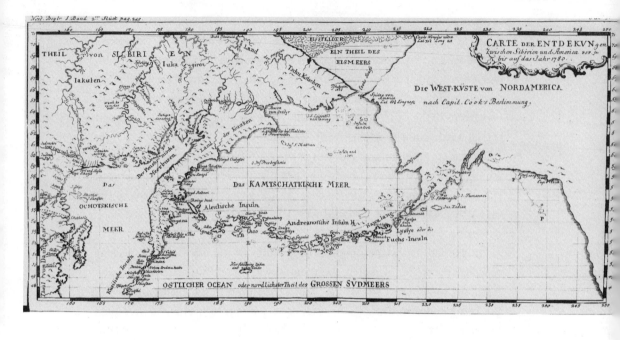

Map 3. P. S. Pallas, "Carte de Entdekungen zwischen Sibirien und America," 1780.

James Ford Bell Library, University of Minnesota

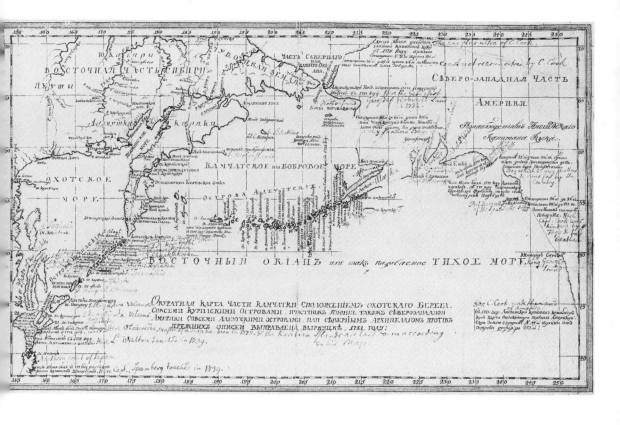

Map 4. Mikhail Tatirinov, "Okuratnaia karta chasti Kamchatki . . . ," 1781. *James Ford Bell Library, University of Minnesota*

Joseph Billings, and a Russian, Gavriil A. Sarychev, led the last official Russian expedition to the North Pacific in the eighteenth century. The expedition lasted from 1785 to 1792. The instructions for it were lengthy, detailed, and related directly to territory. There were several charges, beginning with the order to map all the islands in the North Pacific, including the Kurile Islands and Japan, and to claim for Russia all lands discovered. The instructions stated that the expedition was to complete and perfect the mapping from earlier explorations and that copies of twenty-four maps made by earlier Russian expeditions would be made available for the expedition.[33]

The Billings/Sarychev expedition was also to explore and map the northeast corner of Siberia. The attempt made in 1787 to sail from the mouth of the Kolyma River around the Chukchi Peninsula to the North Pacific failed because of the ice pack. The Billings/Sarychev expedition then set sail for the Aleutians and America. With two ships (three set out but one was wrecked almost immediately) Billings and Sarychev sailed in the fall of 1789 for Unalaska, Kodiak, Chugach Bay, and the Bay of St. Lawrence. The maps and reports made under the supervision of Sarychev added substantially to the available knowledge of these places. In 1791–92, Sarychev attempted to map the Shelagskii Cape area but was unsuccessful due to the weather conditions. The account of the Billings/Sarychev expedition was first published in 1802, and appeared in several translations. The maps of the Aleutian Islands and the nearby mainland made at the close of the eighteenth century by the Russians show extraordinary detail and accuracy (Map 5).[34]

In this brief consideration of selected maps made by the Russians in the eighteenth century, it appears that the Russians were not keeping secrets nearly so much as has been thought.[35] Following their early exploration of the North Pacific, Russians publicized the map resulting from the First Kamchatka Expedition. The Academy of Sciences published an atlas in 1745 that incorporated information from the explorations, though not of the Bering and Chirikov voyages to America in 1741. Müller's map of 1754/58 reflects the knowledge the Russians had of America at that time. In adding coasts with dotted lines, Müller made his map appear more complete than it really was, which fueled the controversy surrounding it. The subsequent maps made by traders demonstrate the difficulties in determining latitude (because of the magnetic variation of the compass) and longitude (because of the difficulties in making astronomical observations). But later in the eighteenth-century, Russian maps resulting from official expeditions show much greater detail and accuracy.

How much did the Russians keep secret? Historians may have misinterpreted the charge to maintain secrecy imposed on the members of the expeditions and the prohibitions about publishing unauthorized accounts and maps. Was the government trying to prevent any reports about the explorations from

Carol
Urness

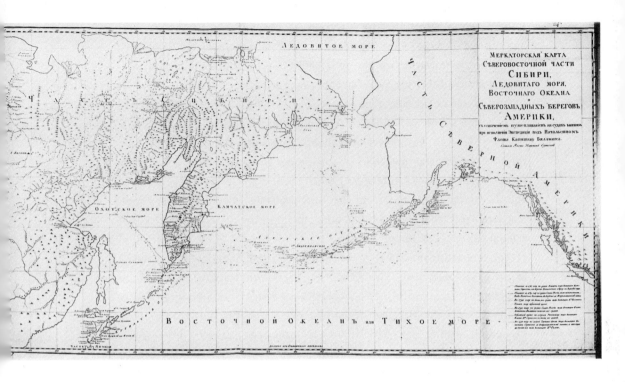

Map 5. General map in G. A. Sarychev, *Puteshestvie . . .* , 1802. *James Ford Bell Library,*
University of Minnesota

reaching western Europe? Or was it trying to maintain control of the quality and content of those reports? If the latter, then the policies about unapproved publication of the results of these explorations were no different from those in effect concerning other expeditions, for example, those of Cook.

Were the concerns about the possible intrusion into the trade on the part of other Europeans enough to have an influence on the policies about map publications? Possibly. But, on the other hand, the European practice of claiming territory was based on discovery and mapping. The problem for the Russians seems to have been the difficulty of getting accurate maps with the personnel and the navigational equipment that were available. In addition, when their maps were published, Russians had difficulty in getting these maps accepted as accurate by other Europeans.

It is interesting that the reception given to Russian maps was almost always negative. The map of the First Kamchatka Expedition was criticized as a plot to discourage attempts to discover a northeast passage by extending the length of Siberia far to the east. The Müller map made from the Second Kamchatka Expedition, with its dotted coastlines, was criticized sharply by some writers because they felt that the purpose of the map was to discourage the search for northern passages. Western European geographers assumed that the Russians were hiding information that was valuable to other Europeans. As it turned out, if the Russians were hiding something, it was the wealth of the fur trade rather than the geography of the North Pacific. Whatever factors governed the release of the Russian maps of the North Pacific, by the time George Vancouver set sail to clear up questions about the geography of the area, Russians had already been exploring and mapping the North Pacific for decades and had shared the best of their maps widely.

NOTES

1. Examples of their maps are reproduced in the *Atlas geografîcheskikh otkrytii v Sibiri i v severo-zapadnoi Amerike XVII–XVIII vv,* edited by A. V. Efimov (Moscow: Nauka, 1964). Efimov has other essential books: *Iz istorii russkikh ekspeditsii na tikhom okeane* (Moscow: Voennoe izdatel'stvo Ministerstva vor uzhennykh sil SSSR, 1948), and *Iz istorii velikikh russkikh geografîcheskikh otkrytii* (Moscow: Nauka, 1971).

2. W. F. Ryan, "Navigation and the Modernization of Petrine Russia: Teachers, Textbooks, Terminology," in *Russia in the Age of the Enlightenment: Essays for Isabel de Madariaga,* ed. Roger Bartlett and Janet Hartley (New York: St. Martin's Press, 1990), pp. 75–105.

3. The early explorations were made under the direction of the governors of Siberia. See Evgenii G. Kushnarev, *Bering's Search for the Strait: The First Kamchatka Expedition, 1725-1730,* ed. and trans. E. A. P. Crownhart-Vaughan (Portland: Oregon Historical Society Press, 1990), p. 6; and Leo Bagrow, *A History of Russian Cartography up to 1800,* ed. Henry Castner, 2 vols. (Wolfe Island, Ont.: Walker Press, 1975), 2:44–46.

Carol
Urness

4. Gerhard Friedrich Müller, *Bering's Voyages: The Reports from Russia,* ed. and trans. Carol Urness (Fairbanks: University of Alaska Press, 1986), pp. 22–27.

5. Kushnarev, *Bering's Search,* pp. 155–56; Marvin Falk, "Vitus Bering," in *Exploration in Alaska: Captain Cook Commemorative Lectures, June-November 1978,* ed. Antoinette Shalkop, et al. (Anchorage: Cook Inlet Historical Society, 1980), pp. 102–13. See also Carol Urness, "Vitus Bering," in *Bering and Chirikov: The American Voyages and Their Impact,* ed. O. W. Frost (Anchorage: Alaska Historical Society, 1992), pp. 11–36.

6. Efimov, *Atlas,* maps 97–102.

7. The manuscript map made of the whole expedition exists in at least fifteen copies. See Kushnarev, *Bering's Search,* p. 153. The James Ford Bell Library at the University of Minnesota, St. Paul, has a copy. The map was first published outside of Russia in 1735, in the massive work of Jean Baptiste Du Halde titled *Description géographique, historique . . . de l'empire de la Chine et de la Tartarie,* 4 vols. (Paris: P. G. Mercier, 1735). It was reprinted many times afterward.

8. Samuel Engel, *Memoires et observations géographiques et critiques sur la situation des pays septentrionaux de l'Asie et de l'Amerique* (Lausanne: Antoine Chapuis, 1765), pp. 228–29.

9. Müller, *Bering's Voyage,* p. 40.

10. *Ibid.,* pp. 38–56.

11. *Ibid.,* pp. 44–50.

12. On this mapping, see L. Breitfuss, "Early Maps of North-Eastern Asia and of the Lands around the North Pacific: Controversy between G. F. Müller and N. Delisle," in *Imago Mundi,* Vol. 3 (1939), pp. 87–99.

13. In the German original edition the map is titled *Nachrichten von Seereisen, und zur See gemachten Entdeckungen, die von Russland aus langst den Kusten des Eismeeres und auf dem ostlichen Weltmeere gegen Japon und America geschehen sind* (St. Petersburg: Kaiserliche Akademie der Wissenschaften, 1758). *Sammlung russischer Geschichte,* v. 3 (St. Petersburg: Academie der Wissenschafften, 1735). A Russian edition, "Opisanie morskikh puteshestvii po ledovitomu i po vostochnomu moriu s rossiiskoi storony uchenennykh," is in volumes 7 and 8 of the *Sochineniia i perevody . . . ,* published by the Academy of Sciences in 1758.

14. Efimov, *Atlas,* number 117.

15. Müller, *Bering's Voyages,* p. 137.

16. John Green, *Remarks in Support of the New Chart of North and South America; In six sheets* (London: For Thomas Jefferys, 1753), p. 25.

17. Müller, *Bering's Voyages,* p. 137. In addition to Delisle's map and publication noted above, Philippe Buache followed it with related maps that showed the same kind of fantastic geography for North America.

18. Arthur Dobbs, *Observations upon the Russian Discoveries* (London: A. Linde, 1754), p. 47.

19. Müller, *Bering's Voyages,* p. 138.

20. Samuel Engel, *Geographische und Kritische Nachrichten und Anmerkungen über die Lage der nordlichen Gegenden von Asien und Amerika,* 2 vols. (Basel: Carl August Serini, 1777), 2:28.

21. Peter Simon Pallas, *A Naturalist in Russia: Letters from Peter Simon Pallas to Thomas Pennant,* ed. Carol Urness (Minneapolis: University of Minnesota Press, 1967), p. 120.

22. Stuart R. Tompkins, "After Bering, Mapping the North Pacific," *British Columbia Historical Quarterly,* Vol. 19 (1955), pp. 1–55.

23. Basil Dmytryshyn, E. A. P. Crownhart-Vaughn, and Thomas Vaughn, eds. and trans., *Russian Penetration of the North Pacific Ocean: A Documentary Record, 1700–1797,* Vol. 2: *To Siberia and Russian America* (Portland: Oregon Historical Society Press, 1988) (hereafter Dmytryshyn, *Russian Penetration*), p. xlii.

24. James R. Masterson and Helen Brower, *Bering's Successors, 1745–1780* (Seattle: University of Washington Press, 1948), pp. 5–6. See also Coolie Verner and Basil Stuart-Stubbs, *The Northpart of America* (Toronto: Academic Press Canada, 1979), pp. 183–84, 186, and map 38. The discussion refers largely to the map of 1754/58, but the reproduction is the map of ca. 1773, which is better for leaving off the large "turtle head," but is worse for putting the second row of islands in the north, as on Sindt's map.

25. This manuscript map, with Müller's notes, is in the James Ford Bell Library at the University of Minnesota, St. Paul.

26. Jakob Stählin von Storcksburg, *Das von den Russen in den Jahren 1765, 66, 67 entdekte nordliche Insel-Meer, zwischen Kamtschatka und Nordamerika* (Stuttgart: Christoph Friedrich Cotta, 1774), and *An Account of the New Northern Archipelago . . .* (London: C. Heydinger, 1774).

27. Pallas, *Naturalist,* p. 55.

28. Tompkins, *After Bering,* p. 21.

29. Glyndwr Williams, "Myth and Reality: James Cook and the Theoretical Geography of Northwest America," in *Captain James Cook and His Times,* ed. Robin Fisher and Hugh Johnston (Seattle: University of Washington Press, 1979), pp. 58–80, esp. p. 77.

30. James R. Gibson, "A Notable Absence: The Lateness and Lameness of Russian Discovery and Exploration in the North Pacific, 1639–1803," in *From Maps to Metaphors: The Pacific World of George Vancouver,* ed. Robin Fisher and Hugh Johnston (Vancouver: University of British Columbia Press, 1993), pp. 85–103 (qtn., p. 101).

31. This manuscript map, in the James Ford Bell Library, was sent by Pallas to Thomas Pennant in England. In 1991 Thomas Clark wrote an excellent student paper at the University of Minnesota on this map, titled "Out of the Fog: Russia's View of the North Pacific after Cook." The paper is unpublished; a copy is in the library.

32. Alexander Walker, *An Account of a Voyage to the North West Coast of America in 1785 & 1786,* ed. Robin Fisher and J. M. Bumsted (Vancouver: Douglas & McIntyre; Seattle: University of Washington Press, 1982), p. 148.

33. Gavriil Andreevich Sarychev, *Puteshestvie flota kapitana Sarycheva,* 2 vols. (St. Petersburg: Shnora, 1802), 1:1–10. An English translation is in Martin Sauer, *An Account of a Geographical and Astronomical Expedition to the Northern Parts of Russia* (London: T. Cadell and W. Davies, 1802), pp. 29–49.

34. See, for example, editions of the *Rossiiskoi Atlas,* published by the Geographical Department of the Academy of Sciences in 1792 and 1800.

35. The policy of secrecy is discussed in Dmytryshyn, *Russian Penetration,* and in Gibson, "A Notable Absence."

Carol
Urness

Part **3** Outcomes and Consequences

J. C. H. KING

Vancouver: Cautious Collector

The ethnographic pursuits of Captain George Vancouver (1757–98) were, like his relations with Native peoples and the results of the voyage itself, a series of paradoxes. First, this was the longest eighteenth-century Pacific voyage and yielded the greatest series of charts of the Northwest Coast, finally disproving the mythical Northwest Passage. Yet Vancouver was disliked by many of the officers and sailors in the unhappy crews that he commanded. Second, he often observed exceptional care in his relations with Native people. But although he treated the Native peoples well by contemporary standards, the surveys of the North American coast were perhaps the single most significant source of information for the colonization of that region, which led to the eventual disruption and dispossession of Native peoples of the region. Finally, one of the effects of Vancouver's overbearing attitude toward discipline was to ensure a correct diet for his crew, with the result that there was little ill health on the expedition due to scurvy. As a direct result of this preventive medicine, the acting surgeon and surgeon's first mate had time to devote to nonmedical pursuits, particularly to ethnography.

The ethnographic collections that resulted were the most extensive, and best documented to the place of acquisition, of any Pacific collection made before 1800. However, in one final paradox, the collections have suffered, more severely than some, from vicissitudes characteristic of the period. Archibald Menzies (1754–1842), the expedition naturalist, made the official collection, which in due course was listed in an inventory. The collection went to the British Museum in 1796, but the list was lost amongst the papers of Sir Joseph Banks, and knowledge of the collection disappeared in the two centuries following the voyage. Yet a dozen, mostly Alaskan, artifacts retained their numerical labels so that they could be keyed to the numbers on the original list of the collection. Although inventories of five other collections have survived, and have been published, none of these were made by the officers most significant in the voyage.[1] Indeed, today little is known of Vancouver's own collection, nor of the collections of Joseph Baker, Edward Bell, William Broughton, Thomas Manby, Peter Puget, or Joseph Whidbey.

The collections of most of the officers must be presumed to have been discarded, sold, or otherwise lost. In contrast, the largest collection to survive is that of a relatively junior participant, the surgeon's mate, George Goodman Hewett. This lowly man, inspired perhaps by his dislike of the captain, created the largest extant single-voyage collection of ethnography from before 1800. He sufficiently inspired his descendants with an idea of its worth that they maintained it for nearly a century until it was acquired by A. W. Franks for the British Museum in 1891. Although the material in the Hewett collection is not magnificent—there is not a single Northwest Coast mask, for instance—it nevertheless contains numerous unique artifacts. When compared to the collections in Madrid, perhaps mostly collected in 1791 by Alejandro Malaspina, its nature becomes obvious. For instance, from the Tlingit there are, in Madrid, a magnificent series of clan helmets, and a slat armor cuirass painted with crests.[2] In contrast, Hewett acquired paint brushes, labrets, and throwing sticks, minor artifacts, but items that became obsolete in the nineteenth century.

The purpose of this paper is to present a preliminary understanding of the Alaskan Native materials obtained on the voyage. This information comes from five Vancouver voyage inventories that have been published in full in an earlier article.[3] The most substantial of these was that made by Archibald Menzies as a list to accompany his collection when it was presented to George III. Thomas Dobson and George Hewett listed their collections, probably in the first decade of the nineteenth century; the lists and artifacts then descended within their respective families and associates. The other two collections, held by Spelman Swaine and James Scott, went to English museums in Wisbech and Exeter in the 1830s and 1860s. They were briefly cataloged by the curators at the time of acquisition.

Vancouver spent three summer seasons (1792–94) mapping the western and northwestern coasts of North America. The first of these summer surveys did not reach as far north as Alaska; during the second year two months at the end of the season were spent in southeast Alaska. In 1794 the whole season of four months was spent in south central and southeastern Alaska. However, while journal references to collecting from Alaskan Natives are quite common, they can only in a very few instances be related to surviving artifacts. Nothing about the collections was published until a century ago, when two articles appeared describing Hewett's collection. In 1951 Richard Dillon published the inventory of Menzies's collection, without the numerical sequence and without reference to the surviving materials.[4] This was followed by Erna Gunther's innovative synthesis of the anthropology of the coast and the history of exploration with a list of surviving artifacts.[5] Later publications analyzed the surviving Menzies's collection and presented all the inventories currently known.[6]

Vancouver had two implicit requirements of Native peoples: they were to allow him to obtain all food and water and other stores needed by the expedition, and they were to permit him to carry out the surveying of the coast without hindrance. The recording of information about these peoples and the systematic collection of material culture were not significant aspects of the voyage. Vancouver was not intellectually engaged with non-Europeans, since he was primarily concerned with the problems of weather, geography, and navigation. He did, of course, record his encounters with Native people, and included occasional descriptions of transactions with Northwest Coast inhabitants.

He is said to have displayed "an uncanny faculty for sifting out the various ranks and relative importance of the native chiefs, and of treating each with the deference due to his rank and position."[7] But he does not seem to have deliberately made detours to Native villages or entered Native houses, nor did he record much of the exchanges and transactions in which he engaged, describing them instead only in formulaic terms. This may have been due to his instructions, which included no passage corresponding to the formidable paragraph in which Cook was directed to report in all possible detail on virtually every aspect of the regions he would be visiting.[8] Instead, Vancouver apparently left ethnography to Menzies.

The instructions issued to the voyage were quite explicit about the treatment of Native people. The British admiralty emphasized the importance of good relations with everyone encountered and to that effect provided what were probably quite astonishing quantities and varieties of trade goods. These were distributed freely. Transactions between the crew and Native peoples were strictly controlled so that no inflationary overpayment for curiosities was permitted, and trading could begin only with the captain's permission.[9]

The relationship between expedition members and Native peoples can be viewed from either the European or Native viewpoint. As always, the latter position is harder to elucidate than the former, since the indigenous people left no written record. Vancouver and his men distinguished among three levels of transactions between themselves and the Natives. During the simplest contacts, the expedition ships, or surveying parties, would give to people in canoes, or leave behind in deserted villages, quantities of trinkets and trade goods of the kind deemed appropriate for the area. This gift might be preceded or followed with a similar action from the people encountered, and on the Northwest Coast the most common goods transferred to the Europeans, in descending order of significance, were food, furs, and ethnographic materials.

The expedition always needed food and water, and obtaining those was the first priority for Vancouver; the second priority was obtaining fur, for private trading purposes; and the third and lowest priority was obtaining items for natural history and ethnographic collections.

At a slightly more complex level, the expedition would specifically trade with Native people for food and for furs. In this type of transaction, open bargaining would take place. Often Vancouver, and other journal writers, would comment on Native abilities in this respect. At the most complex level, particularly in Hawaii and in Spanish settlements, the expedition would be provided with materials as part of a political transaction. However, there were few political transactions of this kind with Russians in south central Alaska, and none with Native leaders. Most of the material culture collected on the voyage was therefore obtained at the first two levels of transactions.

Survey parties encountered Natives in canoes and received fish and sea otter pelts from them. This generosity was repaid with tools, metal, cloth, beads, and trinkets. Occasionally Native materials, particularly bows and arrows, were presented to the sailors. Clearly, from the surviving inventories, large amounts of fishing gear were also obtained. The explanation for this is, quite simply, that bows and arrows and fishing gear represent the material culture most likely to accompany Natives in canoes. Precise description of these items is almost entirely omitted from the written accounts, because it was deemed of little significance by the Europeans. A notable exception to this is Menzies's mention of the acquisition of two arrows [unlocated] tipped with native copper, acquired by Lieutenant James Johnstone on June 5, 1794.[10]

Apart from trading and exchanges of this kind, Vancouver seems to have forbidden the acquisition of ethnography in three other time-honored ways. Most specifically, and best documented in the expedition reports, Vancouver would not allow the looting of graves, although sometimes they were examined. This rule seems to have been mostly, but not entirely, respected. The expedition visited numerous seasonally deserted villages. During the summer, the season for surveying, Native people were away at fishing camps, and while much equipment was taken from the deserted villages to the camps, material suitable for European collecting must also have been left behind. In Alaska nothing seems to have been taken by the expedition members from these villages. Finally, relations with Native people were mostly peaceful. There were apparently no occasions for looting after clashes between the Europeans and Native people, even after the incident with the Tlingit at the end of the 1793 season, the only such difficulty experienced by the expedition in Alaska. Nevertheless, Vancouver's treatment of Native peoples was also sometimes harsh, particularly in meting out punishment in response to petty thefts.

Vancouver had left England in 1791 and voyaged to America via the Cape of Good Hope, Australia, New Zealand, the Society Islands, and Hawaii. During the first season he explored the Strait of Juan de Fuca, Puget Sound, and the Inside Passage between Vancouver Island and the mainland as far north as Queen Charlotte Strait. He then met Juan Francisco de Bodega y Quadra in Nootka Sound to undertake the negotiations for the restitution of property before moving south to California, and then to Hawaii for the winter.

In 1793, the second year, the pattern was repeated. The expedition surveyed the coast between Queen Charlotte Strait and Behm Canal. Upon hearing that further instructions from London had arrived in Nootka Sound, Vancouver proceeded south to resume negotiations with the Spanish.

Vancouver's exploration of present-day Alaska began from the anchorage at Salmon Cove on July 24, 1793, in Observatory Inlet, in what is now British Columbia, near the Alaskan border. The boat expedition lasted twenty-three days and included the exploration of Portland Canal and the circumnavigation of Revillagigedo Island. The first Natives encountered were Tsimshian, but it is likely that their daggers and other accouterments were similar to those of the Tlingit met later on. After contacts with the Tlingit on July 27 in Portland Canal, Vancouver provided a long description of their dress and weapons, never again equaled in his account of the voyage. He wrote:

I did not observe that these people differed from the generality of the North West Americans, otherwise than in the ferocity of their countenances. Their weapons seemed well adapted to their condition. . . . Their bows were well constructed, and their arrows . . . were pointed with bone or iron. Each man was provided with an iron dagger, suspended from his neck in a leather sheath, seemingly intended to be used when in close action. Their war garments were formed of two, three, or more folds, of the strongest hides of the land animals they are able to procure. . . . the body is however tolerably well protected, and both arms are left at liberty for action. . . . the whole is seemingly well contrived, and I doubt not answers the essential purpose of protection against the native weapons.[11]

Then as elsewhere Vancouver manifested no interest in acquiring these materials.

In general terms, encounters with Natives consisted of the ceremonial approach of one or more canoes with at least one high-ranking individual singing and dancing. This was usually followed by a request to trade, which, when not for food, was for sea otter skins. The Natives issued frequent invitations to the explorers to visit the chiefs at home and to trade for sea otter fur; these were always rejected by the explorers. Most of the references to trade mention only "trivial articles." On one occasion sea otter tails were presented in exchange for trade goods, presumably as an inducement for more significant bargaining around the acquisition of firearms, the main *desiderata* of the Tlingit. Later, in Behm Canal, Tlingit again tried to persuade the Europeans to come to visit their village, just before a conflict occurred.[12]

On August 12 a surveying party led by Vancouver was attacked by Tlingit off Revillagigedo Island. During the encounter, one young Indian "put on a mask resembling a wolf's face compounded with the human countenance."[13] It was only with great difficulty that Vancouver extricated himself from this dangerous circumstance, but apparently no artifacts were collected.

To the south, friendly relations were reestablished with the Natives, particularly toward the end of August, when a chief known as Ononnistoy visited Vancouver on August 21.[14] Although he came on board and fur and fish were exchanged for trade goods, no artifacts are recorded as having been acquired by the expedition, either from Ononnistoy or from the Haida who appeared at the same time. Similarly, although numerous villages were encountered during the surveying expeditions, no great carvings were acquired.

Of more interest was the use by women of labrets, or lip plugs, in the lower lips, a mark of high status, of which a number were acquired, probably both in this season and the following one. Most accounts of these, however, are confined to ritualized expressions of horror on the part of the Europeans, accompanied by detailed descriptions, particularly of the unaccustomed sight of the authority of the women who wore them.[15]

In a few places graves were examined. For example, one in Behm Canal consisted of "a box about three feet square, and a foot and a half deep, in which were the remains of a human skeleton." Further to the south, on August 14, Vancouver observed "a sepulchre . . . formed partly by the natural cavity of the rocks, and partly by the rude artists of the country." It was lined with boards, and contained some fragments of warlike implements, so he assumed it "contained the remains of some person of consequence." But following his own proscriptions, he did not disturb it any further.[16]

After wintering in Hawaii, Vancouver returned to Alaska in April 1794. Over the next four months he surveyed what is today south central and southeast Alaska before spending a final two weeks in Nootka Sound in the fall. On April 12 he arrived in Cook's River, which he soon renamed an inlet, and he left Alaska at Port Conclusion, near the southern tip of Baranof Island, on August 24. In starting to the north and working eastwards and southwards, he reversed the previous directions of his survey effort. When he was completed, he finally laid to rest the myth of an open Northwest Passage through the center of North America.

The people encountered in southern Alaska were Aleut and Koniag in the employ of the Russians and Chugach Eskimo and northern Athapaskans in Cook Inlet and Prince William Sound. The first people Vancouver met in Cook Inlet were Chugach Eskimo. On April 26 the expedition was befriended by a young chief, whom Vancouver called Chatidooltz. Twenty-three Natives arrived at the *Discovery* in an *umiak* during the afternoon and were gradually

J. C. H. King

154

allowed on board. Chatidooltz was accompanied by a much-respected younger chief, Kanistooch. There are only occasional mentions of trading, and gift-giving, although this chief presented marten skins to Vancouver after being allowed on board.[17] It is probable, since he is the only chief mentioned in Cook Inlet, that this man provided the painted split spruce root hat in Hewett's collection, probably the finest of the Alaskan objects remaining from the Vancouver expedition.[18]

At the same time, a hunting party on the shore encountered a family of eighteen Natives who Vancouver thought were from a different tribe or society from those with Chatidooltz—possibly Tanaina or Aleut, or perhaps simply another group of Pacific Eskimo. In any case, the sailors fed them and presented the usual gifts of tobacco, iron tools, and beads. More significant than absence of any record of trading in artifacts was a shortage of food, which became apparent on April 27 when Chatidooltz returned, danced, and, when asked for food, made discouraging comments.[19]

A few days later, on April 30, a boat of Russians and Indians visited, along with Chatidooltz's people in a birchbark canoe, suggesting again Athapaskan influence this far west. After other meetings with Russians and Natives, a party visited further dwellings at the end of Cook Inlet, on May 6, where they observed Native men with flat ivory labrets and women decorated with "thongs, & other ornaments over their chin."[20]

At the same time, the *Chatham* encountered similar groups of Natives, some of whom traded materials to the expedition. On April 14 twenty-six Natives approached the *Chatham* at Port Chatham: "They were very eager, expert, and clever in all their commercial dealings. They bartered away their garments, weapons, fishing-tackle, and ornaments in great variety . . . principally for spoons and beads." Later the Russian supervisor of one of these hunting parties presented them with cod and halibut. They came across a larger party of one hundred fifty canoes a few days later.[21]

The *Discovery* encountered a similar if not the same party of hunters, estimated to number four hundred people, on May 16 off Port Dick on the Kenai Peninsula. These people "instantly and very willingly entered into trade, and bartered away their hunting and fishing implements, lines and thread . . . with some fish, and some well executed models of canoes . . . [which] constituted the articles of commerce with these people, as well as our Indian friends in Cook's inlet." Menzies added on May 15 that "their Harpoons, darts, cordage & little Leather bags shew a degree of art that would do credit even to the most civilized nations," and on the following day described trade: "The Canoes were too numerous to get all close along side, they would frequently hand on board their little bags containing the articles to be disposd of from the farthest Canoes, & sufferd as many of us as pleasd to overhaul them, & to fix upon what we likd, whilst the Owners sat composedly in their Canoes."[22] No doubt the numerous examples of fishing gear and canoe models collected on the expedition came from these encounters.

The Europeans spent the end of May and first part of June surveying Prince William Sound. There were many fewer contacts with Natives and, although food was in much demand by the expedition, little in the way of trading took place. For instance, on June 5 eight Natives and a Russian visited the shore tent in the morning. Vancouver explained that he would liberally exchange trade goods for fish. When they returned again that evening with nothing, Vancouver repeated his request for "fish, wild fowl &c." The Natives appeared with four birds the following day, and on other occasions salmon and halibut.[23]

There are few if any records of the acquisition of artifacts. However, on about June 8 in Passage Canal, Whidbey excavated a grave. He found "at the bottom . . . some thin planks, and across them, nearly in the middle of the grave . . . the remains of a dead body, rolled up in a seal skin, and carefully tied with thongs." The remains contained ashes and calcined bones, which Whidbey concluded were human. He reported, "As all the parts of the grave shewed evident signs of the action of fire, it is natural to infer, that consuming their dead by fire is the practice of the inhabitants." The remains were covered by stones, moss, and some old broken paddles, with an eight-foot pole erected at the grave's south end. "The curiosity of the party having been thus satisfied, every thing was restored to its former state."[24]

A greater show of acquisitiveness was displayed later on, when Vancouver's men met with Russians at Port Etches on June 19. Menzies describes a series of transactions, but it is not clear whether the artifacts were Russian or Native:

Soon after we came to anchor a number of Russians came off to us & staid on board till evening, bartering boots made of Seal Skins & articles of curiosity with our people for the former, though rudely executed they found a ready market, as shoes were now from the length of the Voyage become exceedingly scarce amongst us. The articles they chiefly took in exchange were Shirts worsted stockings & other cloathing, but to these they would always prefer spiritous liquors or Tobacco when they could get them.[25]

The boots were likely of Russian manufacture, since Native skin work was usually excellent. Hewett included in his collection, as from Cook Inlet, boots of appropriate description, now lost: "190 Russian Boots or Tourbas." Menzies records the acquisition of Russian boots, "though rudely executed," by the expedition because the sailor's own footwear had worn out during the long voyage.[26]

In general, Vancouver states that they had very little contact with Natives, except off Montague Island, and it was perhaps this group that supplied the few Athapaskan, presumably Tanaina, artifacts collected. Vancouver estimated that he and his men saw two hundred eighty-one Natives, and a few more with the Russians at Port Etches.[27] Puget, in the *Chatham* sailing separately from the *Discovery,* augmented the collection of Pacific Eskimo materials while off Knight Island on June 27, when about fifty canoes came to trade. The Natives acquired "white shirts, stockings, cravats and other parts of the officers' apparel, (which comforts were readily parted with) for such things as were deemed curiosities, consisting of bows, arrows, darts, spears, fish-gigs, whale-gut shirts, and specimens of their very neat and curious needle-work." When the Pacific Eskimo ran out of artifacts for trade, they employed themselves in "making such articles of curiosity as found the most ready market amongst their English friends."[28] The most significant recorded item was a full-size Koniag *baidarka,* which Menzies recorded as being used by William Brown on July 16, 1794.[29] Presumably this was not brought back to Europe.

After the June survey of Prince William Sound, Vancouver spent July and August surveying Tlingit territory in southeast Alaska. The Natives were only too conscious of their territory and the harmful effects of Russian activities there. On July 4 a wood canoe appeared, presumably Tlingit, and the expedition parlayed with the Koniag at the Russian camp on Point Turner: "The native chief exerted his utmost eloquence to point out the extent of their territories, and the injustice of the Russians in killing and taking away their sea otters without making them the smallest recompence."[30] So the relations of these new European intruders with the Tlingit were not easy, as their meetings were accompanied by much ceremonial display on the Native part, and apprehension on the part of the expedition, which resulted on two occasions in firing shots to keep the Tlingit at a distance.

The first significant ceremonial confrontation and description occurred in the upper reaches of the Lynn Canal on July 16. The surveying boats were joined by a large canoe with a chief who was dressed in a much more superb style than any chief they had previously seen.

His external robe was a very fine large garment, that reached from his neck down to his heels, made of wool from the mountain sheep, neatly variegated with several colours, and edged and otherwise decorated with little tufts, or frogs of woollen yarn, dyed of various colours. His head-dress was made of wood, much resembling in its shape a crown, adorned with bright copper and brass plates, from whence hung a number of tails or streamers, composed of wool and fur wrought together, dyed of various colours, and each terminating by a whole ermine skin.

Menzies added that his name was Gincaat, and that after meeting Whidbey he

removd to a little distance, & the Chief equipping himself in his best apparel, stood on a square box in the middle of his canoe, & whilst all his people joind in a song, he dancd and caperd for some time in the most frantic manner that can possibly be conceivd, with a rattle in his hand which now & then he kept twirling backwards & forwards with a quick vibrating motion.[31]

The initial encounter was followed that night by the arrival of further canoes, an attempt at plunder, and, when this failed, a desire to trade. This sequence of events followed the pattern of earlier and later encounters with the Tlingit: a ceremonial approach, which, after failing to elicit an appropriate response from the explorers, was replaced by aggression. This, in turn, when thwarted, was followed by a desire for trade. So while, in theory, there was a good opportunity for the acquisition of ceremonial regalia, in chronology these encounters ensured that transfers of artifacts were rare and seem to have occurred only when the acts of aggression were not avoided. In comparison, the Pacific Eskimo peoples encountered earlier omitted the first two stages of this process, those of ceremonial activity and the aggressive stance, with the result that they traded more artifacts to the expedition than did the Tlingit.

During the boat surveys of the archipelago that followed, numerous further meetings occurred between the Europeans and Tlingit. There are good descriptions of graves and occasionally of the ceremonial presentation of sea otter skins and, rarely, food. As earlier, game seems to have been in short supply, so that the Natives were more willing to dispose of fur than food.[32]

Most of the documented Tlingit artifacts collected were acquired in Cross Sound, where on July 7 a canoe came alongside without much hesitation. Since Vancouver required the passive help of these people to achieve his aim, he behaved in a friendly fashion. None of the Tlingit would come on board without a hostage going into the canoe, so a seaman was exchanged for a Native, who once on board was presented with "such things as were likely to be acceptable." So in a similar fashion the European sailor who had been a hostage in the canoe was, on his return to the ship, presented with a "sea otter skin, and some other trifles, by a person who appeared to be the principal or chief of the party."[33]

At the end of September, Vancouver set off to Nootka Sound for the last time. In the end, the most interesting conclusion about the collecting activities of the expedition is that they were, for the most part, casual and amateur. Earlier expeditions, such as that of Captain James Cook in Alaska in 1778–79, acquired larger and more magnificent items because of orders to study Natives. Other expeditions, from Spain and Russia, seem to have systematically obtained fine ceremonial regalia.

In the second half of the nineteenth century, with the arrival of evolutionary ideas of human development and theories of race, visitors to the region would systematically examine and loot graves, both for human and ceremonial remains. Although Vancouver should be applauded for his restraint in this regard, it would be easy to exaggerate the forbearance of the expedition in collecting artifacts from Natives.

NOTES

1. J. C. H. King, "Vancouver's Ethnography: A Preliminary Description of Five Inventories from the Voyage of 1791-95," *Journal of the History of Collections,* Vol. 9 (1994), pp. 35–58.

2. Paz Cabello Carro, *Coleccionismo Americano Indigena en la España de S. XVIII* (Madrid: Edición Cultura Hispánica, V Centenario, 1989); Araceli Sanchez Garrido, *Indios de America del Norte (Otras Culturas de America),* (Madrid: Ministerio de Cultura, 1991).

3. King, "Vancouver's Ethnography," pp. 35–58.

4. Richard H. Dillon, "Archibald Menzies' Trophies," *British Columbia Historical Quarterly,* Vol. 15 (1951), pp. 151–59.

5. Erna Gunther, *Indian Life on the Northwest Coast of North America* (Chicago: University of Chicago Press, 1972).

6. J. C. H. King, *Artificial Curiosities from the Northwest Coast of America* (London: British Museum Publications, 1981); King, "Vancouver's Ethnography," pp. 35–58.

7. George Vancouver, *A Voyage of Discovery to the North Pacific Ocean and round the World, 1791-1795,* ed. W. Kaye Lamb, 4 vols. (London: Hakluyt Society, 1984), 1:65 (hereafter Lamb, *Vancouver's Voyage*).

8. *Ibid.,* 1:43.

9. *Ibid.,* 1:286, 377.

10. Unfortunately, the arrows have not survived. Wallace M. Olson, *The Alaska Travel Journal of Archibald Menzies, 1793-1794* (Fairbanks: University of Alaska Press, 1993), p. 127 (hereafter Olson, *Menzies's Journal*).

11. Lamb, *Vancouver's Voyage,* 3:995.

12. *Ibid.,* 3:997–98, 1011, 1035, 1006, 1042 (qtn.).

13. *Ibid.,* 3:138, 1011–18 (qtn., 1012).

14. *Ibid.,* 3:1032–43.

15. *Ibid.,* 3:1054.

16. *Ibid.,* 3:1005, 1021.

17. *Ibid.,* 4:1231–32.

18. Van 190, British Museum, London.

19. Lamb, *Vancouver's Voyage,* 4:1232–33.

20. *Ibid.,* 4:1234–35, 1244 (qtn.).

21. *Ibid.,* 4:1249–50, 1253.

22. *Ibid.,* 4:1264–65.

23. *Ibid.,* 4:1274.

24. *Ibid.,* 4:1293–94.

25. Olson, *Menzies's Journal,* p. 141.

26. *Ibid.*

27. Lamb, *Vancouver's Voyage,* 4:1306.

28. *Ibid.*, 4:1332, 1336.

29. Olson, *Menzies's Journal*, p. 172.

30. Lamb, *Vancouver's Voyage*, 4:1337.

31. *Ibid.*, 4:1351.

32. *Ibid.*, 4:1360, 1386, 1320, 1358.

33. *Ibid.*, 4:1319; Olson, *Menzies's Journal*, p. 155.

J. C. H. King

KESLER E. WOODWARD

Images of Native Alaskans in the Work of Explorer Artists, 1741–1805

American, English, French, Spanish, and Russian explorers and traders
made well over one hundred voyages to the North Pacific between
1741 and 1805. During this time Alaska, with its array of natural wonders, its seemingly inexhaustible mineral and animal resources,
and its diverse Native cultures, became an object of great interest to the maritime nations of the world.

Anthropologists, historians, sociologists, political scientists, and many
others have examined the imagery of the artists who accompanied these expeditions. The watercolors, paintings, and drawings made from direct observation provide insights into the cultural schemata of the non-Native artist-
observers. Moreover, the ways those images evolved from rough field sketches
to engravings or lithographs in the published accounts provide a level of insight into the impact of cultural contact and into the cultural capacities of the
European maritime powers to assimilate and portray the essence of others.

There are four principal concerns. First, images in the published accounts
are not the work of the expedition artists but are several steps removed. Many
of the images have been redrawn and cast into other media, typically lithogra-
phy or engraving, and in many cases preparatory steps intervened. The images
were sometimes changed dramatically in that process, and both the conscious
and unconscious motivations and perceptions of various groups and individuals affected the final, widely distributed product.

Second, the majority of the surviving images were produced by trained,
professional artists of some reputation who labored under unvaryingly strict
injunctions against willful distortion, embellishment, and interpretation. The
Russian Imperial Academy of Arts' instructions to Pavel Mikhailov were typical.
He was to strive for accuracy, avoid drawing only from memory, and shun embellishment.[1] Similarly, no term of approbation for explorer artists was greater
than that of accuracy, as evidenced by Alejandro Malaspina's 1793 praise of the
work of one of his artists, Tomás de Suría: "Don Tomás Suría has depicted with
the greatest fidelity to nature all that merits the help of the engraver's art, so

as to secure better understanding in the historical narrative of this voyage."[2] Such praise for accuracy and injunction against personal expression make the variety of explorer artists' images, their range of expression, and the ubiquity of their interpretive cultural biases still more evident.

Third, the few current scholarly discussions of this visual material almost invariably treat the images as ethnographic and/or historical evidence, not as art. When prints from published expedition accounts are shown as something more than decorative illustrations, they are cited as evidence of the kind of clothing, artifacts, housing, ornamentation, and body types found at the time in the North Pacific. Neither their artistic quality nor the information they reveal about the artists' cultural preferences is examined in any detail.

Finally, even when images of Northwest Coast exploration are discussed, they are almost always treated in chronological and geographic isolation. There is no attempt to place them in the context of the artistic conventions of their time, or in the context of other visual images of Native people, either from other parts of the globe or from earlier or later periods of exploration in the circumpolar North. The first European images of northern Natives come from the eastern Arctic, and predate the earliest Alaskan views by two centuries. Few discussions of images from the 1741–1805 period even acknowledge the fact that by this era there were already artistic and illustrative conventions in place that influenced the way European artists portrayed the Alaska Native.

John Frazier Henry's *Early Maritime Artists of the Pacific Northwest Coast, 1741–1841* is the starting point for study of the images of Alaska Natives.[3] Henry's well-illustrated and thoroughly researched account is an excellent source of previously undiscovered and/or uncompiled material about the artists who accompanied early explorers to Alaska. Henry identified a number of the original drawings and compared them with the better-known prints made from those drawings, provided summaries of the expeditions that the artists accompanied, and supplied a wealth of biographical material on the artists themselves.

Henry was also the first to recognize and discuss the differences between the original drawings and the published prints, the evidence of cultural biases on the part of the artists, the artistic quality and significance of these images, and the artistic and historical antecedents and conventions known to the artists. This paper elaborates on his excellent study, examining in more detail a few of the images he interpreted. It illustrates how these well-known images project representative markers of unconscious cultural filters at work.

The first known European image of an Alaskan Native dates from Vitus Bering's voyage of discovery in 1741. It is a sketchy drawing of an Aleut man in a *bidarka*. Attributed to Sven Waxell, Bering's second in command, the figure appears on a 1744 chart of the voyage and closely matches a description of

Kesler E.
Woodward

162

an encounter with the Native recorded by Georg Wilhelm Steller, the expedition naturalist. This and other vignettes on Waxell's charts, along with several views of sea otters, fur seals, and other marine mammals attributed to Friedrich Plenisner (Steller's assistant and Bering's chief clerk) are the only known surviving pictorial views from Bering's expedition.[4]

In order to place this earliest known European image of an Alaska Native in historical and artistic context, it is important to acknowledge the precursors to Waxell's image of the Aleut. In its illustrative attachment to a map, the sketch has something in common with the earliest known image of northern Native people, Eskimos, who appear on Olaus Magnus's *Carta Marina,* a map of Scandinavia and the north Atlantic islands, including Greenland, which was first issued as a woodcut in 1539. The drawing from the Bering expedition is, like the Magnus woodcut, simple and sketchy, but it differs from its sixteenth-century antecedent in at least one crucial aspect: it is drawn from life. The Inuit depicted by Magnus have been extensively discussed by ethnographers, who all conclude that the Native people appear to be products of the artist's imagination, as neither the people nor the vessels depicted have any distinguishable Inuit characteristics.[5]

Sixteenth- and seventeenth-century images of northern Natives from the eastern Arctic, especially those drawn from life, share many characteristics with the earliest Alaskan depictions. There was a common tendency to suppress the individual character of the Native figure in favor of illustrating an activity, closely mirroring a written expedition account. Even a small map, such as the one attributed to Waxell, makes clear the artist's preoccupation.[6]

The discovery by Bering of the marine mammal resources available in Alaskan waters, especially the rich pelts of the sea otter, brought not only Russian expeditions but also those of other nations in the following decades. The first sizable body of pictorial material derives from the voyage of the Russians P. A. Krenitsyn and M. D. Levashov in 1768–70. An atlas containing more than fifty of Levashov's drawings is found in the Soviet Marine Ministry in Petrograd. The drawings include detailed studies of Aleut clothing, housing, and implements. The figures in Levashov's drawings, however, are no more individual than the drawing by Waxell. Interest on the part of the artist lay in the Aleuts' clothing, housing, and implements, and the figures themselves are little more than props that support the dress and hold items of ethnographic interest.

In this respect the conceptual antecedents of the Levashov drawings derive from the earliest images of northern Natives done by an identified artist—a sixteenth-century image by Lucas de Heere, a skilled Flemish costume artist and tapestry designer—of a captured Inuk brought back to Europe from Baffin Island by Martin Frobisher. The image of the Inuk, depicted by de Heere as a European in exotic clothing, is totally at odds with a contemporary description of the man as having a broad face, fat body, and short legs. William Sturte-vant and David Beers Quinn have surmised that de Heere's image comes from a manuscript containing one hundred ninety costumed figures, European and other, in ninety-seven watercolor drawings and, like the other illustrations in the manuscript, uses a standard, mannequin-like figure to display the costume.[7]

The Levashov drawings treat the Aleut figure in the same way, as a manne-quin. They are more elaborate than the drawing attributed to Waxell, but even more clearly documentary in intent. Levashov was a capable draftsman but was evidently not specifically trained as an artist.[8] Like Waxell, he undoubtedly did not think of himself as an artist, or of his drawings as art.

A much better known body of work, indeed by far the best-known body of work from the 1741–1805 period, is that of the artists who accompanied Cap-tain James Cook's third voyage in 1776–80. Cook's official artist was John Web-ber, whose prolific output has been most widely associated with early Alaskan exploration. Several capable draftsmen, including William Bligh and the sur-geon's mate William Ellis, also accompanied the expedition.

Webber was born in London in 1751 to an emigrant Swiss sculptor. He studied art from 1767 to 1770 under J. L. Aberli in Berne. After further train-ing in Paris, he returned to London, where one of his paintings in the annual exhibition of the Royal Academy made a positive impression on the Swedish botanist Daniel Solander. Solander had accompanied Cook on his two previous voyages of discovery, and his recommendation of the young artist eventually led to Webber's employment in the expedition.

The choice was a good one, as Webber produced an astounding number of high-quality images and was retained after the voyage to supervise the produc-tion of the engravings that would illustrate the expedition's published journal. These images have been widely reproduced in subsequent editions of the ex-pedition's journals and in nearly every published book on early Alaskan explo-ration or the search for the Northwest Passage. They are the best-known images of Northwest Coast exploration.

How similar to, and how different from, the earlier images of Waxell and Levashov are Webber's images of Native people? They are more elaborate and more artistically ambitious and accomplished than the earlier drawings. In contrast to Waxell's vignettes, which show no background, and the schematic presentation of costumed figures and objects by Levashov, many of Webber's watercolors, as well as the engravings based on them, feature a fully developed treatment of three-dimensional space. Native people are often shown in the context not only of their dwellings and their clothing but also of their land-scape and environment.

Webber's work on the expedition raised the level of artistic representa-tion of Alaska and Alaskans substantially. He was the first European artist, as opposed to simply competent draftsmen, to make visual images of Alaskan Natives. So his work was a major turning point in the visual images of the 1741–1805 period. If the greater artistic accomplishment and more inclusive environment in Webber's pictures differentiate them from the earlier images of Bering's and Levashov's expeditions, they retain important features in common with those earlier representations. Like Waxell's and Levashov's, Webber's images concern themselves chiefly with documenting the dwellings, clothing, and artifacts of the Native inhabitants. The Native people rarely play a more important role than did the stiffer, less artistically accomplished figures in Levashov's drawings. Webber made a number of so-called portraits of Native men and women, but often attention to clothing and ornament predominates.

Expedition artists apparently had difficulty in knowing how to depict Native people. They solved that problem by making a visual catalog of the Natives' clothing, ornament, habitations, and equipment. The presence of human figures in their work is almost incidental to their job of documentary recording.[9]

Because they became so widely known, Webber's engravings served as models for the conventional representation of Alaskan Natives by other explorer artists for the next quarter-century.[10] Webber was not the originator of these conventions, though he was perhaps the first bona fide European artist on the Northwest Coast. Further, although his are the first published European images of Alaskan Natives, he was undoubtedly aware of many earlier published images of northern Natives from the eastern Arctic. In fact, we know that Cook had a copy of David Crantz's 1767 *History of Greenland* on board during this voyage, which was illustrated with images less artistically sophisticated but essentially identical in format to the watercolors and later engravings after Webber.[11]

Webber's widely disseminated images, nevertheless, became the new standard for images of exploration, and artists from other expeditions followed his much-praised lead. Examination of images from the Billing's expedition in 1785, which followed Cook's voyage, demonstrates Webber's influence, as well as new developments in the evolution of images of Alaska Natives in this early period.

Luka Alekseevich Voronin, a twenty-year-old recent graduate of the Academy of Arts in St. Petersburg, was expedition artist for the Russian expedition led by Joseph Billings.[12] Two engravings based on his drawings show Webber's influence on format and style of presentation, but they also introduce two important new developments. Voronin's *Woman of Unalaskha* is at first glance similar to Webber's portraits of Chugach Eskimos. Both concentrate on ornamentation and clothing detail, and both feature portrait-like representation of the Natives' individual features. But where Webber's engravings effectively capture the typical facial morphology, complexion, and hair texture, Voronin's representation of the young Aleut woman looks like a young European woman

"Man and Woman of Prince William Sound," engraving after John Webber, in James Cook, *A Voyage to the Pacific Ocean . . .* , 1784, Vol. 2, pl. 47. *Rare Book Collection, University of Alaska Fairbanks*

"Woman of Unalashka," 1790, engraving after a drawing by Luka Voronin, in G. A. Sarychev, Atlas to *Puteschestvie . . .* , 1802, pl. 18. *Rare Book Collection, University of Alaska Fairbanks*

playing dress-up. Not only are her facial features European, but her character-istic pulled-back tonsure has been stylized into a slightly askew but still curly-haired version of a European bun. Webber's ability to capture accurately the visual character of these Native people, and Voronin's inability to do so, may be explained by Voronin's lack of artistic skill or ethnocentricism. However, it is far more likely that the difficulty took place after the image left Voronin's hands.

The original Voronin drawing is not extant, but it is certain that the published work was performed by a European engraver who redrew the image, which was a common practice at the time. John Frazier Henry tells us that the contemporary British engraver William Alexander, who worked up Voronin's drawings into engravings for Martin Sauer's 1802 account of the Billings expedition, went so far as to improperly take credit for the original drawings by Voronin on which the engravings were based. He signed on the plates his own name as the delineator of several of the original images, though he was not on this or any other expedition to the North Pacific.

If the loss of fidelity to facial type and character is in fact due to the change from a first-hand artist-observer to an illustrator without first-hand experience, it is but the first of many such instances. Stylization and loss of individuality inevitably occur in the change of medium from drawing or watercolor to engraving, and such multiplication in the influence of stereotype and unconscious cultural bias is regularly observed. Probably already aware of this problem, Webber personally supervised the translation of his drawings into engravings, which perhaps accounts for their close correspondence to his drawings and the relative lack of such subtle but important changes in character. But this practice of close supervision does not appear to have been common, and Voronin apparently did not oversee the engraving process for his drawings.[13]

A similar transformation has taken place in another engraving after Voronin, *View of the Establishment of the Merchant Shelikhov on the Island Kad'iak.* The Native figures who stand in the foreground of the view of the original trading establishment in Three Saints Bay have been somewhat Europeanized, again perhaps by the engraver. This image marks the beginning of another kind of formulaic image of Native Alaskans, the view of an early colonial community, usually with a ship in the harbor, with wondering, fascinated Native people isolated at a distance from the settlement. It is an image that recurs with great regularity in the work of explorer artists for the next half-century. The focus of attention has shifted from the Native and his culture to the pioneering European settlement. Natives are present, not engaged in their own activities nor any longer the subject of inquiry, but foils to emphasize the greater European technology and power. This interpretation of Voronin's image is confirmed by two excerpts from published accounts of the Billings expedition that John

Kesler E.
Woodward

"View of the Establishment of the Merchant Shelikhov on the Island Kad'iak," 1790, engraving after a drawing by Luka Voronin, in G. A. Sarychev, Atlas to *Puteschestvie . . .* , 1802, pl. 36. *Rare Book Collection, University of Alaska Fairbanks*

Frazier Henry juxtaposed with this image. "The islanders flocked to us every day, as curious and wondering spectators, and particularly admired the extraordinary size of our vessel compared with their barges [baidaras]." [14] "About two hundred of the daughters of the chiefs are kept . . . as hostages [apparently] they are perfectly well satisfied." [15]

This constitutes an extraordinary match between image and text. The artist has subconsciously captured in precise visual form the self-satisfied air of superiority and unreflective willfulness inherent in the colonial attitude. Though such a close match between text and visual image in later narratives is not always evident, the visual messages conveyed in succeeding images from the Northwest Coast after Voronin are clear.

To understand the unconscious assumptions made by European artists, just this kind of marker image needs study. Such observations do not discredit the artists of this earlier era. They are the kind of changes that historical and cultural perspective dictate, an apprehension that would have been impossible for the artists themselves. This level of analysis builds on and extends the work of John Frazier Henry.

Probably the most widely reproduced and most striking instance of the multiplication of stereotype and cultural bias between original and published print is *Native Costumes at Port des Français,* by the artist Gaspard Duché de Vancy of the 1786 Lapérouse expedition. John Frazier Henry juxtaposed the original drawing and the published print and briefly noted some of their differences.[16] These two images are worth a closer look, as they reinforce in a slightly different way the conclusions derived from the Voronin image of childlike, admiring Native people surveying the Russian ship and settlement in Three Saints Bay.

The scene in Duché de Vancy's *Native Costumes at Port des Français* depicts a group of Tlingit Natives examining a mirror, beads, cloth, an ax, and a pewter plate acquired by gift from or trade with members of the Lapérouse expedition. Some of the figures are of decidedly European body and facial type, though their clothing is accurately rendered. The prominent distended lips of the foreground figure and the larger female background figure are also consistent with ornamental facial disfiguration characteristic of the time and place. Such distentions and other disfigurations such as facial tattooing are often exaggerated, and almost never left unportrayed, in the work of explorer artists. There is even an attempt in at least two of the figures to render the characteristic Tlingit high cheekbones and general facial structure, all of which makes it all the more remarkable that three of the other figures, also presumably Tlingit, should be so typically European in all but their dress. This is an excellent example of the way the portrayal of the Native Alaskan presented a dilemma for the expedition

"Costumes of the Inhabitants of Port des Français," 1786, drawing by Gaspard Duché de Vancy. *Service historique de la Marine Vincennes*

"Costumes of the Inhabitants of Port des Français," 1786, engraving after a drawing by Duché de Vancy, *Anchorage Museum of History and Art*

artist, one that was solved, however unsatisfactorily, by vacillating between modes of representation, sometimes even within the same composition.[17]

But if the original drawing by Duché de Vancy contains such evidence of cultural bias at work, the engraving based on the drawing takes them much further. The figure at the far left, already European in facial structure and body type in the original drawing, is further transformed in the engraving, as Henry said, into a "statuesque Greek athlete holding a discus."[18] More subtle, perhaps even more telling, he noted, is the transformation of the mood of the scene. In the original drawing, the seated figure who regards his image in the mirror is delighted and amused. In the engraving, he is aghast at his image, and the mood of the entire scene has become one of concern and awe at these magical contrivances of the white man.

It is clear from even this small group of examples that at the outset of the 1741–1805 period the Alaska Native was still an enigma, an exotic and mysterious subject for artist and explorer alike, a subject difficult for the European artist to portray with the objectivity that was demanded of him. These early images are attempts to understand and to describe these new people, to fit them into a more familiar vision of the world. But closer examination also makes it clear that already, by the beginning years of the nineteenth century, the Alaska Native was slipping from enigma to stereotype, a character that would increasingly be portrayed as he was regarded, as an innocent, childlike, underdeveloped foil for European superiority and progress. While that change was still subtle in 1805, the conceptual basis for the stereotype was already evident in the images that were disseminated worldwide by official accounts of these expeditions, accounts that were widely read and that shaped the European and American view of the Alaska Native.

Much more can be learned from these images than ethnographic inferences about Native Alaskan culture at the beginning of European contact, and more can be done to investigate and interpret the artistic and conceptual character of these images than has been done to this date. John Frazier Henry, Douglas Cole, Rüdiger Joppien, and others established a historical and biographical groundwork for many of these artists and their images.[19] More remains to be done, and new examples of original drawings to compare with published prints undoubtedly await discovery. It seems equally important for researchers to examine more closely and in a broader context the images that have been uncovered, to begin to unpack the layers of meaning inherent, but largely unexamined, in even the best-known examples of work by explorer artists.

*Images
of Native
Alaskans*

NOTES

1. Leonid Shur and R. A. Pierce, "Pavel Mikhailov, Artist in Russian America," *Alaska Journal*, Vol. 8 (1978), p. 360.

2. Donald C. Cutter and Mercedes Palau de Iglesias, "Malaspina's Artists," in *The Malaspina Expedition: In the Pursuit of Knowledge* (Santa Fe: Museum of New Mexico Press, 1977), p. 23.

3. John Frazier Henry, *Early Maritime Artists of the Pacific Northwest Coast, 1741-1841* (Seattle: University of Washington Press, 1984).

4. The image and its corresponding written account are reproduced in Henry, *Early Maritime Artists*, p. 9.

5. For more on the *Carta Marina*, see Edward Lynam, *The Carta Marina of Olaus Magnus, Venice 1539 & Rome 1572* (Jenkintown, Pa.: Tall Tree Library, 1949); Kaj Birket-Smith, "The Earliest Eskimo Portraits," *Folk*, Vol. 1 (1959), pp. 5-14; William C. Sturtevant, "First Visual Images of Native America," in *First Images of America*, ed. Fredi Chiappeli et al. (Berkeley: University of California Press, 1976), 1:417-54; Wendell Oswalt, *Eskimos and Explorers* (Novato, Calif.: Chandler & Sharp, 1979).

6. See Kesler E. Woodward, *Painting in the North: Alaskan Art in the Anchorage Museum of History and Art* (Anchorage: Anchorage Museum of History and Art, 1994), pp. 17-19.

7. See William C. Sturdevant and David Beers Quinn, "The New Prey: Eskimos in Europe in 1567, 1576, and 1577," in *Indians and Europe, An Interdisciplinary Collection of Essays*, ed. Christian Feest (Aachen: Rader & Verlag, 1987), pp. 61-140.

8. Henry, *Early Maritime Artists*, p. 11.

9. Kesler E. Woodward, "Enigmas, Dilemmas, and Hidden Agendas: The Evolution of the Image of Native Alaskans in the Work of Explorer Artists, 1741-1990," in *Art and the Native American: Perceptions, Reality, and Influences*, Vol. 10 of *Art History* (University Park: Pennsylvania State University Press, 1996).

10. Webber's watercolors were the finest early record of Native people on the Northwest Coast, without equal until, four decades later, the artists Mikhail Tikhanov and Louis Choris produced their dramatic watercolors during the Russian voyages of von Kotzebue and Golovin in the early nineteenth century. Henry, *Early Maritime Artists*, pp. 38-48. See Dilliara Safaralieva, "M. T. Tikhanov, Artist-Traveler," in *Russian America: The Forgotten Frontier*, ed. Barbara Sweetland Smith and Redmond J. Barnett (Tacoma: Washington State Historical Society, 1990), pp. 33-39, n.16.

11. David Crantz, *The History of Greenland*, 2 vols. (London, 1767); Oswalt, *Eskimos and Explorers*, pp. 249-50. Oswalt not only affirms that Cook had a copy of Crantz aboard but also quotes Cook's references to it as a source of his comparisons of Alaskan Eskimos with their eastern Arctic counterparts.

12. The artist was hired and took part in the overland voyage and Siberian survey portions of the expedition beginning in 1785. Billings did not sail eastward toward Alaska until 1790.

13. A slightly later explorer artist, Friedrich Heinrich von Kittlitz, who was on the Feodor Lutke expedition of 1826-29, was so dismayed by the difficulty in obtaining faithful reproductions from an engraver or lithographer that he took it upon himself to master the art of engraving after the voyage, so as to produce the engravings for his

own account of the trip. The same was true of Louis Choris, the outstanding artist who accompanied Otto von Kotzebue's 1815–18 expedition. Choris's colored lithographs, produced for his own volume *Voyage Pittoresque Autour du Monde* (Paris, 1822), are some of the most artistically impressive images of Alaskan exploration from the early nineteenth century.

14. Henry, *Early Maritime Artists,* p. 19. Gavriil Andreevich Sarychev, *Account of a Voyage of Discovery to the North-east of Siberia, the Frozen Ocean, and the North-east Sea,* 2 vols. (London: J. G. Barnard, 1806), 2:18. This image and the *Woman of Alaskha* engraving originate from the atlas to Sarychev's *Puteshestvie flota kapitana Sarcheva po sieverovostochnoi chasti Sibiri* (St. Petersburg: Shrona, 1802).

15. Martin Sauer, *An Account of a Geographical and Astronomical Expedition . . .* (London: T. Cadell, 1802), p. 171.

16. Henry, *Early Maritime Artists,* pp. 146–47.

17. Woodward, "Enigmas, Dilemmas."

18. Henry, *Early Maritime Artists,* p. 147.

19. See, for instance, Cole's "John Webber, A Sketch of Captain James Cook's Artist," *British Columbia Historical News,* Vol. 13, No. 1 (1979); Rudiger Joppien, *The Art of Captain Cook's Voyages,* 3 vols. (New Haven, Conn., 1985–88).

ANTHONY PAYNE

The Publication and Readership of Voyage Journals in the Age of Vancouver, 1730–1830

P ublished voyage accounts in the Age of Vancouver, from approximately 1730 to 1830, were increasingly addressed to a professional readership— a development that determined the form of their final appearance in print. Travel books in this age had a literary impact, but their more obvious practical uses demand more attention.[1] These books were used, sometimes with desperate concentration. We can imagine Fletcher Christian, having seized the *Bounty,* poring over Bligh's copy of Hawkesworth's *Voyages.* There, in the accounts of the British explorations of the Pacific of the 1760s, he sought a permanent home, a refuge safe from civilization, and consequently from arrest and execution, and found Pitcairn, which was uninhabited, fertile, and difficult of access.[2]

Today, it is difficult to imagine commencing any scientific project without familiarizing oneself with the available information, but in the mid-eighteenth century the navigator had little with which to prepare himself. Further, even if the information was in print, it might, in the days before systematic librarianship and sophisticated bibliographies, be effectively irrecoverable. The French circumnavigator Bougainville wrote that Pernety, who had published an account of the French colony in the Malvinas, spoke of Shelvocke's circumnavigation, but "I [Bougainville] have no knowledge of this voyage."[3] And Shelvocke's *Voyage round the World,* in the English-speaking world at least, enjoyed a wide circulation (it was Coleridges's source for the albatross and other incidents in "The Rime of the Ancient Mariner"), and for an expedition concerned with the coasts of South America and the penetration of the Pacific, as Bougainville's was, it would have been an important narrative to consult whatever its overall reliability.[4]

Shelvocke's account is typical of the early eighteenth-century printed Pacific voyage journal, with a spirited readability, a few engravings, and a small, comfortable format. It appeared in two versions, the first in 1726, and a smartened-up second edition in 1757. The latter was prepared by Shelvocke's son, a senior official in the British post office, and substitutes a rather stilted pompous style for the father's more direct seaman-like language and brings pretension to parts of the original text.[5] The well-known voyage journals of Dampier were similar in appearance, and their physical characteristics were imitated by the early editions of *Gulliver's Travels,* as Swift's text itself imitated and satirized the accounts of real-life voyagers.[6]

In 1748 the journal of the voyage of George Anson, one of the most popular voyage books of the epoch, appeared in print.[7] It went through at least fifteen editions by 1776. Unlike Shelvocke's privateering venture, Anson's was a naval expedition, and he went on to achieve high rank. His book, although private in a strict sense, may be considered an official account, and its extensive list of subscribers is witness to widespread support in high political and social circles. It is a good, thorough narrative, well illustrated with useful charts and views, but, as with any text, it has a particular point of view, so that anyone consulting it should remember Anson's perspective was not universally shared. This is apparent from a recently discovered manuscript critique of his book by the East India Company's representative in Canton, which reveals how Anson's arrogant behavior there threatened the Company's pragmatic, commercially prudent *modus vivendi* with Chinese officialdom.[8]

A few years later there began the first of a series of British naval exploring expeditions to the South Seas, soon after the accession in 1760 of George III, whose interest in science, and through it the assertion of national power and glory, is an important strand in all subsequent voyages in the Age of Vancouver. The advancement of knowledge and the celebration of these achievements combined to emphasize the desirability of publishing an official record of these voyages, which had been undertaken by Byron, Wallis, Carteret, and Cook. John Hawkesworth, a prominent literary figure of the day, was commissioned to edit the journals of the various commanders and of Joseph Banks, Cook's companion. The resulting three-volume *Account of the Voyages Undertaken by the Order of His Present Majesty for Making Discoveries in the Southern Hemisphere,* which appeared in 1773, was an enormous success. Some indication can be found in the record of borrowings from the Bristol Library for 1773–84, during which period Hawkesworth was borrowed no fewer than two hundred one times.[9]

The
Publication
and
Readership
of Voyage
Journals

177

This interest was no doubt partly due to curiosity and fashion, as the Pacific was the new world of the eighteenth century.[10] But, like many other bestsellers, the book also provoked substantial controversy, with a confused mixture of moral and theological outrage and salacious titillation. As a brief indication of the commotion sparked off by the publication of Hawkesworth's book, mention can be made of his denial of the particular workings of Providence in saving the expeditions from danger, his descriptions of Tahitian life and love, and the satirists' field day over Banks's behavior in Tahiti, Horace Walpole's witticisms ("at best it [Hawkesworth] is an account of the fishermen on the coasts of forty islands"), Alexander Dalrymple's trenchant editorial criticisms, and the desire of Hawkesworth's friend, Samuel Johnson, to join the next expedition to the Pacific.[11]

It is the failure of Hawkesworth in technical terms that is most significant to our theme. His rendering of the various journals created an exciting narrative, the structure of which he justified by appealing to Samuel Richardson's novel *Pamela,* but to the detriment of the strict scientific and navigational record.[12] To illustrate this we must go to Capetown, South Africa, in April 1775, where on the homeward stretch of his second Pacific voyage, Cook saw Hawkesworth's book for the first time. To put it bluntly, he was horrified, and in his journal Cook particularized the misrepresentation of society in the colony of St. Helena that Hawkesworth seemed to put into his mouth:

It is no wonder that the account which is given of [St. Helena] in the narrative of my former voyage should have given offence to all the principal inhabitants. It was not less mortifying to me when I first read it, which was not till I arrived now at the Cape of Good Hope; for I never had the perusal of the manuscript nor did I hear the whole of it read in the mode it was written, notwithstanding what Dr Hawkesworth has said to the contrary in the introduction.

Cook goes on to specify the misleading data in Hawkesworth with care, for his next port of call on the homeward course was St. Helena itself, where his hosts of four years earlier awaited him. "How these things came to be thus misrepresented, I cannot say, as they came not from me, but if they had I should have been equally open to conviction and ready to have contradicted anything, that upon proof, appeared to be ill-founded, and I am not a little obliged to some people in the isle for the obliging manner they pointed out these mistakes."[13]

Most embarrassing for Cook was the fact that his host, the governor of St. Helena, was John Skottowe, son of Thomas Skottowe, the very landowner of Great Ayton, Yorkshire, who, as employer of Cook's father, had recognized the abilities of the future explorer in early life and volunteered his fees at the Postgate School.[14] With "great good humour and pleasant raillery," Cook "was called upon to defend himself." To tease Cook about the remarks Hawkesworth attributed to him that there were no wheeled vehicles on the island, several wheelbarrows and carts were "studiously placed before Captain Cook's lodgings every day."[15]

Hawkesworth's £6,000 contract and his death soon after publication, which was supposed to have been brought on by the torrent of criticism, are well known. However, his book's influence should not be disparaged, as it found a place in the libraries of the literary and navigators alike (as noted above, a copy was available for reference on the *Bounty*). As Beaglehole remarks, "For a hundred and twenty years, so far as the first voyage was concerned, Hawkesworth was Cook." [16]

The account of Cook's second voyage, entitled *A Voyage towards the South Pole and round the World,* discreetly edited by Dr. John Douglas, was very much Cook's own book, "a work for information and not for amusement" in his words, and, in many ways, of the official accounts of his three voyages, it is the most satisfying in format. It contains two neat quartos with more than sixty engravings bound in.[17] In narrative terms it is satisfying to the reader not just because of Cook's personal involvement in its composition but also because the story has a beginning, a middle, and an end. The author leaves home, experiences many adventures and tribulations, and returns safely. Its best known literary influence was on Coleridge, whose "Argument," or plot, of the "Ancient Mariner" was inspired by the story of Cook's second voyage, "a voyage in which science, adventure and the strange wonders of the deep were blended in a marvellous unity." [18]

The wider readership of the second voyage account is more difficult to gauge, but it is reasonable to suppose that it was less popular than Hawkesworth, and, at the Bristol Library, for example, there were only forty-five borrowings in the three-year period following its acquisition (1777–79), in contrast to one hundred fifteen for Hawksworth (1773–75), and one hundred thirteen borrowings in total for the years 1777–84.[19] Not least this was because its highly competent, responsible composition could not spark the sort of sensational controversies that irritated the professionals but attracted the public. It should also be remembered that at this time Cook was not especially famous, as the first voyage was very much associated with Joseph Banks.[20]

Although Cook was increasingly esteemed in naval, political, and scientific circles, the general reading public would not necessarily have sought out the second voyage account on the basis of Cook's reputation alone. Some evidence for this may be found in surviving sets of Cook's three voyages in undisturbed contemporary bindings, of which a number exist with Hawkesworth in one style of binding and the second and third voyages bound uniformly with each other but not matching the Hawkesworth. In these instances, it is likely that Hawkesworth was bought on publication, but the second voyage, published originally in 1777, was not acquired until after the third voyage, which, when it appeared in 1784, consolidated and confirmed Cook's reputation.[21]

Publication of the third voyage account, entitled *A Voyage to the Pacific Ocean, undertaken by the Command of His Majesty, for Making Discoveries in the Northern Hemisphere,* was carefully overseen by the admiralty and the Royal Society.[22] Its publication history is unusually well documented, including details of print runs, and the first and second editions were of 2,000 copies each. The editors and publishers of Cook's third voyage account were confident of

The
Publication
and
Readership
of Voyage
Journals

179

its success, so print-runs of this size may be inferred as being relatively high. The first edition sold out within three days and, although the published price was £4 14s. 6d., as much as 10 guineas was apparently offered by disappointed would-be purchasers.[23] It was generally praised, but there was clearly some dissatisfaction behind the scenes from a "junto of Captn. Cook's declared enemies," suspected the editor John Douglas.[24]

The second edition was entrusted to the admiralty's own stationers, and the contract for printing it was given to a different printer.[25] Beaglehole remarked that the second edition was "much better printed than the first." [26] The revision of the text was undertaken by William Wales, Cook's astronomer.[27] It is of interest to note here that Lapérouse, whose expedition was provided with an extensive reference library, took special care to obtain the second edition of Cook's third voyage because it was the best, not so much for its appearance but for the reliability of its text.[28]

There were unofficial published narratives of Cook's three voyages written by several of his officers and men. Published in contravention of naval orders, which required that all logs be surrendered, the number of unofficial accounts shows that whatever the demands of naval discipline, popular demand for these books, and therefore profit, was clearly greater.[29] The civilians attached to the expeditions were not subject to naval regulations in publishing their accounts.[30] All these published narratives are indicative of the degree of literacy of the ships' companies. Indeed, James Burney, who sailed on Cook's second and third voyages and who was later to publish *A Chronological History of the Discoveries in the South Sea or Pacific Ocean*,[31] records that on the third voyage a weekly newspaper was prepared on each ship, such was "the literary ambition and disposition to authorship" amongst many of the crew.[32]

Mention should also be made of the periodical literature, abridgements, popularizations, and translations, all of which helped disseminate knowledge of the new discoveries and reflect the immense proliferation of the printed word as the eighteenth century progressed.[33] As to the publication of official accounts, Cook's third voyage record established high standards that were emulated by the French in their government's history of Lapérouse's voyage and would have been by the Spanish for Malaspina's expedition had it not been for his untimely disgrace and exile.[34]

The compilation of the official account of Lapérouse's voyage was a remarkable achievement, since the expedition vanished without trace in 1788, with the loss of its captain's logs, a mass of other documents, and the bulk of its natural history collections. Fortunately, Lapérouse had dispatched home portions of his journal whenever the opportunity presented itself. It is clear that he had written this journal in the expectation that it would be published and that he was conscious that his predecessor, Bougainville, had produced a highly regarded account of his circumnavigation. The editor, Milet-Mureau, acquitted himself remarkably well given the political turmoil of revolutionary France, which not only caused considerable administrative disruption but also necessitated tailoring the text to avoid offending "the austere principles of republicanism." Louis XVI, who had taken a close interest in the planning of the expedition, is not mentioned in the book. Milet-Mureau was no Hawkesworth, and Lapérouse's latest editor, John Dunmore, commends Milet-Mureau's respect for Lapérouse's text and his generally unintrusive editorship.[35]

In writing the account of his voyage Vancouver stated explicitly that it was "calculated to *instruct*, even though it should fail to *entertain*," and, echoing Cook's sentiments, he emphasized that he had spent most of his life in naval service and consequently begged the public's indulgence of his unpolished literary style.[36] Based on his own journals, which are now lost, the *Voyage of Discovery* was prepared for publication by his brother John after Vancouver's untimely death in May 1798. It went through a second edition and foreign translations but never captured the imagination of a wide audience: one critic, the midshipman Robert Barrie, thought it was "one of the most tedious books I ever read." It was the highly professional record of a highly professional expedition, and if at times the text resembles a set of sailing instructions, this was intentional, for the book was as much a navigational aid as a historical record of the expedition's course.[37]

A few years later, in 1813, the English translator of Krusenstern's circumnavigation account wrote that the "characteristic feature of the work is that of accuracy, rather than elegance of description." He explained he had no alternative but "to follow the original, with that precision which he conceives to be absolutely necessary in translating a work of this nature, and on which, indeed, its value so mainly depends." Krusenstern himself insisted on the importance of giving longitudes and latitudes at every point, "a plan adopted by Vancouver; and it should be the duty of every navigator to follow him," and laments the failure of the British to publish accounts of some important recent voyages.

It might almost be believed that the English government had purposely cast a veil over the voyages of Colnett and Broughton on the coast of Japan, were it not that the liberality which they have shewn in publishing every voyage that has been undertaken during the last half century, a period so brilliant in the history of discoveries, completely controverts this suspicion.[38]

A footnote qualifies these remarks, as Broughton's voyage was published in 1804, while Krusenstern was absent on his expedition. Krusenstern's sentiments are evidence of the growing insistence on accuracy and accessibility of information and the assumption that the readership of such narratives would be primarily professional in its interests.

The
Publication
and
Readership
of Voyage
Journals

181

As a particular instance of voyage journals being used in a working context it may be noted that Krusenstern writes that his expedition set sail with an "excellent collection of charts, and a well chosen library," of which he made extensive use.[39] Aside from the immediate practical uses of a ship's library, it should be remembered that these great oceanic voyages would have had hours of tedium that could be relieved through access to the printed word. In Krusenstern's case, he used his ship's library to undertake an exhaustive study of Tasman's discoveries, which he published in a scientific journal soon after his return home.[40]

The last voyage to be considered here is that of the *Beagle*. The publishing history of this voyage neatly draws together the themes of this paper. The official account of the voyage, under the general editorship of Robert FitzRoy, appeared in three volumes and an appendix, with the suitably ponderous title *Narrative of the Surveying Voyages of His Majesty's Ships Adventure and Beagle, between the Years 1826 and 1836, Describing Their Examination of the Southern Shores of South America, and the Beagle's Circumnavigation of the Globe.*[41] Volume 3 was subtitled *Journal and Remarks, 1832–1836, by Charles Darwin, Esq.*, and it is by his account that the voyage of the *Beagle* is generally known. Demand was such that Darwin's volume was also issued separately and has gone through numerous editions to the present day, when it is readily available in paperback.[42]

It is significant that Darwin devoted much effort and thought to the literary composition of his volume and abandoned a strict chronological narrative in favor of a geographical organization. He also omitted or abridged much of his original diary and added a great deal of scientific information based on jottings in his field notebooks.[43] The effect is literary in the best sense, and, unlike Hawkesworth, the book benefits from being compiled by the journal writer himself. But the hydrography was relegated safely to the mariners' department, and FitzRoy's volumes went through but one edition, as indeed did the separately published scientific zoology, which was edited by Darwin.[44]

In the final analysis, the specialist and general reader had to be addressed separately, and the voyage of the *Beagle,* which sowed the seeds of one of the most important scientific theories of all time, harks back to the literary appeal of Hawkesworth rather than forward to the modern scientific monograph.[45]

NOTES

1. See Percy G. Adams, *Travelers and Travel Liars, 1660–1800* (Berkeley and Los Angeles: University of California Press, 1962); Percy G. Adams, *Travel Literature and the Evolution of the Novel* (Lexington: University Press of Kentucky, 1983); and, for a study of Coleridge, whose poetic imagination was steeped in travelers' tales, John Livingstone Lowes, *The Road to Xanadu: A Study in the Ways of the Imagination* (London: Houghton

Anthony
Payne

Mifflin, 1927). See also P. J. Marshall and Glyndwr Williams, *The Great Map of Mankind: British Perceptions of the World in the Age of Enlightenment* (London: Cambridge University Press, 1982), which contains much of relevance for the broader context of this paper.

2. H. E. Maude, "In Search of a Home: From the Mutiny to Pitcairn Island, 1789–1790," *Studies in Pacific History,* Vol. 14 (1968), p. 32. The evidence that Christian consulted John Hawkesworth's *Account of the Voyages Undertaken by the Order of His Present Majesty for Making Discoveries in the Southern Hemisphere* (3 vols. [London, 1773]) is found in John Shillibeer, *A Narrative of the "Briton's" Voyage to Pitcairn's Island* (Taunton, 1817), pp. 97–98, and F. W. Beechey, *Narrative of a Voyage to the Pacific and Beering's Strait,* Part 1 (London: H. Colburn and R. Bentley, 1831), p. 59 (quarto edition; p. 80 in the octavo), both of which are first-hand accounts of expeditions that visited Pitcairn and interviewed John Adams, the last surviving *Bounty* mutineer.

3. Louis Antoine de Bougainville, *A Voyage round the World,* trans. J. R. Forster (London: J. Exshar, 1772), p. xvii.

4. George Shelvocke, *A Voyage round the World by Way of the Great South Sea* (London: J. Senek, 1726); James Burney, *A Chronological History of the Voyages and Discoveries in the South Sea or Pacific Ocean* (London: L. Hansard, 1816), 4:527.

5. W. G. Perrin, ed., *A Voyage round the World [by] Captain George Shelvocke* (London: L. Hansard, 1928), p. xx. Where Shelvocke senior states that he and his officers "were drinking together," Shelvocke junior, mindful of his father's reputation in matters alcoholic, says "sitting together."

6. William Dampier, *A New Voyage round the World* (London, 1697); *A Voyage to New Holland* (London, 1703), with numerous subsequent editions; *Travels into Several Remote Nations of the World . . . by Lemuel Gulliver,* 2 vols. (London: B. Motte, 1727). (Jonathan Swift's authorship was not given on the title page).

7. George Anson, *A Voyage round the World* (London: J. and P. Knapton, 1748).

8. Glyndwr Williams, "Anson at Canton, 1743: 'A Little Secret History,' " in *The European Outthrust and Encounter . . . Essays in tribute to David Beers Quinn on his 85th Birthday,* ed. C. H. Clough and P. E. H. Hair (Liverpool: Liverpool University Press, 1994).

9. Paul Kaufman, *Borrowings from the Bristol Library, 1773-1784: A Unique Record of Reading Vogues* (Charlottesville: University of Virginia, 1960), pp. 39, 122. The Bristol Library was a private institution with 137 subscribing members in 1782, drawn from the middle to upper middle class. From 900 titles and 13,497 borrowings, the most popular book from 1773 to 1784 was Hawkesworth's *Voyages,* which was borrowed 201 times, 115 times in 1773-75 alone, comfortably ahead of all other titles in all subjects.

10. Alan Frost, "The Pacific Ocean—the Eighteenth Century's 'New World,' " in *Captain James Cook: Image and Impact,* ed. Walter Veit, Vol. 2 (Melbourne: Hawthorne Press, 1972).

11. Helen Wallis, "Publication of Cook's Journals: Some New Sources and Assessments," *Pacific Studies,* Vol. 2 (Spring 1978), pp. 163–73 (hereafter Wallis, "Cook Publications"); J. C. Beaglehole, ed., *The Journals of Captain James Cook,* Vol. 1: *The Voyage of the Endeavour, 1768-1771* (Cambridge: Cambridge University Press, 1955), pp. ccxlii–ccliii (hereafter Beaglehole, *The Voyage of the Endeavour*); J. C. Beaglehole, ed., *The Endeavour Journal of Joseph Banks* (Sydney: Trustees of the Public Library of New South Wales, Angus and Robertson, 1962), 1:101; Horace Walpole, *Correspondence with John*

The
Publication
and
Readership
of Voyage
Journals

183

Chute . . . , ed. W. S. Lewis et al. (London: Oxford University Press, 1973), p. 421; Thomas Curley, *Samuel Johnson and the Age of Travel* (Athens: University of Georgia Press, 1976), p. 221.

12. Curley, *Samuel Johnson,* p. 51.

13. J. C. Beaglehole, ed., *The Journals of Captain James Cook,* Vol. 2: *The Voyage of the Resolution and Adventure, 1772–1775* (Cambridge: Cambridge University Press, 1961), pp. 661–62 (spelling modernized) (hereafter Beaglehole, *The Voyage of the Resolution and Adventure*). Cook's dissatisfaction was shared by the commanders of the other expeditions narrated in Hawkesworth's book, but only Philip Carteret had the opportunity (or inclination) to write a new version of his voyage to supersede Hawkesworth's; however, it remained unpublished. See Helen Wallis, ed., *Carteret's Voyage round the World, 1766–1769* (London: Hakluyt Society, 1965), p. 475.

14. J. C. Beaglehole, *The Life of Captain James Cook* (London: A. and C. Black, 1974), pp. 4, 440.

15. Beaglehole, *The Voyage of the Resolution and Adventure,* p. 662 notes.

16. Beaglehole, *The Voyage of the Endeavour,* p. ccliii.

17. James Cook, *A Voyage towards the South Pole and round the World,* ed. John Douglas (London, 1777); the title page states unequivocally, "By James Cook, Commander of the Resolution." Beaglehole, *The Voyage of the Resolution and Adventure,* pp. cxxv, cxliii–cxlviii, 2; Wallis, *Cook Publications,* pp. 173–75.

18. Bernard Smith, "Coleridge's 'Ancient Mariner' and Cook's Second Voyage," in *Imagining the Pacific,* ed. Bernard Smith (New Haven, Conn.: Yale University Press, 1992), p. 169.

19. Kaufman, *Borrowings,* p. 32.

20. Beaglehole, *Life of Captain Cook,* pp. 273–74.

21. For example, one set sold at Christie's, London, May 1, 1991, lot 111 ("The property of a nobleman," bought by Bernard Quaritch Limited). The second voyage account in this set was the fourth edition, published in 1784, the third voyage was the third edition, 1785. It is not unusual to find Hawkesworth without mention of Cook on the spine labels, and sometimes it is labeled "Banks's Voyage."

22. Three volumes, "Vol. I and II written by Captain James Cook, F.R.S. Vol. III by Captain James King, LL.D. and F.R.S. . . . Published by Order of the Lords Commmissioners of the Admiralty," and an atlas of engravings (London, 1784). J. C. Beaglehole, *The Journals of Captain James Cook,* Vol. 3: *The Voyage of the Resolution and Discovery, 1776–1780* (Cambridge: Cambridge University Press, 1967), pp. cxcviii–cciv (hereafter Beaglehole, *The Voyage of the Resolution and Discovery*); Rudiger Joppien and Bernard Smith, *The Art of Captain Cook's Voyages* (Melbourne: University Press for the Australian Academy of the Humanities, 1987), 3:161–9; Wallis, *Cook Publications,* pp. 177–92. The first two volumes of the official account are based on Cook's journals and the third, covering the period after his death in Hawaii in 1779, was compiled by James King.

23. Sir Maurice Holmes, *Captain James Cook, R.N. F.R.S.: A Bibliographical Excursion* (London: Francis Edwards, 1952), p. 52. Joppien and Smith (*Art of Captain Cook's Voyages,* p. 169) indicate that the original selling price might actually have been £3.5.0.

24. Quoted by Beaglehole, *The Voyage of the Resolution and Discovery,* p. cxcix.

25. Wallis, "Cook Publications," p. 188.

26. Beaglehole, *The Voyage of the Resolution and Discovery*, p. cciv.

27. Wallis, "Cook Publications," p. 189.

28. Catherine Gaziello, *L'Expédition de Lapérouse, 1785-1788: Réplique française aux Voyages de Cook* (Paris: Comité des Travaux Historiques et Scientifiques, 1984), p. 155 ("beaucoup plus complète"). Annexe 5 is a catalog of the expedition's library.

29. These include, for the first voyage, *A Journal of a Voyage round the World* (London, 1771), anonymous, often attributed to the midshipman James Magra; for the second voyage, *Journal of the Resolution's Voyage* (1775), also anonymous but found by Cook to be by the gunner's mate John Marra; and for the third voyage, *Journal of Captain Cook's Last Voyage* (London, 1781), anonymous but conclusively attributed to Lieutenant John Rickman; *Reise um die Welt* (Mannheim, 1781), by the coxswain Heinrich Zimmermann; *An Authentic Narrative of a Voyage Performed by Captain Cook and Captain Clerke*, 2 vols. (London: G. Robinson, J. Sewell and J. Debrelt, 1782), by the surgeon's mate William Ellis; and *A Journal of Captain Cook's Last Voyage to the Pacific Ocean* (Hartford, Conn.: Nathaniel Patten, 1783), by the marine corporal John Ledyard.

30. Civilian accounts include *A Journal of a Voyage to the South Seas* (London: Calaban Books, 1773), by Sydney Parkinson, botanical draftsman on the first voyage, and *A Voyage round the World*, 2 vols. (London: W. Whitestone, 1777), by Georg Forster, naturalist on the second voyage.

31. James Burney, *A Chronological History of the Discourses in the South Sea or Pacific Ocean*, 5 vols. (London, 1803-17). See G. R. Crone and R. A. Skelton, "English Collections of Voyages and Travels, 1625-1846," in *Richard Hakluyt and His Successors*, ed. Edward Lynam (London: Hakluyt Society, 1946), pp. 127-29.

32. None of these newspapers is known to survive. James Burney, *A Chronological History of North-Eastern Voyages of Discovery and of the Early Eastern Navigations of the Russians* (London: Payne and Foss, 1819), p. 280. See also Beaglehole, *The Voyage of the Resolution and Discovery*, p. ccx.

33. See M. K. Beddie, ed., *Bibliography of Captain James Cook*, 2d ed. (Sydney: Council of the Library of New South Wales, 1970).

34. Joppien and Smith, *Art of Captain Cook's Voyages*, p. 169; Warren L. Cook, *Flood Tide of Empire: Spain and the Pacific Northwest, 1543-1819* (New Haven, Conn.: Yale University Press, 1973), p. 318.

35. John Dunmore, ed., *The Journal of Jean-François de Galaup de La Pérouse, 1785-1788* (London: Hakluyt Society, 1994), pp. 571-77; Bougainville, *A Voyage round the World*.

36. George Vancouver, *A Voyage of Discovery to the Pacific Ocean and round the World*, 4 vols. (London: G. G. and J. Robinson, 1798), introduction; George Vancouver, *A Voyage of Discovery to the North Pacific Ocean and round the World, 1791-1795*, ed. W. Kaye Lamb, 4 vols. (London: Hakluyt Society, 1984), 1:290-91 (hereafter Lamb, *Vancouver's Voyage*). For Cook's remarks, see Beaglehole, *The Voyage of the Resolution and Adventure*, pp. cxxv, 2. Vancouver sailed on Cook's second and third voyages.

37. Lamb, *Vancouver's Voyage*, pp. 240-45, 267-69 (qtn. 244).

38. A. J. von Krusenstern, *Voyage round the World by Order of His Imperial Maiesty Alexander I*, trans. Richard Belgrave Hoppner (London: C. Roworth for J. Murray, 1813), 1: iii-iv, 2:55, 1:222-23.

39. *Ibid.*, 1:9. Vancouver was similarly well equipped with books, including accounts

The
Publication
and
Readership
of Voyage
Journals

185

by Cook, Portlock, Dixon, Meares, and Bougainville. See Lamb, *Vancouver's Voyage,* p. 47.

40. Glynn Barratt, *The Russians and Australia* (Vancouver: University of British Columbia Press, 1988), pp. 208–11.

41. Robert Fitzroy, ed., *Narrative of the Surveying Voyages of His Majesty's Ships Adventure and Beagle* (London, 1839). The first volume concerns the first expedition (1826–30), under Phillip Parker King. FitzRoy was commander of the second expedition (1831–36), the famous voyage of the *Beagle,* which Darwin accompanied as supernumerary naturalist.

42. See R. B. Freeman, *The Works of Charles Darwin: An Annotated Bibliographical Handlist,* 2d ed. (Folkestone: Dawson, 1977), pp. 31–54 (hereafter, Freeman, *Darwin's Works*).

43. R. D. Keynes, ed., *Charles Darwin's Beagle Diary* (Cambridge: Cambridge University Press, 1988), p. xx.

44. *The Zoology of the Voyage of H.M.S. Beagle,* 5 parts (London, 1838–43; New York: New York University Press, 1987). The geological researches, separately published in three parts (London, 1842–46, issued collectively as *Geological Observations on Coral Reefs, Volcanic Islands, and on South America* [London, 1851]), did go through more than one edition (see Freeman, *Darwin's Works,* pp. 58–63), but this reflects their scientific import rather than the broader popular appeal of the voyage.

45. Any assessment of the massive circulation of the *Origin of Species* (first published London, 1859) must take into account that its final format, length, and title were carefully thought out in terms of public appeal by Darwin, his advisers, and the publisher, John Murray. See Adrian Desmond and James Moore, *Darwin* (London: Michael Joseph, 1991), pp. 474–75.

Anthony
Payne

STEPHEN J. LANGDON

Efforts at Humane Engagement: Indian-Spanish Encounters in Bucareli Bay, 1779

I n the late eighteenth century, Spanish explorers pushed northward up the Pacific coast of North America in an effort to extend Spanish imperial claims, preempt expanding Russian interests from western Alaska, and blunt English designs on the region. In a series of voyages from 1774 to 1792, Spanish explorers encountered Tlingit and Haida groups from Salisbury Sound to Bucareli Bay, and from Yakutat Bay to the Queen Charlotte Islands. The explorers found not simple societies but complex, highly developed cultures with seasonal settlement patterns, stratified social relations, far-ranging trading capabilities, sophisticated artistry, elaborate military equipment and fortifications, and religious beliefs based on mutual respect between humans and animal spirits.

The most extensive interaction between the Europeans and the people of the northern Northwest Coast region occurred at Bucareli Bay, in southeast Alaska, during the summer of 1779. Spanish behavior and expectations that summer need to be understood in the context of earlier experiences with Natives of the Northwest Coast, for those encounters provided the framework for Spanish policies and procedures on the coast.[1] In 1774, an expedition led by Juan Pérez encountered Haida off the north end of the Queen Charlotte Islands.[2] A number of Haida came offshore from Langara Island in canoes, near the large northern island of the Queen Charlottes, and some trade occurred. The Spaniards noted the presence of iron among the Haida, as well as their strong interest in acquiring more. The Natives manifested an eminently pragmatic and aggressive desire to trade. The Haida rowed out in their impressive wooden plank canoes to meet Pérez's ship, the *Santiago,* and some boarded the vessel for trade. Some Spanish sailors, presumably not officers, dropped down into the Haida canoes, where they were greeted warmly.[3]

In 1775, a second expedition, commanded by Bruno de Hezeta, was sent out, initially with three vessels, although only the *Sonora,* under the command of Juan Francisco de Bodega y Quadra, assisted by Don Francisco Antonio Maurelle, eventually made it to Alaska. A notable catastrophe occurred early in the voyage when six Spaniards sent ashore from the *Sonora* to get wood and water were killed by Native people in the vicinity of Point Grenville on the west coast of the Olympic Peninsula.[4] This event likely established an atmosphere of uncertainty and caution in dealings with other indigenous groups later in the voyage.

The journals of Bodega y Quadra and Maurelle record the first contact between the Tlingit and Europeans. The *Sonora* was a tiny two-masted schooner, thirty-eight feet long, with just fourteen men, only four of whom had sailed before. They left Hezeta at Point Grenville and sailed north under very arduous circumstances, making landfall off Mount Edgecumbe on August 15, 1775. The Spaniards proceeded inshore probably into what is now called Sea Lion Bay, on the west coast of Kruzof Island. They noticed Tlingits on the shore immediately south of a placid river and described a single dwelling that may have been fortified. The description indicates that this was probably a seasonal camp and that the intensive season of salmon harvesting and processing was about to begin. Bodega y Quadra's comment on the presence of fortifications is puzzling, as these are unlikely at a seasonal camp, and the terrain described does not fit the topographic profile of Tlingit fortified sites, which were usually found in steep bluff areas.[5]

As they attempted to acquire supplies, the Spaniards had a brief encounter with the Tlingit, who brandished lances tipped with stone blades in an apparent assertion of property rights to the nearby river. The Spanish weighed anchor. On August 24, the vessel entered an open, placid sound that they named Entrada de Bucareli (Bucareli Bay), after the Mexican Viceroy Antonio María de Bucareli, who sponsored the mission. Maurelle went ashore and conducted a claiming ceremony, and he raised a cross. He noted habitations and trails in the area but encountered no Indians.

Spanish contacts on the northern Northwest Coast in these first two voyages revealed a relatively sparsely settled outer coast occupied by active and able groups, some of whom exhibited strong trading interests and others who demonstrated an aggressive, proprietary sense accompanied by a willingness to defend against intrusions. The ambush and loss of life at the hands of the Natives near Point Grenville suggested to the Spanish that maintaining peaceful relations and protecting members of future exploration parties would require considerable arms and manpower.

Despite a desire by Viceroy Bucareli to continue exploration in the North Pacific, other matters, including European conflicts, lack of ships, and a shortage of funds, delayed the next voyage until 1779. When this third Spanish voyage was sent to the north from Mexico, it followed James Cook's voyage of 1778. British entry into the sweepstakes for the Northwest Coast deeply concerned the Spanish.

Stephen J. Langdon

The 1779 Spanish expedition was headed by Ignacio de Arteaga and Bodega y Quadra, with Maurelle responsible for detailed mapmaking.[6] The possible presence of British and Russian expeditions and previous experiences with Native inhabitants of the region led the Spanish to prepare for this expedition carefully and to provide it with superior equipment. The objectives were still primarily exploration and observation, but the Spanish also wanted to determine if Bucareli Bay was suitable for the establishment of a colonial outpost.[7]

The expedition comprised two vessels of three hundred tons each, the *Princesa* and *Favorita*. The former had a crew of one hundred seven and the latter, ninety-eight. Soldiers, chaplains, surgeons, and a botanist accompanied the expedition, which carried food for fifteen months, as well as cannon, muskets, and pistols capable of defending the voyagers against Natives or Europeans. In addition, the ships transported substantial quantities of trade goods. The directions given to Arteaga by Viceroy Bucareli stressed the necessity of maintaining peaceful relations with the Indians and of avoiding provocation at all costs.[8]

The two vessels made landfall at Bucareli Bay within ten hours of each other on May 3, 1779. In the midst of some nasty spring squalls, they finally anchored in today's Port Santa Cruz on May 5. Anchorage appears to have been established near the southern shore of the bay by a freshwater source, Rio de la Aguada. This early May arrival fell at the time when Tlingit and Haida groups were in the area for various spring activities, including fishing for halibut and salmon, collecting seaweed, hunting seals, and collecting sea-bird eggs.

Some time during those first two or three days, several large plank canoes with Natives came into view of the Spanish ships. They were described as impressive vessels that approached in what was interpreted as a solemn fashion, slowly, with the rowers singing to a drummed beat. A man stood in the bow of one of the vessels crossing his chest with his arms and then extending them. He was dressed in a cloak with designs and appeared to have white down attached to his face. Other persons in the boat tossed what appeared to be down into the air above this man, and the feathers drifted over his head and onto his shoulders.[9] This behavior is indicative of a noble person of high rank presenting himself to another person of similar or perhaps higher standing. It could apply to either Tlingit or Haida culture; a similar scene had been reported by Pérez among the Haida off Langara Island in 1774.[10]

On May 18, Maurelle headed a party of twenty men in two longboats equipped with cannon and armaments to explore the inner reaches of Bucareli Bay. After taking soundings, naming places, observing the landscape, including at least one Tlingit settlement site, and engaging in some not especially friendly interactions, Maurelle and his party returned to Port Santa Cruz on June 12.

This expedition provided the first extensive interaction between Europeans and Tlingit. The products of the expedition include a number of maps showing placenames and soundings throughout the bays and nine or ten different journals by the participants.[11] Most of the journals remain to be compiled and fully translated into English. One of the priests on board, Father Riobo, described a series of trading activites, suggesting that a number of objects of Tlingit manufacture, such as hats, mats, woven robes, hooks, small boxes, and perhaps suits of armor and helmets, were acquired by expedition members and returned to Mexico.[12]

From the journals, it is possible to trace the daily movements of Maurelle's longboats (see map). Virtually all of the longboat survey occurred in Tlingit territory, with only a slight dip into Haida territory in what is now known as Ulloa Channel. The Spanish located one fortified village, saw Tlingits at another lookout or fort, and had a number of encounters with several canoes of Tlingits. They also identified mortuary platforms and likely shamans' graves on islands in Real Marina off Baker Island.

Initially the Tlingits apparently watched the Spaniards while hidden in the woods, as the Spanish did not find any Natives at La Ranchería, the fortified site, when they visited. The placenames the Spanish bestowed, as they traveled in the area, help identify the location of certain activities they observed. Noteworthy in this respect are the Ladrones (Thieves) Islands, where the sail from one of the longboats was stolen by the Tlingits after the boat was left momentarily unattended on shore. Bodega y Quadra reports that Maurelle "found himself obliged to punish one Indian, and to put the others who came with him to flight." [13] This likely refers to the theft of the sail, which was recovered. According to Riobo, the punishment was a lashing with a rod, which might have been taken as an insult demanding reprisal by the Tlingit.

The Spaniards, as their logs and maps indicate, took samples of materials and in particular looked for precious minerals or metals. Comments were made about the possibility of copper and silver occurring in the stones in Port San Antonio. Punta de Mineral was a name given a point in the bay where copper was located. Such mineral investigations may have been regarded by the Tlingit as uncompensated takings. On several occasions Tlingit came in their canoes to the longboats to indicate their displeasure with the Spanish presence and activities. At one time they even erected temporary shelters in a location where the Spaniards were attempting to land.[14]

While Maurelle's party was surveying the islands and inlets, a much larger group of Natives, probably Tlingit and Haida together, started to appear around the two expedition vessels anchored in Port Santa Cruz. By early June it was estimated that more than one hundred canoes and over 1,300 people were in the vicinity of the two vessels. These numbers had been gradually building during the period when the longboats were away on their survey.[15] Reports of tense moments between the residents and visitors, as well as the large num-

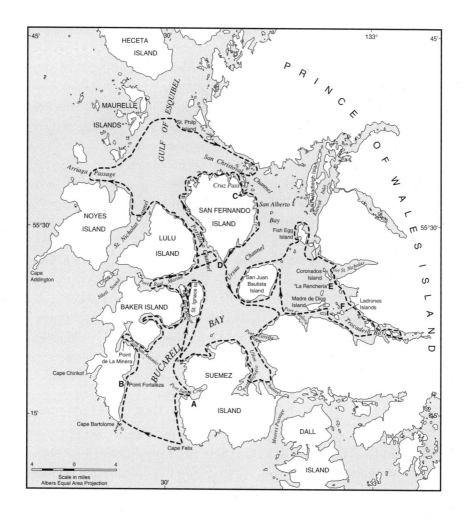

Reconstructed route of Spanish longboat exploration in Bucareli Bay,
May 18–June 12, 1779

A   Anchorage of Spanish ships *Favorita* and *Princessa*

B   Spaniards report seeing Indians high up on shoreline

C   Spaniards overnight in Cruz Pass, May 24, 1779

D   Spaniards spend two nights at Point Amargura because of storms

E   Discover fortified village (probably Tlingit) called "La Ranchería"

F   Probable location of acrimonious encounter between Spaniards and Tlingits bers of Indians gathering, suggest that there were clans and probably *kwaans*, or tribes, of both Tlingit and Haida present at the time.

In Port Santa Cruz, Indian interests in acquiring Spanish commodities emerged. At least two nobles or chiefs were recognized by the Spaniards, based on their appearance in woven robes and the dance and accompanying song that was sung as their canoes approached the larger vessels. After an exchange of simple goods, the Indians brought fish, mats, and a variety of other objects in an effort to trade for iron, the main object of indigenous interest. The chiefs and several of their party were invited on board the Spanish ships on several occasions, where they were treated with respect, fed, and given gifts by the Spaniards. Some Natives pilfered items lying about the vessels, probably because they, not being chiefs, were unlikely to receive items in gift exchanges.[16]

The Spanish located several Native seasonal camps during this visit to the region. In addition, other camps, termed "rancheros" by the Spaniards, were quickly established along the shores of Port Santa Cruz by outlying groups of Indians attracted to the area. Daily interactions began amicably, largely to trade fish, mainly salmon and halibut, for beads, iron, and cloth. Maurelle even commented on the establishment of a "market," which may refer to a specific location where daily trade took place.[17] The Spaniards complained about the disappearance of many of their objects, as the Indians carefully watched their movements and took items left lying about.

One Spanish sailor, separated from his shore party while collecting wood, had all of his clothing and gear taken from him but was released unharmed. These incidents were initially taken in stride by the Spaniards, mindful of their instructions from Viceroy Bucareli to eschew violence. But the tone of Bodega y Quadra's account shifted, as he wrote first of "gentle behavior," then "audacity," and later spoke of the "shamelessness" of the Indians, which stretched "our limit of endurance." The Spaniards came to bitterly resent the petty Indian pilfering.[18]

Some of the trade reveals social structure and group relations. Among the trade items offered by the Natives were several young persons who most subsequent observers have assumed were slaves or those with severe handicaps.[19] The actions of one boy obtained in trade can be interpreted as an indication of the presence in Port Santa Cruz of separate groups, as well as their animosity toward one another. According to Maurelle, when a particular group approached in a canoe, the boy grasped a Spanish officer's hand and led him to the arms chest so that he would take up muskets against his enemies, perhaps even those who enslaved him.[20]

One of the most significant and lasting effects of the Spanish expedition on the Tlingit may have been the appearance of an unidentified disease that rapidly gripped many of the Spanish crew. To aid recovery of the afflicted crew members, the Spanish constructed a barracks onshore and sent several of the most sick there. Two of the Spaniards subsequently died and were buried in Port Santa Cruz. The remainder recovered. The journals indicate that the Tlingits brought fresh fish, water, mats, and robes to the sick and otherwise ministered to them and expressed concern for their welfare. Bodega y Quadra remarked that the sailors' "recovery, like all our work on shore, was much assisted by the gentle behavior of the Indians since our occupation." [21]

Another illuminating event occurred when two of the Spanish crew jumped ship and apparently sought to be accepted into Tlingit or Haida society.[22] According to Bodega y Quadra, the men disappeared from a work party and the captain initially thought they had been captured. The priest Riobo, however, indicated that the men later admitted they had jumped ship. When they approached the Spanish vessels the next day in Indian canoes, the crewmen attempted to return but were prevented from doing so by the Native people who accompanied them. The two crewmen were then taken to separate villages, where they spent at least one night. Riobo reported that the men were kept up all night with "horrible dancing" and continous song.[23] These descriptions suggest that the Spaniards may have been treated as "deer hostages" in the ceremony used by the Tlingits to create a category of cleansed intermediaries as a prelude to peaceful exchange. This explanation was offered by de Laguna for the treatment received by one of Malaspina's men, who was briefly held by the Yakutat Tlingit in 1791.[24]

In response to the loss of his men, Arteaga ordered his crew to capture one of the Indian nobles he had been dealing with, to hold him for exchange. This was accomplished by successfully luring one of the adult men aboard the *Princesa* and holding his canoe. Unfortunately, the indigenous political order interfered with this stratagem, as the Natives who held the deserters were apparently not interested in seeing the captured noble returned. It is likely that the noble was Haida, since almost assuredly those holding the two Spanish crewmen were Tlingit. Following Tlingit rejection of the exchange, the Spanish randomly took as many as twenty more hostages. Unfortunately, in the process of rounding up the hostages, two Tlingits died, one by gunshot and one by drowning. Arteaga was apparently distressed by the Indian deaths and provided presents to the relatives of the deceased.[25] Since this act of indemnification paralleled indigenous practices of dispute settlement, Arteaga's action may have been a significant factor in the subsequent resolution of the impasse.

After a day and a half of diplomacy, duplicity, display, and discussion, during which at one point the Tlingit donned their armor and brandished their weapons, a solution was negotiated. An exchange was conducted when Maurelle took the hostages to the proximity of the "ranchero" where the Spanish crewmen were being held. In return for his two crewmen, Maurelle also gave presents of cloth, beads, and metal.[26]

The day after the exchange, the Spaniards attempted to depart Bucareli Bay, but a southwest gale forced them to anchor in Port San Antonio on Baker Island, directly across Bucareli Bay from Port Santa Cruz on Suemez Island. Here they remained for over two weeks waiting for favorable winds. According to Bodega y Quadra, several groups of Indians established camps in Port San Antonio during this time, visited the ships, and traded fresh fish.[27]

The Tlingit and Haida acquired a substantial amount of information about European characteristics and practices during the Spanish visit to Bucareli Bay. They became aware of armaments, as muskets and cannons were deployed against them, although they were not intimidated by them. They found that iron and metals were in great abundance and that the Spaniards possessed desirable clothing, hats, beads, buttons, and mirrors.

On the social side, the Natives probably also found Spaniards to be relatively underdeveloped in their protocol and gift-giving mechanisms. By Tlingit standards, they were uncouth and rude, in addition to being stingy. The Natives discovered that the Spaniards did not respect local property rights and were highly acquisitive, taking from the land without providing any recompense to the proper owners.

The Natives must also have wondered about the lack of women in the Spanish entourage, although we have no evidence about this, as the Spanish did a poor job with the language, making little effort to record names or words. Unlike later British and American voyagers, the Spanish attempted to keep a sharp rein on sexual relations between members of their party and the Natives, and there is no documentary evidence to indicate violation of this principle in Bucareli Bay in 1779.

There is little doubt that the length of the Spaniards' stay quickened the indigenous groups' fears that their territories were being invaded with little regard for their rights. The linguistic barrier inhibited communication of Spanish intentions. Nevertheless, the range of contacts and relationships between the Europeans and Natives went far beyond the hostility and mutual exploitation that might be expected in the encounters of peoples equally "haughty and possessive."[28] Noteworthy in this respect is that, following the exchange of hostages, the first Indian hostage returned in his canoe to one of the ships and received additional compensation. This indicates both the reestablishment of trust in the Native man for Spanish action and the desire of the Spanish to demonstrate their desire for positive relations. The ability of the Spanish commanders to maintain peace and leave Bucareli Bay on good terms commends their ability to work through conflicts with the Native people despite limited linguistic and cultural understanding.

Furthermore, despite considerable cross-cultural misunderstanding and mutual ethnocentricity, a continuing stream of efforts to establish humane relations and understanding is evident in the Spanish actions, and was reciprocated in much of the reported Native behavior. This is shown in the Spanish journals through the admiring and respectful descriptions of the women, the recognition of the quality of the woven robes obtained in trade, the appreciation of the Native choral music, and the perception, perhaps not warranted, that the observation by the Indians of the processional, cross raising, and performance of mass demonstrated "great respect and admirable silence."[29]

On the Native side, the Spaniards' reported the pleasure that the chiefs exhibited for the range of objects on the ships, as well as with the food and music that they experienced while spending a night on the vessels. Taken together, these statements indicate an intersection of peoples that truly had at its core a humane grappling with "the Other" from both vantage points.

Subsequent events eclipsed Bucareli Bay in the geopolitics of the Northwest Coast, shifting European interest south to Nootka Sound. These events, beyond the reach of the political worlds of the Tlingit and Haida, placed the people of the western part of the Prince of Wales Archipelago on a side stage from the main saga of European penetration of the North Pacific littoral.

For the Tlingit and Haida in the area, their attention must have turned regularly to the outer coast to see if any more vessels were on the horizon. The next time they encountered such vessels in Bucareli Bay was when the British merchants John Meares and William Douglas came to the area in 1787. They were later followed by British and American merchants who seemed preoccupied with the trading of arms for sea otter furs. As a result of these trading missions, arms were unevenly distributed, occasionally sabotaged, and always in great demand, and traditional intergroup rivalries and territorial principles were under constant stress from warfare due to the new weaponry and competition for control of the new trade.[30]

Spanish entry into the world of the Tlingit and Haida provided the local people a degree of information about the nature of the European outsiders and their capabilities. It also gave Europeans the first glimpse into the unique world of the Tlingit and Haida. For the Native people, this first contact may have helped prepare them for the struggle to retain their autonomy that lay ahead, a struggle that they steadfastly pursued with remarkable success in the century to follow.

NOTES

1. See Christon I. Archer, "The Making of Spanish Indian Policy on the Northwest Coast," *New Mexico Historical Review,* Vol. 52 (1977), pp. 45-67, for a discussion of how Spanish policy toward indigenous groups in this new theater was designed to eliminate the "misrepresentations by some Europeans that Spain invariably destroyed Indian societies." To that end, he suggests that Viceroy Bucareli's instructions required the prevention of bloodshed, even if "sentiments of self-preservation and revenge were to be suppressed" (p. 48).

2. Herbert K. Beals, trans., *Juan Pérez on the Northwest Coast* (Portland: Oregon Historical Society, 1989), p. 33 (hereafter Beals, *Pérez on the Northwest Coast*); Donald C. Cutter, *The California Coast* (Norman: University of Oklahoma Press, 1969), pp. 135-278.

3. Beals, *Pérez on the Northwest Coast,* pp. 75-79.

4. Herbert K. Beals, *For Honor and Country: The Diary of Bruno de Hezeta* (Portland: Western Imprints, 1985), pp. 77-78.

5. Madonna Moss and Jon Erlandson, "Forts, Refuge Rocks, and Defensive Sites: The Antiquity of Warfare along the North Pacific Coast of North America," *Arctic Anthropology,* Vol. 29, No. 2 (1992), pp. 75-76.

6. Mercedes Palau, "The Spanish Presence on the Northwest Coast: Sea-going Expeditions (1774-1793)," in *To the Totem Shore: The Spanish Presence on the Northwest Coast* (Ediciones El Viso, 1986), pp. 45-46.

7. Henry Wagner, *The Cartography of the Northwest Coast of America to the Year 1800* (Amsterdam: N. Israel, 1968), 1:193; Warren L. Cook, *Flood Tide of Empire: Spain and the Pacific Northwest, 1543-1819* (New Haven: Yale University Press, 1973), p. 81.

8. Archer, "Making of Spanish Indian Policy," pp. 45-46.

9. Cook, *Flood Tide,* p. 94.

10. Beals, *Pérez on the Northwest Coast,* p. 77.

11. Wagner, *Cartography of the Northwest Coast,* p. 195.

12. Walter Thornton, trans., "An Account of the Voyage Made by Fr. John Riobo as Chaplain of His Majesty's Frigates the *Princesa* and *Favorita* to Discover New Lands and Seas North of the Settlements of the Ports of Monterey and of Our Father, San Francisco," *Catholic Historical Review,* Vol. 4 (1918), pp. 222-29 (hereafter Thornton, "Voyage Made by Fr. John Riobo").

13. "Expeditions in the Years 1775 to 1779 towards the West Coast of North America by Captain Juan Francisco de la Bodega y Quadra," anon. trans., Anuario de la Direccion de Hidrografia, Ano. III. 1865, Seccion Historica, Miscelanea, p. 33, British Columbia Archives, Victoria (hereafter Bodega y Quadra, "Expeditions to the West Coast of North America").

14. Palau, "Spanish Presence on the Northwest Coast," p. 54.

15. Cook, *Flood Tide,* pp. 95-97.

16. *Ibid.*

17. Don Francisco Antonio Maurelle, "Extract from 'The Account of a Voyage Made in 1779 by . . . Don Francisco Antonio Maurelle . . . ,' " in Jean François de Galaup, Comte de La Pérouse, *A Voyage round the World, Performed in the Years 1785, 1786, 1787, and 1788 . . .* (London: A. Hamilton, 1799), 1:242-56 (hereafter Maurelle, "Account of a Voyage Made in 1779").

Stephen J. Langdon

18. *Ibid.*, pp. 249–50.

19. Mary Gormly, "Tlingits of Bucareli Bay, Alaska, 1774–1792," *Northwest Anthropological Research Notes,* Vol. 5, No. 2 (1977), pp. 157–80; Christon I. Archer, "Seduction before Sovereignty: Spanish Efforts to Manipulate the Natives in Their Claims to the Northwest Coast," unpublished paper delivered at the Vancouver Bicentennial Conference, Simon Fraser University, Vancouver, B.C., 1992, p. 15. See also Cook, *Flood Tide,* p. 97.

20. Maurelle, "Account of a Voyage Made in 1779," p. 250.

21. Bodega y Quadra, "Expeditions to the West Coast of North America," p. 29.

22. Thornton, "Voyage Made by Fr. John Riobo," p. 225.

23. *Ibid.*, p. 228 (qtn.).

24. Frederica de Laguna, *Under Mount St. Elias: The History and Culture of the Yakutat Tlingit* (Washington: Smithsonian Institution Press, 1972), p. 89.

25. Cook, *Flood Tide,* p. 96.

26. *Ibid.*

27. Bodega y Quadra, "Expeditions to the West Coast of North America," p. 38.

28. Archer, "Seduction before Sovereignty," p. 14.

29. Bodega y Quadra, "Expeditions to the West Coast of North America," p. 28.

30. James R. Gibson, *Otter Skins, Boston Ships, and China Goods: Maritime Fur Trade of the Northwest Coast, 1785–1841* (Montreal: McGill-Queen's University Press, 1992), p. 171.

ROBIN FISHER

George Vancouver and the Native Peoples of the Northwest Coast

Much of the history of European encounters with indigenous peoples continues to be written in terms of the clash of opposites. Certainly this was the view in much of the writing in North America during the Columbus quincentenary of 1992. In a book entitled *Stolen Continents,* which was on the bestseller list for months, Ronald Wright adopted a conceit that was far greater than anything imagined by Columbus. Wright presumed to see "the 'New World' through Indian Eyes since 1492." And what he saw were two cultures meeting in incomprehension, with the inevitable result of violent encounters and the dispossession of the Native people.[1]

In Canada the Native rights advocate Thomas Berger wrote a book called *A Long and Terrible Shadow* and argued that the history of Native people in North America has been a straight downhill run from 1492 to the present day.[2] A similar view is perhaps implicit in Anne Salmond's concept of "two worlds" as applied to the first meetings of Maori and Europeans.[3] It is certainly explicit in the current academic fascination with the notion of "the Other" and its emphasis on the distinctions between peoples.

This dichotomous construct—of two completely different cultures meeting at an absolute line of contact, failing to communicate, and often resorting to violence—has a long and persistent history. The notion of the "fatal impact" was popularized by Alan Moorehead and, to some extent, it goes back to the accounts of the European explorers themselves.[4] To have a fatal impact one must, of course, first have a noble savage, a perfidious European, and the whole bundle of ideas that go with such naïve distinctions. The purpose of this paper is to look at George Vancouver's experience with the Native people of the Northwest Coast and to ask: Was the past ever quite as simple as we would like to make it?

Adding the period spent with Cook's second and third expedition between 1772 and 1780 to his own voyage of four and a half years, George Vancouver had probably spent more time in the Pacific and among its peoples than any European of his generation. At the end of the instructions for his own voyage Vancouver was required, in addition to carrying out his primary tasks, to do all he could to avoid disputes with the Native people and "to conciliate their friendship and confidence."[5] He knew from experience the extent to which a successful voyage of discovery was dependent on the good will of Native people. Yet during the summers of 1792, 1793, and 1794, which he spent meticulously charting the western coast of North America, he was not a particularly perceptive observer of the coastal cultures.[6] And being constantly on the move, he did not establish close relations with any group. His experiences with the Native people of the coast were therefore varied and discursive, and historians should be careful about making generalizations.

It is not surprising, given the variety of cultures on the coast, that Vancouver had a variety of experiences among them. The Northwest Coast was one of the most densely populated parts of the continent, and, over thousands of years, the people had developed distinctive lifestyles. They were both unique to the coast and distinct among themselves. So for Vancouver, experience with one group did not necessarily help in dealings with another. Nor were the people of the coast diffident in their approach to Europeans.

Vancouver was on the coast at a critical time in the history of the Native people. The presence of newcomers on the coast would change their way of life forever as they were drawn into the wider world of trade and empire. Yet their cultures did not suddenly collapse. As elsewhere in North America, the people of the coast responded decisively to the European presence and shaped it to their needs. The coast was not a new world; its civilizations were as old as Europe's. The people of the coast had already changed and adapted over thousands of years, and their cultures were dynamic and evolving at the point of contact. Trade was not new to these people who had well-defined patterns of commerce amongst themselves long before the Europeans arrived. Many quickly adjusted to this new tribe of traders, and, at least in the south, the fur trade soon settled down into a regular pattern over which the Indians exercised a great deal of control. The Native people were confident and assured, while the newcomers, as aliens on a foreign shore, were often tense and uncomfortable.

The variety of cultures and the assertiveness of the people meant that navigating the often turbulent waters of intercultural relations could be more hazardous than charting a coastline. Here voyagers had neither precise science nor navigational instruments to guide them, and experience on one section of coast did not necessarily help on another. Nevertheless, Vancouver's *Voyage of Discovery* tells us as much about his view of, and relations with, the people of the Pacific as it does about the relatively straightforward task of mapping coastlines.

The Vancouver expedition's first encounter with the Native people of the

Northwest Coast was with a group of Tututnis who lived along the lower reaches of the Rogue River in southern Oregon. They paddled out to the passing ship, appeared to be open and friendly, and were interested in trade. Vancouver wrote a rather perfunctory account of their physical appearance and showed little enthusiasm for their presence. Not all crew members were as scathing as Thomas Manby, who commented: "The eye received them with disgust: in stature small and in person filthy and stinking, we considered them the nastyest race of people under the Sun."[7] The naturalist, Archibald Menzies, as he would do throughout the voyage, recorded a much more detailed ethnographic description of these people.[8] Yet this first meeting was hardly auspicious and it was not the prelude to close encounters of any kind on the Northwest Coast.

Two months later on a beach on Hood Canal in Puget Sound there was a revealing moment. Vancouver and his boat crews went ashore to rest, eat breakfast, and dry their equipment. A group of Native people landed a short distance away and walked along the beach toward Vancouver's party. They approached with confidence, were apparently unarmed, "and behaved in the most respectful and orderly manner."[9] But Vancouver wanted to control the encounter and prevent too much familiarity. As the Native people drew near, he had a line drawn in the sand between the two groups. He would not allow anyone to cross it without first requesting permission.

Vancouver's own boundary lines were both physical and mental. He kept some physical distance between his men and the people of the coast largely out of fear and the desire to avoid conflict. His first encounters were with Native people who were friendly enough, and yet he expected hostility and often exaggerated perceived threats. His mental distance came from lack of curiosity about the people of the coast. Unlike other European visitors of the time, he took little interest in ethnography. During his first weeks back on the coast he drew on his earlier experience with Cook and compared all the Native groups to those of Nootka Sound. In spite of the point of comparison, he was slow to appreciate the diversity of languages, and therefore of cultures, even on the relatively short stretch of coastline between Puget Sound and the north end of Vancouver Island.

He did not put much credence in Native testimony. His skepticism arose from his notion of "the little respect which most Indians bear to the truth, and their readiness to assert what they think is most agreeable for the moment, . . . although they could have no motive for deceiving us."[10] And Vancouver was particularly struck by cultural features that were unusual and different from his preconceived expectations, once again emphasizing the lines of distinction between the Native people and Europeans.

Even Vancouver's men who did look across the boundary lines recognized the limits of their understanding. Archibald Menzies, who was both a more interested and a more perceptive observer than his commander, made up to some extent for Vancouver's lack of interest in the cultures of the Northwest Coast. When time permitted, he tried to understand the indigenous languages, and he was quick to recognize that there were significant linguistic differences over short distances.

Yet even Menzies was conscious of the limitations to his comprehension. Both he and Vancouver were interested in the possibility of population decline among the Native people in the Puget Sound and Strait of Georgia area. Noticing large burial sites and deserted villages, they began to speculate about causes. Menzies felt that on the southern coast the population seemed "too small for such a fine territory." So he wondered if a hunting way of life could not sustain large numbers of people. In addition to the impact of disease, he contemplated the impact of warfare, and considered the possibility that people had moved to be near the centers of trade. Though these were interesting hypotheses, in the end Menzies maintained a caution that recent students of the issue would do well to emulate. He had to admit that "they could form no conjecture or opinion on the cause of this apparent depopulation which had an equal chance of proving fallacious from their circumscribed knowledge of the manners & modes of living of the Natives." [11]

The artistic record of the Vancouver expedition's time on the Northwest Coast is also of limited ethnographic interest. Vancouver's artists were midshipmen trained in drawing coastlines for navigational purposes. Most of the drawings, and therefore most of the engravings in Vancouver's *Voyage of Discovery,* have little human interest. With a couple of exceptions, such as John Sykes's watercolor *View of Indian Village on Cape Mudge . . . ,* or the engraving of *Cheslakee's Village* at the mouth of the Nimpkish River, there is little evidence of the presence of Native people. [12] The engravers for the published voyage accounts sometimes added a flotilla of Native canoes to the otherwise uninhabited drawings done by the expedition artists. [13] But none of the visual record from Vancouver's voyage has anything like the ethnographic detail of John Webber's drawings and engravings from Cook's stay at Nootka Sound or his various stops in Alaska.

Vancouver found little to appreciate in Native culture, even at Nootka Sound, where he had been with Cook and where he returned at the end of each survey season to negotiate with the Spanish. Vancouver's dealings were mostly with the Nuu-chah-nulth groups who lived on the west side of Nootka Sound. They had a major winter village at the head of Tahsis Inlet, and Yuquot, or Friendly Cove as it was known to the Europeans, at the opening of the Sound was one of their summer dwelling places. The ranking leader among these people was Maquinna, who had led them through the difficult years of European contact since his meeting with Cook in 1778. [14] Maquinna had become

Vancouver
and the
Native
Peoples
of the
Northwest
Coast

201

both wealthy and powerful through his ability to manipulate the fur trade, but at the same time the international rivalry over Nootka Sound threatened to undermine his leadership. As a diplomat, Maquinna was as skilled as any European who came to his territory, but he too was navigating in some difficult waters.[15]

Vancouver's relations with Maquinna got off to a bad start and did not improve much. When the Native leader first tried to come aboard the *Discovery* he was stopped by the deck officer who did not realize who he was. This was a serious gaffe in protocol that had to be smoothed over by Bodega y Quadra, the Spanish commander, who had established a rapport with Maquinna. Particularly when they were among the Salish and Nuu-chah-nulth groups on the southern coast of what is now British Columbia, Vancouver and his men commented that they could not tell who were the leaders. There were chiefs by name, but they appeared to have little authority and there was little apparent subordination on the part of the people.[16] It was difficult, from a European perspective, to figure out the indigenous political system.

Yet even when Vancouver realized Maquinna's preeminence among his own people, he was unimpressed. Bodega arranged a visit to Maquinna's village at Tahsis. The two commanders were served a meal, followed by dancing and ceremonies. Vancouver was unmoved by the ritual of the occasion, commenting when Maquinna danced with a mask that the presentation was "ridiculously laughable." Later, Maquinna and his retinue made a return visit to the *Discovery,* and Vancouver dismissed them "as the most consummate beggars I had ever seen."[17]

In September 1794, Vancouver once again visited Maquinna's village with the Spanish representative at Nootka Sound. They were given an effusive welcome and led to Maquinna's house, where they were seated according to their rank. This time Vancouver was a less critical and more perceptive observer of the proceedings. Maquinna made a speech in which he apparently said that he was honored by the visit, which he saw as the outcome of the peaceful relations that he and his people had maintained with the Europeans. When dancing followed, Vancouver still found the music "as offensive to the ear" as the dancing was "to the eye." He did acknowledge the skill with which Maquinna changed masks, the enthusiasm of the performance, and the need, at least in the interests of diplomacy, to enter into the spirit of the occasion.[18] But he had little idea that he was being used as a pawn in indigenous politics as Maquinna capitalized on these European visits to his village and enhanced his prestige. After three visits to Nootka, Vancouver left none the wiser about the role he had played in indigenous power relations.[19]

Though Vancouver and his men had limited ethnographic curiosity, he did recognize that charting the Northwest Coast involved more than hydrography.

Robin
Fisher

202

He arrived on the coast determined to avoid violence, and he soon realized that his survey could not be carried out without the cooperation of, or at least the tacit acceptance of his presence by, the coastal people. His men were very vulnerable in their little boats, and they depended to some extent on the local people for food. Vancouver's wish to avoid violence was not just a matter of self-interest, for he also believed that no Native people should lose their lives because of his expedition.

Throughout the first and most of his second season on the coast, Vancouver maintained peaceful relations with people there. He assumed that he was the determining factor in avoiding violence, but the Native people had their own reasons for tolerating his presence. As well as charting the coast, Vancouver's men also traded for furs on the side. At one village at the mouth of the Nimpkish River on the east coast of Vancouver Island, they acquired more than two hundred sea otter pelts.[20] This was a business that the Native people could understand, and it provided the basis for mutual and peaceful relations.

But it was not to last. Later, in the north, perhaps because the trade goods had run out, the tenor of things seemed to change, and there were violent skirmishes with the Tlingit. Vancouver was leading a boat expedition near the entrance of Portland Canal when a small group of Native people approached in two canoes. Initial offers to trade did not go smoothly and they seemed to be preparing their weapons. It was not clear whether they intended to attack or were merely preparing to defend themselves, and, in the event, violence was avoided. But the incident should have warned Vancouver that tense situations could easily get out of hand.

Several days later there was a more serious incident. Rowing down Behm Canal on the west side of Revillagigedo Island, the Europeans were once again approached by some Native people, who seemed friendly enough. They were now in Tlingit territory. Vancouver went ashore, leaving Puget offshore in the launch. Having taken his readings, he returned to his yawl to find Native people pressing around on all sides. He became concerned and ordered a quick retreat. They got the boat out onto the water but were immediately surrounded by Tlingit threatening violence and apparently intent on plunder. Puget was too far off to offer immediate help so Vancouver tried to calm the situation. Each time he seemed to pacify one group of Tlingit a new wave of hostility surged from another quarter. Suddenly, the situation was out of control and it looked as though they would be overwhelmed. Puget had now drawn in close enough to be within gunshot range. Without much hope that they could extricate themselves, Vancouver gave the order to fire on the Tlingit. To his surprise, the assailants immediately retreated, heading for the shore and then up into the high rocks. Perhaps as many as twelve were killed and others were injured.[21]

Vancouver had come very close to losing his life on a remote shoreline. If, in

Vancouver
and the
Native
Peoples
of the
Northwest
Coast

203

that wild moment, he thought of Cook, he does not appear to have committed the recollection to paper. He did reflect on the incident afterward, wondering if they had inadvertently given offense to the Tlingit. He did not think they had, so he was more inclined to the view that the Tlingit were trying to take revenge for some former insult from another European. Maritime fur traders had already been in the area. The Tlingit indicated that they had been given defective firearms that sometimes blew up in their faces. Vancouver deplored the trade in guns and the havoc that he thought they created.

In the end, however, he had to admit that the conflict with the Tlingit had erupted because they had relaxed their guard. As he put it: "That attentive wariness which had been the first object of my concern on coming among these rude nations, had latterly been much neglected."[22] If they were to avoid further violence, they would have to be more careful. By keeping their distance they were able to avoid further bloodshed, but Vancouver still felt that the killings had marred his record on the coast. He had hoped to complete the survey without firing a single shot in anger and was exasperated that he had failed.

These experiences with Native people at the end of the second season made Vancouver more cautious at the beginning of the third. In Alaskan waters, he was more concerned with the problems of weather and geography than with the people of the coast. In Cook Inlet and, to a lesser extent, Prince William Sound, the expedition made contact with a number of Native groups. They mostly seemed to be mild-mannered people who showed no hostility toward Vancouver's men. On one occasion Johnstone was a bit edgy when he camped for the night near a large group of Native people, but, in the event, there were no violent incidents. Vancouver had some inkling of the cultural diversity of the area, but it is difficult to tell which specific group he met at each encounter. The area was a meeting place of cultures. There were Chugach Eskimo groups, as Prince William Sound was the easternmost region inhabited by Eskimo on the south coast of Alaska. The Tanaina, an Athapaskan group, had moved into the area prior to European contact and adopted some aspects of Chugach culture. Tlingit Indians from the south sometimes traded this far north, and the cultural pattern was made even more complex by the fact that Russian fur traders imported Aleuts as laborers.[23]

Vancouver was impressed with the degree of Russian influence on all of these people. The first group to come aboard the *Discovery* showed that they were acquainted with European manners by "bowing very respectfully on coming upon deck." Vancouver was also fairly sure that many of them knew a number of Russian words, though he could not be certain since he knew neither the native language nor Russian. He later claimed that many of these Native people were very much under the thumbs of "their Russian masters."[24]

The Russians had recently established permanent fur trading posts on the

Robin
Fisher

204

coast. The *promyshlenniki* (fur traders) had initially come to the islands and coast of the Gulf of Alaska only as temporary residents for the fur hunting season. Then, between Vancouver's first visit to the area with Cook in 1778 and his return in 1794, permanent fur trading posts were established in both Cook Inlet and Prince William Sound. It appeared that the Russians had not yet established any posts beyond Prince William Sound, but they were making trading excursions eastward to Cape Suckling and beyond. They were already finding, as would Vancouver, that the northern Tlingit were a good deal more aggressive than the Native people of Cook Inlet and Prince William Sound, and there had been at least one serious dispute with the people of Yakutat Bay.

In the north, the Russian fur trade developed along different lines from the maritime fur trade on the southern coast. Rather than trading through middlemen, the Russians coerced the Native hunters into working directly for them. These hunters were forced to give up their furs and, the Aleuts particularly, became virtual serfs. Initially the Russians were able to impose this system of compulsory labor and Vancouver saw little sign of hostility, but eventually it would lead to conflict.

Members of the expedition visited some of the Russian posts. The Russians were friendly enough, though they wanted to make it clear from the start that the area "belonged exclusively to the Russian empire."[25] The British, however, were wholly unimpressed with these tenuous outposts of empire, commenting mostly on the filth and stink around the settlements. Vancouver was also critical of the fact that they had made no effort to cultivate the soil, which he presumed to be capable of producing food in summer. He commented revealingly, "They appeared to be perfectly content to live after the manner of the native Indians of the country." In fact, he went on, it was difficult to see much difference between the two groups. Vancouver's men did not tarry at any of these Russian settlements. They paid one last visit to a post in Port Etches at the entrance to Prince William Sound, but, according to Vancouver, it "afforded little worthy of attention besides what has already been described."[26] With that parting comment, he proceeded down the coast.

Farther south, in Tlingit territory again, Vancouver's boat crews felt threatened but avoided direct conflict by firing warning shots at Native canoes. Back at the *Discovery*, Vancouver worried about the fate of his men and reflected on the possible causes of this hostility. He was still inclined to blame the behavior of Europeans rather than to entertain the idea that the Indians may have had their own reasons for harassing the intruders. By this late stage, Vancouver's men were anxious to move along and finish the survey, and they cannot have had many trade items left. Smooth relations were not being fostered by the exchange of goods and so the Tlingit tried to get what they could by plunder.

Vancouver's explanation had more to do with his faith in the superiority of

Vancouver
and the
Native
Peoples
of the
Northwest
Coast

205

European technology, particularly when it came to weapons. He, once again, berated those fur traders who had provided the coastal Indians with firearms. He argued that Native people would not normally have had the courage to attack Europeans, but, once they became familiar with guns, they were emboldened to do so. Somewhat contradictorily, Vancouver claimed that the Indians now knew the destructive power of firearms in their own hands and, at the same time, no longer feared them in the hands of white men. In fact, firearms do not seem to have been a critical factor on the Indian side of these violent encounters. Though some had guns, they seemed to prefer to get close enough to use traditional hand-to-hand weapons. Still, Vancouver was convinced that, given the growing antagonism of Native people and its causes as he saw them, a survey such as his, conducted from small, vulnerable boats, would be impossible just one year later.[27]

Though there may have been moments of comprehension and communication, Vancouver left the Northwest Coast without having established close contact with any Native group or appreciating the strength and diversity of the coastal civilizations. By keeping their distance, with only a few exceptions to prove the rule, Vancouver and his men avoided violent encounters with the Native people. This was a point that went unnoticed during the Columbus quincentenary, as instant historians made continental generalizations about the nature of early culture contact in North America. There were vast differences between the North American east coast in the 1490s and the west coast in the 1790s. And yet, like most Europeans who came to the Northwest Coast in the late eighteenth century, Vancouver stuck to his predetermined agenda. He was there to pursue his own instructions and objectives, so his contact with Native people was limited by self-interest, and he found little to appreciate in their cultures.

When he was on the coast, Vancouver was preoccupied with the difficult and often dangerous work of the survey. The coast seemed endless, the seasons imposed deadlines, so he was constantly on the move. Most of Vancouver's contacts with the coastal people were brief encounters, as Native people paddled out to the vessels or when boat crews put ashore for a short respite. Vancouver seldom stayed in one place for long enough to learn much about any one group. Like many European observers, he thought that the people of the northern coast were more interesting and attractive than those to the south.[28]

Yet, even with his curiosity quickened, there was much that he could not know. At some places on the northern coast he noticed Native women taking an active, and sometimes even a determining, role in trading with his men. He wondered whether this was a matriarchal society but concluded that he could

Robin

Fisher

206

not be sure, because "the knowledge we obtained of their manners and customs, in our short acquaintance, was however too superficial to establish this or any other fact, that did not admit of ocular demonstration."[29]

To map an area is, of course, to appropriate it. Vancouver's task on the coast was not simply a matter of disinterested science. To fix the convolutions of the Northwest Coast on a grid made up of straight lines of latitude and longitude is to begin to bring it under control. Vancouver's charts were part of a process of economic exploitation and, eventually, cultural disruption. The Native people of the coast had, in the long run, little reason to celebrate Vancouver's coming, as they were diminished and dispossessed by the forces that his survey unleashed. Yet we should be careful about holding George Vancouver responsible for all of this, as the city of Vancouver tried to do during commemorative events in 1992, when the organizers of public events made every effort not to even mention the name of Vancouver. Laundering the past for public consumption is not the same thing as understanding history.

In North America at least, the recent anniversary commemorations of European contact have not resulted in a rethinking of the hard issues of history. Rather, they have produced a shift from one simple-minded view to another. European explorers have been transformed from heros to villains, and their coming is seen as an unmitigated disaster for the Native people. As the past is called upon to serve the present, the distinctions among different times and places get lost in the big generalizations. If we must draw lessons from the past, we would do well to remember that in North America European contact did not lead simply to confrontation and violence. There were fleeting moments as well as long periods of reciprocity and accommodation between First Nations people and the newcomers. And this last thought might be a better basis for coming to terms with our mutual history on this continent.

NOTES

1. Ronald Wright, *Stolen Continents: The New World through Indian Eyes since 1492* (New York: Viking, 1992).

2. Thomas R. Berger, *A Long and Terrible Shadow: White Values, Native Rights in the Americas, 1492-1992* (Vancouver and Toronto: Douglas & McIntyre, 1991).

3. Anne Salmond, *Two Worlds: First Meetings between Maori and Europeans, 1642-1772* (Auckland: Viking, 1991).

4. Morehead's book was first published in 1966, came out in a Penguin paperback in 1968, and continues to appear in popular editions. See Alan Moorehead, *The Fatal Impact: The Invasion of the South Pacific, 1767-1840* (London and Melbourne: Hamish Hamilton, 1987).

5. Vancouver's instructions, March 8, 1791, in George Vancouver, *A Voyage of*

Vancouver
and the
Native
Peoples
of the
Northwest
Coast

207

Discovery to the North Pacific Ocean and round the World, 1791–1795, ed. W. Kaye Lamb, 4 vols. (London: Hakluyt Society, 1984), 1:286 (hereafter Lamb, *Vancouver's Voyage*).

6. In Hawaii, by contrast, where Vancouver wintered over after the first two summers on the coast, he learned much about the culture and was engaged with the people.

7. Thomas Manby, "Journal of Vancouver's Voyage, 1790–1793," April 24, 1792, f. 70, photocopy, University of British Columbia Library, Vancouver (hereafter Manby Journal).

8. Archibald Menzies, "Journal of Vancouver's Voyage, 1790–1794," April 24, 1792, f. 109, Ad. ms. 32641, British Library, London (hereafter Menzies Journal).

9. Lamb, *Vancouver's Voyage,* 2:524.

10. *Ibid.,* 2:551.

11. Menzies Journal, June 6, 23, 1792, ff. 139, 147.

12. *View of Indian Village on Cape Mudge, Gulf of Georgia,* monochrome watercolor by J. Sykes, view no. 44, Hyrographic Office, Ministry of Defence, Taunton, England; *Cheslakee's Village in Johnstone's Straits,* sketch by J. Sykes, engraved by J. Landseer, in George Vancouver, *A Voyage of Discovery to the North Pacific Ocean and round the World . . .* (London: G. G. and J. Robinson, 1798), 1:346. For reproductions of these drawings and engravings, see Robin Fisher, *Vancouver's Voyage: Charting the Northwest Coast, 1791–1795* (Vancouver and Toronto: Douglas & McIntyre, 1992), pp. 41, 42.

13. Compare, for example, *Port Dick,* monochrome watercolor by H. Humphreys, view no. 34, Hydrographic Office, Taunton, and *Port Dick, near Cook's Inlet,* sketch by H. Humphreys, engraved by B. T. Pouncy, in Vancouver, *A Voyage of Discovery,* 3:151. See cover illustration and frontispiece of this book. See also Fisher, *Vancouver's Voyage,* pp. 86, 89.

14. Robin Fisher, "Cook and the Nootka" and "Maquinna," in *Dictionary of Canadian Biography,* Vol. 5 (Toronto: University of Toronto Press, 1983), pp. 618–19.

15. Yvonne Marshall, "Dangerous Liaisons: Maquinna, Quadra, and Vancouver," in *From Maps to Metaphors: The Pacific World of George Vancouver,* ed. Robin Fisher and Hugh Johnston (Vancouver: University of British Columbia Press, 1993), pp. 160–75.

16. Manby Journal, July 1792, f. 96.

17. Lamb, *Vancouver's Voyage,* 2:671–72.

18. *Ibid.,* 4:1403.

19. Marshall, "Dangerous Liaisons," pp. 160–75.

20. Lamb, *Vancouver's Voyage,* 2:627.

21. *Ibid.,* Introduction, 1:137–38, 3:1011–17.

22. *Ibid.,* 3:1017.

23. See Erna Gunther, *Indian Life on the Northwest Coast of North America as Seen by the Early Explorers and Fur Traders during the Last Decades of the Eighteenth Century* (Chicago: University of Chicago Press, 1972), pp. 182–83; and Kaj Birket-Smith, *The Chugach Eskimo,* Nationalmuseets Skrifter Etnografisk Roekke no. 6 (Copenhagen, 1952), pp. 7–8.

24. Lamb, *Vancouver's Voyage,* 3:1219, 1224, 1255.

25. *Ibid.,* 3:1235.

26. *Ibid.,* 4:1256, 1241, 1302.

27. *Ibid.*, 4:1370, 1382.

28. For this tendency in European attitudes, see Robin Fisher, *Contact and Conflict: Indian-European Relations in British Columbia, 1774–1890* (Vancouver: University of British Columbia Press, 1977), pp. 81–82, 85.

29. Lamb, *Vancouver's Voyage,* 3:1055.

Vancouver

and the

Native

Peoples

of the

Northwest

Coast

209

Contributors

Andrew David is Retired Commander, Royal Navy, and Qualified Hydrographic Surveyor, Taunton, Somerset, England.

Alun C. Davies is Professor of Economic and Social History, The Queen's University of Belfast, Northern Ireland.

Iris H. W. Engstrand is Professor of History, University of San Diego, California.

James Barnett is an attorney in Anchorage, Alaska.

Robin Fisher is Professor of History, University of Northern British Columbia, Prince George.

Stephen Haycox is Professor of History, University of Alaska Anchorage.

Phylis Herda is Associate Professor of Anthropology, Victoria University of Wellington, New Zealand.

Robin Inglis is Director, North Vancouver Museum and Archives, Vancouver, BC.

J. C. H. King is a member of the Department of Ethnography, Museum of Mankind, The British Museum, London.

John Kendrick is a historian in Vancouver, BC.

Steven Langdon is Professor of Anthropology, University of Alaska Anchorage.

Caedmon Liburd is Associate Professor of History, University of Alaska Anchorage.

John Naish MD lives in Iron Acton, Bristol, England.

Anthony Payne is a Director of Bernard Quaritch Ltd. and a Council Member of the Hakluyt Society, London.

Carol Urness is Curator, James Ford Bell Library, University of Minnesota, Minneapolis.

Glyndwr Williams is Professor of History, Queen Mary and Westfield College, University of London.

Kesler Woodward is Associate Professor of Art, University of Alaska Fairbanks.

Index

Academy of Arts (St. Petersburg), 165
Academy of Sciences (Paris), 31, 134
Academy of Sciences (Russian), 133, 134,
   137, 142
Acapulco, 66, 88
*Account of the Voyages in the Southern
   Hemisphere* (Hawkesworth), 177
Admiralty Bay, 127
Admiralty Island, 128
Adventure, 93, 96
Agattu, 137
Album de Colbert, 89, 97, 99
Aleutian Islands, 133–42 *passim*
Aleuts, 154, 155; drawing of, by Levashov,
   164
Alexander, William, 168
Alexander Archipelago, 61
Anchorage: future site of, 3
Andreanof Islands, 137
Anglo-Russian Convention (1825), 129
Anson, George, 81, 177
Archangel, 133
Architectura navalis mercator (Chapman),
   91
Argonaut, 124
Argüello, Doña Concepcíon, 16, 18
Arnold, John, 104, 110
Arrowsmith's Chart of the Pacific Ocean,
   128
Arteaga, Ignacio de, 11, 189, 193
Ascorbic acid: and scurvy, 82, 84
Astor, John Jacob, 18
Astrée, 52
Astrolabe, 52, 57, 61, 93, 96

Athapaskans, 154
Atlas (Efimov), 134
Atrevida, 11, 66, 93
Attu, 137
Australia, 42, 71

Baffin Island, 163
Baja California: transit of Venus in, 31
Banks, Joseph, 42–52 *passim,* 149, 177, 179;
   failure to publish botanical data from
   Cook voyage, 30; president of Royal
   Society, 41; image of "noble savage," 72
Baker, Joseph, 150
Baker Island, 190, 194
Baranov, Alexander, 15
Baranov Island, 128
Barren Islands, 122
Barrie, Robert, 181
Barrington, Daines, 40
Basov, Emelian, 6
Bayly, William, 112, 120, 121
Bay of St. Lawrence, 142
Beagle, 182
Beaglehole, J. C., 178, 180
Behm Canal, 126, 153, 154, 203
Bell, Edward, 150
Berger, Thomas, 198
Bering, Vitus, 5, 116, 132–37 *passim,* 142,
   162, 165; death of, 6
Bering Land Bridge, 4
Bering Strait, 40, 116, 120, 121, 132
Bhering's Bay, 127
Billings, Joseph, 8, 13, 142, 165, 168
Blane, Sir Gilbert, 85

Bligh, William, 8, 10, 41, 94, 121; explores Cook Inlet, 119; draftsman with Cook, 164
Bligh's River (Knik Arm), 122
Bolts, William, 51
Botany Bay, 32, 41
Bougainville, Louis Antoine de, 30, 44, 51, 59, 176; journals published, 34, 39; image of "noble savage," 72; and scurvy, 81
Bounty, 8, 41, 94, 96, 121, 176
Boussole, 52, 57, 61, 93
Brady Glacier, 127
Bristol Bay, 120, 121
Bristol Library, 177, 179
British Museum, 149, 150
Brosses, Charles de, 30
Broughton, William, 150, 181
Brown, William, 157
Buache, Philippe, 52, 58, 136
Bucareli, Antonio María de, 11, 188, 192
Bucareli Bay, 187, 188, 194; Quadra's 1775 voyage to, 7; Arteaga visits (1779), 11; interaction between Europeans and Tlingit at, 189
Bucareli Sound, 54
Buffon, Georges Louis Leclerc: Natural History of Animals, 27
Burke Inlet, 125
Burney, James, 121, 180
Byron, John, 38, 177

Caamaño, Jacinto, 18
Cabo San Lucas, 109
Callao, 66
Canton, 177
Cape Decision, 108, 126, 128
Cape Douglas, 108
Cape Edgecumbe, 123
Cape of Good Hope, 30, 105
Cape Ommaney, 119
Cape Prince of Wales, 120, 121
Cape Suckling, 205
Capetown, 178
Captain Cook (ship), 122
Caribbean, 79, 80, 85

Carlos III, 27, 54, 68
Carlos IV, 27, 32, 33, 68
Carta Marina (Olaus Magnus), 163
Castries, Maréchal de, 51
Catherine II, the Great, 54, 137
Cenotaph Island, Lituya Bay, 60
Chapman, Fredrik Henrick, 91
Chatham, 14, 43, 84, 92, 107, 124, 126, 127, 155, 157
Chatham Strait, 128
Chatidooltz (Chugach Eskimo), 154, 155
China, 57, 139
Chirikov, Aleksei, 5, 116, 133, 134, 137, 142
Chirikov Island, 126
Christian, Fletcher, 176
Chronometer, 88, 104, 125; invention and development, 103; difficulty with, 105
Chugach Bay (Prince William Sound), 142
Chugach Eskimos, 154, 165, 204
Chukchi Peninsula, 137, 142
Chukchi Sea, 120
Cleeve, T. L., 85
Clerke, Charles, 8, 120
Climatorial theory of infectious disease, 79
Coal Cove, 123
Cocos Islands, 84
Colbert, Jean Baptiste, 89, 97, 99
Cole, Douglas, 173
Coleridge, Samuel Taylor, 176, 179
Colnett, James, 42, 123, 124; confrontation with Martínez, 13–14
Columbia, 14, 123
Columbia River, 14
Columbus, Christopher, 27
Commander Islands, 133, 137
Commerson, Philibert de, 30, 51
Cook, James, 39, 41, 45, 46, 49, 61, 65, 93, 103, 116, 120, 122, 144, 164, 165, 177, 188, 200, 201, 204; career, 8; significance of third voyage, 10; interception attempted by Bucareli, 11; and the transit of Venus, 30; search for Terra Australis, 30; death of, 31; journals published, 34; voyage linked to Vancouver, 38; Span-

ish reaction to plans for third voyage, 40; at Tonga, 67; and scurvy, 81, 83; and Müller/Stählin map, 139; and Native artifacts, 158; and Hawkesworth's volumes, 178; account of second and third voyages, 179

Cook Inlet, 121–27 *passim*, 155, 156, 204; naming of, 3; Cook enters, 10; Vancouver at, 15; Vancouver sets chronometer in, 106

Cook's River (Cook Inlet), 154

Coppermine River, 58

Crantz, David (*History of Greenland*), 165

Crimean War, 18

Cross Sound, 107, 121, 127, 128, 129; Vancouver sets chronometer in, 106; Tlingit artifacts collected at, 158

Daedalus, 43

Dageler, Joseph, 52

d'Alembert, Jean le Rond, 27

Dall, William, 15

Dalrymple, Alexander, 41–45 *passim*, 122, 178

Dampier, William, 38, 177

Dana, Richard Henry, 82

Darwin, Charles, 182

D'Auteroche, Jean-Baptiste Chappe, 31

Delisle, Joseph Nicholas, 134, 136

Delisle de la Croyère, 134

Denning, Greg, 72

D'Entrecasteaux, Joseph Antoine Bruni, 81

Descubierta, 11, 66, 93, 96

De Zulueta, J., 81

Díaz, Bartolomew, 80

Diderot, Denis, 27

Diet: shipboard, 79–86 *passim*

Dillon, Richard, 150

Discovery, 14, 41, 43, 84, 93, 96, 107, 108, 116, 121, 124, 126, 154, 155, 157, 204, 205; design of vessel, 92; as observatory, 106; Maquinna visits, 202

Dixon, George, 8, 13, 42, 61, 122, 124

Dixon Entrance, 123

Dobbs, Arthur, 136

Dobson, Thomas, 150

Dombey, Joseph, 31

Douglas, John, 179, 180; publishes Cook's journal, 40

Douglas, William, 195

Doz, Vincente, 31

Du Halde, Jean Baptiste, 133

Duncan, Charles, 42, 123

Dundas, Henry, 43

Dunmore, John, 181

Dusky Sound (New Zealand), 105

Eagle River (Anchorage), 126

Early Maritime Artists . . . (Henry), 162

Earnshaw, Thomas, 104, 110

East India Company, 41, 177

Edgar, Thomas, 121

Efimov, Aleksei V., 134

Egmont, Earl of, 39, 46

Elizabeth, Empress, 133

Ellis, William, 164

Encyclopédie; ou, dictionaire raisoné . . . (Diderot and d'Alembert), 27, 51, 92

Endeavour, 30, 93, 96

Engel, Samuel, 133, 136

English Bay, 119, 121

Eskimos, 163. *See also* Chugach Eskimos

Etches, John Cadman, 42

Eveinov, Ivan M., 132

Experiment, 122

Fairweather Mountain, 121

Falkland Islands, 40, 66

Favorita, 189

Felipe V, 27

Fernando VI, 27

FitzRoy, Robert, 182

Fleurieu, Claret de, 51

Flinders, Matthew, 110

Flora americae septentrionalis (Pursh), 34

Flora peruviana et chilensis (Ruiz and Pavón), 32

Floridablanca, Count, 43

Foggy Island (Chirikov Island), 126

Fonte, Bartholomew de, 41, 134

Fort Ross, 18

Fox Islands, 137
Franks, A. W., 150
French Revolution, 51
Friendly Cove (Nootka Sound), 31, 128
Frobisher, Martin, 163
Fuca, Juan de, 41
Funk, Casimir, 82
Fur trade, 13

Galaup, Jean François. *See* Lapérouse
Galiano, Alcalá, 18
Gama, Vasco da, 80
Garrote, Antonio, 89
Gaztañeta, Antonio, 91
Geodesists, 132, 133
George III, 46, 150, 177
Gincaat (Tlingit chief), 157
Glacier Bay, 127
Godoy, Manuel, 68
Gooch, William, 112
Gore, John, 121
Gray, Robert, 14, 123
Green, Charles, 112
Green, John, 136
Grenville, William Wyndham, 42, 43, 45
Guadeloupe, 109
Guayaquil, 66
Guerra, José Bustamante y, 65, 66, 70
Gulf of Good Hope (Turnagain Arm), 122
Gulliver's Travels (Swift), 177
Gunther, Erna, 150

Haida, 7, 154, 187, 189
Halley, Edmond, 38
Hanna, James, 13
Hawaii, 32, 154
Hawkesworth, John, 39, 176–79 *passim*
The Health of Seamen (Lind), 82
Hearne, Samuel, 58
Heere, Lucas de, 163
Henry, John Frazier (*Early Maritime Artists of the Pacific Northwest Coast*), 162, 168, 170, 173
Hewett, George Goodman, 150, 155, 156
Hezeta, Bruno de, 7, 187
Histoire des navigations aux terres austraes (Brosses), 30

Holst, A., 82
Homann, Johann Baptist, 132
Home Office, 41
Hood Canal, 200
Hopkins, Gowland, 82
Hornsby, Thomas, 31
Hudson's Bay Company, 18, 41
Hughes, Elwyn, 84
Hutchinson, William, 93

Icy Cape, 122
Icy Strait, 128
Inuit, 163
Izmailov, Gerasim Grigorovich, 120, 121

Jay, John, 54
Jefferson, Thomas, 54, 136
Johnson, Samuel, 80, 178
Johnstone, James, 126, 127, 152, 204
Jones, John Paul, 54
Jappien, Rudiger, 173
Juno, 16

Kamchatka, 49, 116, 120; First Expedition, 132, 133, 134, 142, 144; Second Expedition, 132, 133, 144
Kanistooch (Chugach Eskimo), 155
Kealakekua Bay (Hawaii), 31, 105, 106
Kenai Peninsula, 15, 155
Kendall, Larcum, 104
King, James, 10, 40, 41, 119
King George (ship), 122
King George Sound (Australia), 105
King George's Sound Company, 42, 122
Kirilov, Ivan K., 132
Kiska, 137
Knight Island, 157
Knik Arm, 122, 127
Kodiak, 142
Kodiak Island, 121, 122, 126, 127, 128
Kolyma River, 142
Koniag, 154, 157
Krasil'nikov, Semen, 137
Krenitsyn, P. A., 121, 163
Krusenstern, Adam J. von, 181
Kruzof Island, 188
Kurile Islands, 132, 142

Labrets, 154, 155
Ladrones (Marianas Islands), 67
Ladrones (Thieves) Islands, 190
Laguna, Frederica de, 193
Lamartinière, Joseph, 52
Lammanon, Robert, 52
Langara Island, 187
Langle, Paul Antoine Fleuriot de, 52
Langsdorff, G. H. von, 16
Lapérouse, Jean François Galaup, Count of, 10–11, 32, 34, 44, 49–62, 81, 93, 103, 170, 180
La Ranchería, 190
León, Joaquín Velázquez de, 31
Lesseps, Barthelemy de, 49
Lettre d'un Officier de la Marine Russienne . . . 1753 (Müller), 134
Levashov, M. D., 163, 164
Lewis and Clark expedition, 34
"Limeys," 85
Lind, Dr. James, 81, 82
Linnaeus, Carolus, 25–31 passim
Lisiansky, Urey, 16
Lituya Bay, 53, 58
Lomonosov, Mikhail, 139
Long and Terrible Shadow (Berger), 198
Longitude: computation of, 103–11 passim
Louis XIV, 99
Louis XVI, 49, 52, 181
Lunar method, 104
Luzhin, Fedor F., 132
Lynn Canal, 128, 157

Mackenzie, Alexander, 42
Macleod Harbor, 124
Malaspina, Alejandro, 27, 34, 44, 65, 66, 103, 150, 193; 1791 voyage of, 11; 1790–92 voyage of, 33; arrested, 67; publication of journal banned, 68; analysis of Tongan society, 69; use of violence, 72; image of "noble savage," 72; and ship design, 93; praises Suría, 161
Manby, Thomas, 150
Maquinna, 13, 201, 202
Marchand, Etienne, 61
Maria Luisa, Queen, 68
Martínez, Estéban José, 13–14, 124

Maskelyne, Nevil, 104
Maurelle, Don Francisco Antonio, 49, 187–94 passim
McCloud Harbor, 123
Meares, John, 13, 85, 122, 124, 195
Medina, Salvador, 31
Menzies, Archibald, 33, 44, 46, 126, 156, 157, 200, 201; appointed by Banks, 43; and scurvy, 85; and Native artifacts, 149, 150, 155
Mexicana, 14
Middleton, Christopher, 38
Mikhailov, Pavel, 161
Moorehead, Alan, 198
Monneron, Paul, 52
Montague Island, 121, 123, 127, 156
Monterey, 105, 109, 128
Montevideo, 66
Mount Augustine, 126
Mount Edgecumbe, 8, 121, 188
Mount Fairweather, 53
Mount St. Elias, 5, 8, 53, 122
Moziño, José Mariano, 32, 33, 34
Mulgrave Sound, 71
Müller, Gerhard Friedrich, 116, 133, 134, 136, 137, 139, 142, 144
Mutis, José Celestino, 32

Napoleonic Wars, 110
Native art and artifacts, 149–58 passim
Native Costumes at Port des Français (de Vancy), 170
Natives: and European explorers, 10, 55, 151, 155–57, 187–207 passim. See also individual tribes
Natural History of Animals (Buffon), 27
Nautical Almanac, 111, 120
Nepean, Evan, 42, 46
Neue nordische Beyträge (Pallas), 139
Neuville, Jean Bauche de la, 51
Neva, 16
Nevodchikov, Mikhail, 137
New Caledonia, 67
New Eddystone, 126
New Guinea, 30, 67
New Hebrides, 30
Newhouse, Daniel, 89

New South Wales, 67

New South Wales Corps, 42

New Zealand, 67

Nimkish River, 201, 203

Nootka, 13, 44, 49, 54, 68

Nootka (ship), 122

Nootka Indians, 8. *See also* Nuu-chah-
nulth

Nootka Sound, 8, 11, 13, 31–42 *passim*, 67,
105, 108, 119–25 *passim*, 153, 154, 158,
195–202 *passim*

Nootka Sound Convention, 42

Norfolk Sound (Sitka Sound), 123

Northwest Passage, 15, 32, 33, 39, 44, 45,
52, 58, 67, 116, 136, 149, 154, 164

Norton Sound, 121

Noticias de Nutka (Moziño), 33

Nouvelle carte des découvertes (Müller), 134

Nueva Granada, 32

Nuu-chah-nulth, 201, 202

Observatory Inlet, 125, 126, 153

Olaus Magnus, 163

Ononnistoy (Tlingit chief), 154

"Other," 69, 71, 74, 195

Pallas, Peter Simon (*Neue nordische
Beyträge*), 139

Pamela (Richardson), 178

Paramore, 38

Parkinson, Sydney, 30

Passage Canal, 156

Pavón, José Antonio, 31, 32

Peas: and scurvy, 85

Pérez, Juan, 7, 187

Peter the Great, 132

Petropavlovsk, 49, 120

Philippines, 67, 88

Plenisner, Friedrich, 163

Point Grenville, 188

Point Turner, 157

Pond, Peter, 42

Ponomarev, 137

Port Althorp, 107, 127, 128

Port Banks, 123

Port Bucareli, 61

Port Chalmers, 106, 107

Port Conclusion, 106, 107, 128, 129, 154

Port des Français, 10, 53, 54, 55, 58

Port Dick, 155

Port Etches, 123, 124, 156, 157

Port Graham, 123

Portland Canal, 126, 153, 203

Portlock, Nathaniel, 8, 13, 42, 43, 61, 122,
124

Portlock's and Goulding's Harbor, 123

Port Mulgrave, 11, 123, 124

Portola, Gaspar de, 6

Port Protection, 126, 128

Port San Antonio, 190, 194

Port Santa Cruz, 189–94 *passim*

Port Stewart, 126

Prince of Wales, 123

Prince of Wales Archipelago, 195

Prince of Wales Island, 126

Princesa, 189, 193

Princess Royal, 123

Prince William Sound, 8, 15, 119–29
passim, 154, 156, 157, 204, 205

Promyshlenniki, 132, 133, 205

Providence Bay, 121

Puerto Deseado, 66

Puget, Lt. Peter, 14, 45, 125, 127, 150, 157,
203

Puget Sound, 14, 200, 201

Punta de Mineral, 190

Pursh, Frederick, 34

Purtov, George, 15

Pushkarev, Sgt. Aleksei, 134

Quadra, Juan Francisco de la Bodega
y, 7, 11, 14, 32, 33, 49, 61, 153, 187–94
passim, 202

Quadrant, 104, 125

Queen Charlotte (ship), 122, 123

Queen Charlotte Islands, 42, 53, 124, 128,
187

Queen Charlotte's River (Knik Arm), 122

Queen Charlotte Strait, 153

Quicksilver, 125

Quinault River, 7

Quinn, David Beers, 164

Raper, Lt. Henry, 110
Real Gabinete, 66
Real Jardín Botanico, 66
Real Marina, 190
Rennel, James, 43
Resolution, 41, 93, 96, 116, 121
Restoration Bay, 125
Revillagigedo Island, 126, 153, 154, 203
Rezanov, Nicholas, 16, 18
Richardson, Samuel (*Pamela*), 178
Riobo, Father, 190, 193
Rio de la Aguada, 189
Roberts, Henry, 42, 44, 121
Rogue River, 200
Romantick Isles (Barren Islands), 122
Rousseau, Jean Jacques, 59
Royal Academy (London), 164
Royal Academy of Medicine (Madrid), 27
Royal Botanical Garden (Madrid), 27
Royal Dockyards (London), 99
Royal Scientific Expedition to New Spain, 32
Royal Society of London, 25, 39, 40
Ruiz, Hipólito, 31, 32
Running survey, 120
Russian American Company, 8, 15
Russian Imperial Academy of Arts, 161
Russian Orthodox, 7
Russians, 6, 155, 156, 157, 204, 205

St. Helena, 105, 178
Saint Matthew Island, 120
St. Paul (ship), 5
St. Peter (ship), 5, 6
St. Petersburg, 49
Salisbury, 82
Salisbury Sound, 187
Salish, 202
Salmon Cove, 125, 128, 153
Salmond, Anne, 198
Samgoonoodha, 119
Samoa, 30
Sandwich, John Montagu, Earl of, 39, 40, 41
Sandwich Sound (Prince William Sound), 119

San José del Cabo, 31
Santiago, 7, 187
Sarychev, Gavriil A., 142
Sauer, Martin, 168
Sceptre, 52
School of Navigation (Russian), 132
Scott, James, 150
Scurvy, 4, 6, 7, 15, 53, 79–86 *passim*
Sea Lion Bay, 188
Sea of Okhotsk, 120, 132
Sea Otter, 13, 122
Seduction River (Knik Arm), 122
Semichi, 137
Serra, Junipero, 6
Sextant, 104, 125
Shelagskii Cape, 142
Shelikov, Grigor Ivanovich, 7
Shelvocke, George, 177; *Voyage round the World,* 176
Shumagin Islands, 122, 123
Siberia, 132, 133, 134, 142
Sindt, Ivan, 119, 137
Sitka, 16
Sitka Sound, 123
Skottowe, Thomas, 178
Slave Lake, 123
Snug Corner Cove, 10, 119, 122
Solander, Daniel Carl, 30, 31, 164
Solomon Islands, 67
Sonora, 7, 187, 188
Soviet Marine Ministry, 163
Spain, 4, 6, 7, 187
Spanberg, Martin, 133
Spanker, 94, 99
Spruce beer, 84
Stählin, Jacob von, 116, 137
Steller, Georg Wilhelm, 5, 6, 133, 134, 163
Stephens, Philip, 44, 46
Strait, Clarence, 126
Strait of Admiral de Fonte, 119
Strait of Anian, 33
Strait of Georgia, 201
Strait of Juan de Fuca, 54, 123
Strait of Maldonado, 33, 58, 67
Strange, James, 13, 122
Stolen Continents (Wright), 198

Sturtevant, William, 164
Suemez Island, 194
Sumner Strait, 126
Suría, Tomás de, 161
Sútil, 14
Swaine, Spelman, 150
Swift, Jonathan, 177
Sykes, John, 201

Tables Requisite, 111, 120, 124
Tahiti, 30, 31, 105, 177
Tahsis Inlet, 201, 202
Tanaina, 155, 156, 204
Tasman, Abel Janszoon, 182
Tatarinov, Mikhail, 139
Theodolite, 125
Thompson, David, 42
Three Saints Bay, 7, 13, 170
Tlingit, 11, 55, 59, 126, 153–54, 157–58, 170, 187–94 *passim*
Tompkins, Stuart R., 137
Tonga, 69, 70, 72
Tongan Islands, 65
Toulon, 97
Treatise of the Scurvy (Lind), 81
Treaty of Tordesillas, 54
Tsimshian, 153
Turnagain Arm (River), 3, 10, 22, 119
Tututnis, 200

Ugak Island, 126
Ulloa Channel, 190
Umnak, 137
Unalaska, 120, 122, 142
Unalaska Island, 119

Valdés, Antonio, 33, 66
Valdés, Cayetano, 18
Valparaíso, 66, 105

Vancouver, George, 43, 61, 103, 124, 127, 198, 207; and Cook, 8, 38; account of voyages, 14, 34, 45, 181, 199; at Vancouver Island with Quadra, 33; relations with crew, 45, 149; and scurvy, 83–85, 149; and navigational technology, 103–12 *passim*, 125; survey methods and charts, 112, 124–29 *passim*, 207; and Russians, 127, 205; and Natives, 149, 151, 154, 155, 156, 158, 198–207 *passim;* and collection of Native artifacts, 149–58
Vancouver, John, 109, 181
Vancouver, B.C., 207
Vancy, Gaspar Duché de, 53, 170, 173
Vanikoro, 32
Vava'u Archipelago, 65
Venus: transit of, 25, 31, 39, 109
Verón, Pierre Antoine, 30
View of the Establishment of the Merchant Shelikhov on the Island Kad'iak (Voronin), 168
Voronin, Luba Alekseevich, 165, 168, 170

Wales, William, 112, 180
Walker, Alexander, 139
Wallis, Samuel, 177
Walpole, Horace, 177
Waxell, Sven, 162, 163, 165
Webber, John, 8, 164, 165, 168, 201
Whidbey, Joseph, 3, 126, 127, 128, 150, 156
White, W. H., 94
Wisbech, 150
Women of Unalaska (Voronin), 165
Woodall, John, 81
Wright, Ronald, 198

Yakutat Bay, 11, 15, 53, 67, 68, 127, 187, 193, 205
Yuquot (Friendly Cove), 201